On Assignment with Adama

Susan Isabelle with Joshua Summer's rendition of Adama based on the Adama revealed photo of March 2000. Adama is a pan-ethnic personage that embodies all cultures and races of the earth. 2005

Mt. Shasta, Telos, Lemuria, and Sacred Earth Sites, Book I

by
Susan Isabelle

authorHOUSE™

1663 Liberty Drive, Suite 200
Bloomington, Indiana 47403
(800) 839-8640
www.AuthorHouse.com

This book is a work of non-fiction. Unless otherwise noted, the author and the publisher make no explicit guarantees as to the accuracy of the information contained in this book and in some cases, names of people and places have been altered to protect their privacy.

© 2005 Susan Isabelle. All Rights Reserved.

All rights reserved. No part of this book may be reproduced in any form or by any electronic or mechanical means, including information and retrieval systems, without permission in writing from the publisher, except by a reviewer who may quote brief passages in a review.

First published by AuthorHouse 06/07/05

ISBN: 1-4208-6338-X (e)
ISBN: 1-4208-4278-1 (sc)

Library of Congress Control Number: 2005902584

Printed in the United States of America
Bloomington, Indiana

This book is printed on acid-free paper.

SECOND EDITION 2005
Revised Dolphin Priestess

To Melchizedek:

Light of Life
Giver of the Way
Illuminator of the Mind
Dedicated to the Progression of Worlds
The High Priest of El Elyon,
The God Most High of All Universes

To Adama;

My Friend
High Priest of Lemuria
Patient Guide
Friend of Humanity
Dedicated to the Way Of Progression of Worlds

To the Ancients;

My Companions
On an Unwavering Path of Truth
Leading to Ascension of All Sentient Beings
Together We Travel
As Written and Foretold So Long Ago

From an Ancient One Returned

You are our Past
You are our Future,

We are your Past
We are your Future,

There is no Time
No Past
No Future
There is only Now

We come to you
To Secure the Past
The Present
And the
Now

Adama
A Da Na Mos
High Priest of Telos

"Just give me one moment in time,
to be all I can be"

As sung by Whitney Houston and was the 1980 Olympic Theme,
It was then and is now
My song and my prayer.

Susan Isabelle

A Channel from Adama, A DaNaMos
Adama Channel

To those who seek and are meek
We come, we thrive and are alive
Yea, to those who have chosen a way to stay
Come here before the snow,
 So that you forever may know.

Our lives of peace and of glory
Oh, long is our story
My child, on Earth is wild
We cannot come for us to die,
That IS WHY
Our death not that of physical form:
Spirit, that is our form.

Long ago, oh we shall show
How and why to know
Long ago we fled:
Those on surface lost their head
War and famine and progress
Caused us all to regress.

Seeking shelter from the coming storm
Became the norm
We, an endangered race,
Our survival had to face
We rose our voices on high,
But insanity was neigh.

We from planets, so vast
Our return there long past
Sought the Creator of All
During Earth's planetary fall
A vision strong came in the night
Now no longer any fright.

For was shown a way
To wait for yet another day
Our race not lost,
But must seek frost.

A Northern realm,
Far from the kiln
Burning, raging in mind
Of those not our kind.

Our steps were guided to the towers
Above the lands, not formerly ours
Tears of sorrow
For our tomorrow.

Bound our hearts:
To save our people, yea to start
The long trek to higher land
There our race to take a stand
There, upon Creator's sacred ground
A solace would be found.

A dream, a vision in the night,
Again removed our fright
A way to stay, safe secure
Our souls a place to nurture.

Creator showed a passageway
Here within we were to stay
Yea, the mountain
Became the fountain
Of eternity.

My peoples and me
Immortal being,
Forever seeing
Events of strife
Cut as a knife
Upon the surface
Not our place.

Remember now, oh my friend,
You, who we now send
To bring again a message sure
So many once again secure.

Now we tell you as we were
No longer, that is sure.
We no longer in body be
Our souls forever free.
We not imprisoned as one thought
Expanded beyond we have sought
A higher plane, beyond our frame
Encompass Earth, in full girth.

How you ask?
Oh, long past the land, the sea
Turned upside down and we
Hidden beneath the turning soil
We, sought the Holy Oil.
Prayers raising high
Brought the Spirit neigh.

Ages passing by in that state
One day opened the Holy Gate.
Seeing its Glory passing through
To Creator: To you...

Sought the Shining Face
This to become our abiding place.
Ever watching, ever there
You our brothers, desiring to share.

Our words and our knowledge wait
And offer you the Holy Gate.
Established long ago
A race did forego.

To you who remember, we
Come for all to see.
Soon, and at
Even mid day noon.

Seek not our Presence
But rather use your sense.
Spirit's hand reaches out
Her voice, not a shout
Through our ascended being
For your freeing.

Learn our way,
Hear all we have to say;
Not of war
That's not what we are for.

But Peace,
For your soul's release
To fly on high, that is why
We come to you this day.
Hear, oh hear, what we say
Bring many this way.

For upon the Earth,
The entire girth;
The waves, the waters
Throughout all the quarters,

Once again are come.
To spare some,

> Your task:
> In this our story be
> Teach the way,
> So some to free

To Susan Isabelle
As channeled to her by Adama
Feb 21, 2005

Table of Contents

To Melchizedeck, Adama and the Ancients v
You Are vii
Adama Channel viii
Introduction xiii
Foreword xvii

Part I Revealing the Feminine Melchizedek

Call of the Dolphin 1
What's an OBED? 12
Transformation Begins 32
Faith and Family 48
Heaven and Earth 57
Discovering Shambhala 63
Meeting Adama 71
Telos and Lemurians 71
Al'lat Le Andro 81
All My Steps Directed 96
Many Are Called 105
Maya Magical Mystery Tour 108
A Gift of Vision 116
The New Hampshire Telos Portal Return 131

Part II The Mayan Magical Mystery Tour

The First Temple 141
Maya Miracles 145
Don't Make Him Angry! 164
What Did You Say? 170
It Is All Illusion 173
Muluc Speaks: Remember! 186
The Atlantean 193
One With Open Mouth 207
And So It Is, Ixchel 212
Tikal Magic 220
Just Ask 224
The Maya: Lords of Light 231
Activation of the Skulls 241
Plumed Serpent's Return 246
Telos Portal 248
Heed the Message 252
Sastun 256
Red Resonant Skywalker 260
White Galactic Wizard 264
Word of Melchizedek 266
Codex 271
Bibliography 274

Introduction

On Assignment With Adama
By Susan Isabelle, Al'lat Le Andro Melchizedek

This book is taken from my personal journal and is an almost daily record of events. It documents the meeting I had with Adama, The High Priest of the Lemurians while on a trip to Mt Shasta, California in 1999. I was later to find out that Adama was well known to peoples who lived in the area and was supposedly a fabled being who lived in a society of ascended beings beneath the mountain. It was rumored that occasionally, Adama and other beings from their underground city called Telos, made surface visits to rescue lost hikers on the mountain or bring messages to the people living on the surface.

My meeting with Adama was a very real experience. He is real. He is powerful. He is Holy and the people of Telos are an ascended people. You will learn much about them and the culture of Lemuria, their history and their hopes for humanity. I heard him speak to me while I was on the mountain doing sacred ceremony at dawn of Novemeber 9, 1999. That was just the beginning.

Later that same day, I was literally taken out of body to meet with the inhabitants of Telos, or Shambhala, within the dimensional space around the mountain. On that day I agreed to begin a work on behalf of humanity with Adama to assist the earth in its transition, or ascension. There were to be thirty six sites I was to visit, seal and dedicate to the Light of The Highest, El Elyon, God Most High, the God above All Gods. These sites were also to be used by humanity in the ascension as they have become sacred sites upon the earth. In this agreement, the Lemurian peoples will come at the time of our ascension to hold the integrity of the earth, the wholeness, and stabilize the time for us.

I was also to discover many things about my own path, my destiny, and my reason for coming to this planet from a Universe far away and from the distant future. I have time traveled here to do this work. For what reason? To bring about the highest probable reality for all future generations. At the beginning I did not know what was to come. I had no idea the extent of my mission, Mission Earth, or the danger and challenges I would encounter along the way. Many events were kept secret even from me, until the last moment and then I was given everything I needed to do the job.

In this book, you will journey with me to the first two sites Adama sent me to open and secure for humanity. You will also evolve along with me as this writing has been taken directly from my journals and reflects my own transformation. I would ask the reader to consider the synchronistic events and make a direct correlation to events that are, or may have happened in your own past. I ask this because many of us are receiving the information, but are missing the clues. It is vital now that we all learn how to put all the pieces together, because without the fully functioning human operation, our work of Light on the earth is more difficult. You are all vital to the whole.

This writing and release is also for education. Much has been taken from a sacred transcript, or the **Codex** as the Lemurians call it. These teaching have been hidden for ages and come to life through the experiences and events in this writing. They are universal truths, they are forfuture meditation upon them . They are noted in the text and will be listed in the back for you.

The sacred words of the Codex come alive and they are personalized through my experiences so they become the living Shambhala Mastery we all seek within ourselves. It is through life initiations, as circumstances and daily challenges are presented to us, we pass our initiations for self mastery and enter into Shambhala. We may need to repeat the same challenges until we do master them. To enter Shambhala, the Heavenly Holy City of Light spoken of by the Tibetans and many other cultures and called by many names in different languages, one must master certain aspects of oneself and become Light Body. The Principles of Shambhala were taught to me along my journey, in my experiences and personal challenges, and I share some of them with you in the beginning of the book.

My first assignment took me to my own backyard to the Eastern summit called Mt Washington. There the earth quaked at the opening! On the second assignment I traveled to the land of the Maya in Belize, Central America. I went to carry out and complete a sacred task: To activate several ancient sites in Belize, as prophesied and directed by Adama, the High Priest of the Lemurians and Melchizedek, the High Priest of El Elyon, or God Most High.

The restoration of these sites was foretold long ago in many global indigenous tribal legends, and written about in Dr. J. J. Hurtak's The Keys of Enoch, the Ancient Secret of the Flower of Life by Drunvalo Melchizedek, and the Bible. The sites are to be opened by the Melchizedek line. This time, however, the coming was the Feminine Aspect of the Melchizedek energies and restoration of the Olive Branch of Peace to the world through the Belize sites.

While reading , you will personally experience the multidimensional power and excitement of the Shambhala Energy. Experience the manifestation of gifts and what the Lemurians, the dwellers of the Inner Earth the and the Ancients offer to the world, interwoven with the revelations of higher Truths and their teachings. In reading this adventure, you will experience the activation of the new Shambhala and Melchizedek energies on Earth. After reading, you will know this energy transcends all that has been previously written about or experienced. There are within, answers to many New Age questions as to how we will use our gifts in the coming dimensional transition of the Earth and how we will one day live on this new planet in the making!

The Secrets are revealed! You are there as we perform on-site Earth Healing, activation of the Crystal Skulls of the Maya, purification and activation of the sacred sites as we were directed by the Lemurians. You will also see how we worked with the dolphin energy to complete our task.

The incredible synchronicity of events that occurred throughout our journey will astound you, as it did us. The ancient Mayan Gods and Spirits interacted with us to assist us in the completion of our previously-predicted tasks. They also had a few surprises planned for us not even hinted at prior to our journey!

Foreword

Many today are hungry for the higher Truths on their personal path and know, at least intuitively, we are facing major earth and personal changes. The Feminine Aspect of the Melchizedek is here now for the restoration of the planet Earth. The opening of the ancient sites to the Divine Feminine Energies will aid the Earth transition.

This is a true story, but it is also the precursor of many other transitional challenges and life alterations we will have to make. They may be perceived by us as tragedies or as miracles. It is all in our perception, in our knowledge base and our abilities to deal with our situation at any given moment. We are all participating in these events. Whether or not we are aware of it, we are all hurtling towards the end of the fourth sun and are about to enter the fifth sun as foretold by the Maya and many cultures across our planet.

Many will want to know what's really going on out there, how it will affect them, as well as how to prepare for transition. These energies are being made available to all that desire them.

This begins the story; the final event will be in 2012. There were to be 36 sites to open. With the gifts the Maya and the Ancient Lemurians gave to us, we are now preparing for our next journey. As of this revision, 27 of the sites have already been opened. Each one has been a challenge, an education in the Principles of Shambhala, an adventure, and a life changing event for me and those around me.

In February of 2004 I was awakened by Adama's voice in the night. He said, "Go to Shasta, don't return!" I said back to him, "What do you mean? You can't mean that I am to leave the beautiful Shambhala Temple housing over a hundred persons and twelve therapists and teachers of Shambhala in New Hampshire we have established there, my students, friends and family-leave fifteen years of work????" Again I heard Adama say,

"Go to Shasta, don't return!"

I was given four options that night. I choose to come to Mt Shasta where it all began in 1999. I now live in Mc Cloud, California beneath the holy mountain of Mt Shasta. I have begun a new work here and will be teaching many from all over the world. I have already established a global network of Shambhala teachers and Melchizedek Priests and Priestesses who will carry on the global work, to the delight of the Lemurians! I serve to help direct efforts and provide information and the Teachings as they are given to all of us through the Lemurians.

Currently, I am channeling and writing as the messages still come in the middle of the night. I have nine more sites to open and seal for humanity.

I am completing the second book, We The Lemurians Shall Come outlining the second half of the journey through 2003 and the time space experiments the Lemurians interrupted for the protection of humanity. It shall be released as soon as possible for it contains more of the information needed for humanity and ascension.

Now I await the next assignment and I await the arrival of the Lemurians,
For they shall come.

Susan Isabelle

Part I

Revealing the Feminine Melchizedek

1

Call of the Dolphin

Date: September 1999

"Now, just keep sending the energy round and round as
I've shown you.
Form the vortex
That's it. Feel the breeze of the energy as it passes your
fingertips,
Stronger, stronger, keep pushing
In a moment- we'll enter the vortex
Go to the beach for a period of three minutes
Now, I am sending the symbols for us to go;
The symbols to enter the vortex are going in,
Chant with me! Sing the ancient song!
Feel, allow yourself, lift up through the top of your head
and now,
"GO"!

I felt myself flow out the top of my head, a white, flowing mist and enter the waiting, spiraling mouth of the vortex! Spinning down, down, down through the tunnel and suddenly --pop! I emerged onto a dark seashore, lit only by the moon. Hovering over the moonlit sandy beach, I could see my "body," now a shimmering glow, star-like, and swift in its movement. This is fun! Skimming the lapping water shining on the sands, I sped along the shoreline. Freedom, pure joy filled me! I love this! I thought.

I could see two human forms up ahead. Soaring in closer, I saw a petite woman with short dark hair, and a large man who seemed to be shouting something at her. I was unable to hear what was being said but saw that she cowered before him, frightened. Tears flowed down her face. The burly man raised his hand high and then with great downward force, hit the woman solidly across her face!

"Hey, you can't do that! Leave her alone!" I screamed, but no human voice was heard. Inwardly, I raged and began to buzz around him as an angry bee buzzes an intruder. Frustrated and powerless to physically intervene, I flew at him time and again. Suddenly there were others there with me, flying at his face. My students! They had come! His startled eyes glowed in our light and a look of sheer terror contorted his face. He backed off, swatting at us like flies, and ran away from the woman, up the dunes and away. She fell to the sands weeping as we viewed her from above.

Triumphant, I felt myself being lifted up to view the scene below. I watched as the woman seemed to shrink upon the beach beneath me. The moonlight glistened on the tops of gentle rolling waves, softly stroking the silvery sands. Oh, how I love to travel like this! I thought. Another advantage of becoming a teacher! Suddenly from my high perch, I was unexpectedly propelled through the air, flung down uncontrollably.

"What's happening?!" my mind screamed out. Drawn downwards at such incredible speed my own thought was barely completed. I was plunged beneath the waters of the ocean and submerged, seeing only the bottom sands of the ocean floor.

"I'll drown!" was my initial panic, then, Oh, I don't need to breathe!" I spoke to only myself. "Wow, this is cool!" I watched in amazement as a whole school of dolphins swimming gracefully came toward me. As they drew closer they watched, observing and studying me, their silvery gray bodies sparkling in the sea. They began to swim in a circle around me, staring at me as if waiting for me to do something.

From my position in the center of the dolphin ring, I commanded with determination:

"Tell them we are coming!" Then the pulling began, drawing me upwards toward the gaping hole, the swirling vortex of time and space.

"Oh, no! Not yet!" I cried out to the darkness. I could see the dolphins below, shrinking and disappearing, in the ocean waters as I was lifted above them.

Speeding back up through the tunnel, I was instantly back up above my body. I looked about the room at seemingly empty bodies seated there, motionless upon their chairs, suspended in time. Then I slipped back into my inert body through the top of my head, like a mist entering a cavern. Sliding down in and touching my feet to the glowing Earth Star beneath my feet, I became physical once again. I spoke to my students,

"Time to return. That's it
Now time to come back
Now touch your feet to the Earth Star!
Draw in a deep breath!
Focus on your breath
Come back!"

As I stated the commands firmly to my students, one by one they returned and with incredulous eyes looked at each other.

"Did you see THAT? " someone asked.

"Boy, was he scared! " another gleefully exclaimed.

"That was the most incredible thing I've ever done!"

My students excitedly discussed their experiences. They each told what they had done, and tried to do, as I listened to each story.

No one mentioned the dolphins; did they see them? I was puzzled by the appearance of the dolphins. Why did I say that to them?

"Did anyone see the dolphins?" I asked my students. The room went silent as they stared back at me. Seeing their inquisitive looks, I continued, "I saw dolphins all around me and said the strangest thing to them. I told them we were coming! I haven't a clue as to what that means".

Little did I know I had just contracted with a school of dolphins to work with them. I was beginning a journey that would take me to another country, and the experience of a lifetime. A few other things had to be in place first, however, and I was soon to find out.

My last student from my weekend class had just departed for home. Saying my goodbyes I looked out after them. I wondered and realized they were newly enlivened beings, distinct creations of energy and spirit as they had now integrated the two. They would never be the same, nor view their lives as they had previously. The experience we had on the beach had taught all of us how much power and impact we could have on the earth. Responsibility hit me.

I piled up the multicolored cushions that lay all over the floor of the Center. Soft scent of incense still hung in the air, and the energy of the class still held a white glow in the room. Taking advantage of the opportune moment, I jumped into the pile of mats and cushions, snuggled in, and lay back as I considered the events. What could those dolphins have wanted from me? Why did I tell them I was coming to them? Another mystery! Was this to be another adventure? How incredible my life has been over these last seven years, I thought. Here I am now, a teaching Shambhala Master and having these unbelievable experiences and leading others into their highest potentials. My mind traveled back to the events leading up to this new life, to Shambhala and the Melchizedek Energies. Lying back and staring up at the ceiling, I suddenly found myself traveling back in time, to a very difficult time of my life.

1989. The injury was crippling and I was left totally disabled. The spasms were so constricting my left leg was much shorter than my right. My spine was twisted; each step became a shuffle. Unable to move my head from side to side or lift my arms, I was so afraid that the rest of my life would be in that crippled condition. I missed my work as a social worker. I had been working for disabled children and their families, helping them and I loved each one. I was lonely, my friends had all disappeared as quickly as the months had gone by. I was unable to participate in any normal activities, and I missed my church and friends there. As time went on, I suffered even more. I experienced nine months of physical therapy, stretching traction, painful massage, manipulation, and many medications. Life was very depressing at that point. Then, in just one morning, my life changed.

"Susan, there is someone here at the hospital clinic who thinks she may be able to help you, the massage therapist mentioned casually. We would like to try a new method to relax the spasms known as 'Reiki'." I thought about it for a moment, then said,

"I'll try anything!" I moaned in pain; I knew even then there would be consequences. My church didn't allow this. As soon as I was under the warmth of Reiki, my body just seemed to somehow absorb its warmth and soothing comfort. She worked on my neck and shoulders and it felt so wonderful. Twisted muscles relaxed and I could feel my shoulders coming down closer to their normal position. I left that day able to move my head from side to side. That was the first time in over nine months! I had instant relief in *one* treatment!

"Why didn't anyone tell me about Reiki sooner?" I complained to the therapist. I now had over ten thousand dollars in uninsured medical therapy bills to pay.

"Well, it's not really accepted by the medical community," she answered.

After three weeks of Reiki treatments—a total of nine sessions—I was able to return to work part-time. Soon after I was back to my normal schedule. For me, this was a miracle!

Shortly after I returned to work, my newfound friend and Reiki therapist moved to another state. I didn't know where to find Reiki again. In 1989 in the northeast United States, Reiki was not something you'd just look up in the phone book. I had experienced something truly wonderful and healing; now it was gone. I desired to have more Reiki, even though I had been healed and didn't require it for pain management.

I also had come from a very strict fundamentalist Christian background. The concept of hands-on healing in my particular sect was taboo, forbidden as witchcraft. This presented a moral and spiritual dilemma. I felt this healing was a gift from God to me.

"How can this be? I wondered, I am healed. Totally and completely healed! I said to myself. Perhaps the concepts I hold so intensely have not being accurately interpreted?"

I thought long and hard at that time. I asked the Sunday school teachers and the Pastor of my church about this, only to be told it was the deception of the New Age Movement, but I knew I had been touched by an Angel of Mercy. I have to find out and resolve this one way or another for my own peace of mind. So I set out to discover for myself what this was.

For the next two years I studied scripture with new eyes. I soon realized my mind had been clouded with others' interpretations and indoctrination. I researched all cultural religious beliefs. I began to see a core of beliefs that seemed to run throughout all religions. I became a sponge, absorbing all the knowledge I could to help me understand.

To further my understanding, I went to Indian reservations in Arizona, New Mexico, and to Prince Edward Island to the Micmac Indians to research the American Indian culture. I came to believe through my studies that they held some of the highest understanding of spirituality on the planet. I visited many pueblos, and sought out information about their healing methods.

Coming back, I felt that I had learned much, but knew that this, too, was only a piece of the puzzle. I had slowly begun to understand the Universal concepts of Light and total Love that are interwoven throughout all cultures and belief systems. Scripture and ancient writings from many cultures were filled with passages that spoke of light, sound, tone and vibration. The Koran is sacred tone and measure. Karma and reincarnation were new concepts for me and I was challenged to understand through study. Imagine my amazement at the discovery that the very disciples of Christ thought the He, Christ, was a reincarnation of Elias or a walk in of John the Baptist! Brahma, Vishnu and Shiva became precious as I recognized the Divine in a new language. Each time I passed a hurdle in my formerly closed mind, I found there was more to learn. Christ's words "Seek and you will find" took on a totally new meaning: *And you will keep on finding*! I also began to understand we have a wonderful inheritance as the Children of Light. I also learned that the time of that inheritance was fast approaching. I needed to be ready! Christians called it the Rapture, and New Age people called it the Ascension. No matter what, humanity was about to undergo a dramatic and world changing event.

All the cultures were saying the same thing, but in different languages and terms of expression.

After coming back from one of my new passions, a "research vacation", I opened my local newspaper and there was an ad for Reiki right in my own back yard! It is amazing to me now that the whole time I was in Sedona, a New Age energy Mecca, I never once had seen a Reiki ad or sign. I must have been blind. But, all is in Divine order. I hadn't been ready before, now I had opened my mind to new possibilities. At last I was ready, remade in all my thought processes, and the Universe had provided a teacher at just the right time. I called and spoke to a wonderful woman who informed me that there would be a Reiki class the very next morning!

Arriving at the class the next morning, I was still uncertain. My church would not be accepting of me or this! I remember praying,

"Dear Jesus, don't let anything happen to me that is not of your Light and Beauty of the Highest!" As soon as the Reiki Master stood behind me for Reiki attunement, I was flooded with Light, incredible Love, and Joy. Finally, I felt as though I'd come home. I was at last connected to the Ultimate Divine Source, and like rivers of Light, that flowed though me. I felt peace and total contentment. This had been the right decision., my soul was at peace. As soon as I began to give Reiki to another student, tears of joy flowed from both of us.

"Can you feel that I asked tearfully?" She nodded as tears rolled down her face. Pure joy, pure love was all I felt!

During the next few weeks, my experience of the Reiki attunement totally changed my life. This new pulsing energy within me opened floodgates of love. I became Divine Love. Now I understood. I am the totality of who I AM. Now I was to find out who that really is.

2

What's an OBED?

I had been told I would have a Reiki Guide to help me on my path. (UT) I really wanted to meet this Guide, and heard I could do so through meditation guided by a Reiki Master. I arranged a private session with my new Reiki Master Teacher.

As I settled into the big comfortable chair, the Master Teacher sat beside me and began to speak softly. As she did, I became aware of a bright light with colors that seemed to swirl about. I wasn't sure what I was actually seeing. I couldn't make out any features at all. In semi-trance, I softly explained to the Master,

"I think I am seeing an Angel; the lights just keep swirling around." I said.

I heard the Master say, "Ask if there is a name." I did as instructed and asked,

"Do you have a name?" Instantly I heard something, a voice in my head say,

"OMMMMBMYGOD!" "What? What did you say?" I asked astonished. Recovering, I mentally asked again, astounded that I'd heard anything at all. Again an answer shot back at me in my mind,

"OMMMBMYGOD." I had heard the same thing again, but I didn't feel I was getting anything intelligible. I asked aloud this time, speaking slowly to the voice in my head, saying to it, "Oh -My- God?"

An answer quickly shot back, more loudly this time.

"NO! OBEDBYGOD!" Then more, powerfully, more distinctly , the voice inside my head nearly shouted at me repeating what it had said before, "OBED-BY-GOD!"

The power and strength of the voice startled me. Clearly, I was trying the patience of an Angel! I shut down. I was afraid, confused in mind and spirit. The rest of the meditation didn't go any better. I was really disappointed, in myself for being rather slow at these things and that I hadn't been able to communicate better. What was an 'OBED' anyway? I would find out soon!

I went to my church the following Sunday and casually picked up my Bible. I watched in amazement as the pages turned by unseen hand and it somehow opened to the Book of Chronicles. As though the verse jumped out of the Bible and levitated above the scripture, my attention was drawn to Chapter 11, Verse 47. I read the verse, "Eliel, and OBED, and Jasiel, now these are they who came to King David, and they are among the mighty men." OBED! There was such a thing as an Obed! Was Obed trying to tell me who he was? If so, he had once been a man, or maybe an angel in human form , but certainly a servant of King David. You can imagine my excitement! I had never heard of a name like Obed and now here it was in front of me. Was this really Obed? Was this confirming my guide's name? Was this a coincidence? So many questions!

After going home, I looked up the name Obed in my Hebrew concordance. It meant "Serving" , so the angel named Obed was serving by God. I began to hear my own words-Obed was a serving angel, one who was by God. I instantly felt humble. WOW! That's quite an angel! I realized I'd been pretty impatient with Obed and spoke to him,

"Obed, if you are really as real as I think you are, I want to get to know you a whole lot better!" I began to feel loved and an unseen embrace of warmth around me.

A few weeks later, I was again in church. I felt and saw a great flood of Light all around me. I raised my hands in song and felt the Reiki energy flow out in a great arc of light. I watched as a rainbow raised from my hands out over the congregation. I suddenly became aware of a Presence beside me which glowed like the sun. Obed was standing beside me! The light was so bright. I felt such love! Although not seen by others, he came to be with me that day and has been beside me ever since. I even have aura pictures that clearly show him standing with me. They are so clear you can even see the folds in his robe. I was, and still am, deliriously happy!

    I was initially trained for Reiki I & II in the Radiance style of Reiki, using colored symbols that corresponded to the Chakras, the spinning wheels of light energy that are within every human being., and bring life and energy to us all. I began volunteering in two small local Reiki clinics to practice. I met many wonderful, supportive people who encouraged my use of Reiki, as well as participated in many miracles of Reiki similar to my own healing experience. Seeing people come up off the massage tables glowing with the energy with big smiles and relief of pain is very rewarding . People were being healed by the wonderful energy that flowed through me. I loved it! I wanted more, and to learn more! I became a Reiki sponge.

    Mastery in Usui Reiki came quickly, and then I took the Tibetan Usui Reiki courses to become a Master Teacher. One day a few months later, I had a phone call from one of my former massage therapists.

    "Susan, I just wanted to wish you a Merry Christmas!"

    "Oh, it has been a wonderful year! I began. I am now a Tibetan Usui Master Teacher! I'd love to teach you this someday," I added.

    "You're a Master Teacher! she exclaimed. Wait just a moment!" She said she'd call back shortly, and she did.

    "Guess what? she bubbled. I've just set you up to teach every month for the next year at the largest Naturopathic Clinic in the state! They want you! You'll start in three weeks! Will you do it?"

    "Yes, I suppose I, -I'd love to!" I answered.

    "Great!"

That's how it all began, but it didn't stop there. I later became an Independent Master Teacher. I desired, as a teaching Master, to present the finest training material possible to my students. I wanted to ensure a standard of quality and progression of Reiki throughout the world for health benefits and pain relief for everyone. Seeking advanced skills, I became fully trained in the International Center for Reiki Training methods under William Rand. I became a licensed teacher for that organization. Licensure required I document one hundred sessions with clients, write three papers, and complete an internship with other teachers. This was excellent training, and I am ever grateful for all of my learning experiences there, but the Universe had other plans for me. Through a strange series of incidents, I was shown my path was not to be part of an organization. (UT) I became an Independent Master Teacher once again, but with my Guides as my teachers. I now realized that was the plan all along.

My own spiritual needs began to grow as well. I kept the extracurricular activities of my Reiki practice a private, personal matter. But now, I had to face another hurdle. Soon after people were being healed through my work at the clinics, I knew it would just be a matter of time that someone would find out at my church. I loved my friends at my church and knew that they just would not understand and I was experiencing such soul conflict at that time. I remembered the woman who had had a crippled hand, all twisted and bent. I was as astounded as she was that after her session with me at the clinic, her hand was straight and completely healed.

"I am going to tell everyone about you!" She exclaimed! She did.

Soon, I had the dreaded, but expected, evening visit from the pastor of my church.

"I hear rumors that you are doing healings," he said.

Answering truthfully, I explained the wonderful gift I had received and, yes, there had been instant healings at the clinics and, yes, I had been a participant in those healings. I explained to him, my belief that this was one of the Gifts of Spirit as described in the scriptures.

"Well, Susan, under the by-laws of our church, healing is not allowed. Only the Elders, the men, of the church may bring healing with oils and prayers. All such laying- on of hands healing were suspended after the Apostles died and there are no such 'Gifts of the Spirit' these days," he said.

I listened patiently as he explained the process. He continued to say that if I did not stop using Reiki, I would lose all membership rights. Also, I would only be reinstated back into the church after I had made a public apology and confession of my sins for already having used the Reiki energy. I would be expected to go in front of the whole congregation and deny my gifts from God. This I could not do, not ever, and I told him so.

"You know personally the people who have been healed through this gift I have been given, I answered. I was healed, too. How can that be denied or explained away? It is God that heals. God has chosen to do this, to share Universal love through us to one another," I explained to no avail. UT

After our little talk had ended, my church membership was revoked. I was told I would lose my marriage, my job, my family and all blessings from God by him. As the minister went out the door he looked directly at me and stated maliciously,

"Your healings won't last; only healings from God will last. We are not of the same spirit." UT

I felt frustrated as he went out the door, and I thought , "No, we are not of the same Spirit. I thank God we're not!" I would never return to his teaching again. I realized they were *his* teachings-not the teachings of the Spirit of Love. " How could I have been so blind all those years?" I wonder aloud.

In one night, I had instantly lost my church fellowship and all my former friends. This would mean the church body could not fellowship, as it is called, with me. This dis-fellowshipping-was designed to bring the sinner into a realization of their 'sin'. My friends didn't know or understand and they were still blinded, it is not their fault, I realized. This Reiki , and teaching of giving love through one's self is so new, how could they know? II went through a short period of depression. I also had to explain Reiki and my excommunication to my family. I called my daughter and my three sons. They were all married with children and also deeply involved in fundamentalist church beliefs. I told them what had happened, and explained my own healing miracle. They didn't know what to think, I could tell.

I also told them of the day at work when I had come into a client's home to find a baby stiff in seizure. I touched the baby and warm glowing love energy flowed from me to the child. The baby instantly relaxed, opened her eyes and was well once again. I also told them about the woman who had come to a clinic for the first time, whose hand had been crippled in spasms for many years. That night her hand was restored to normal functioning. I told them many things, but felt the horrified reaction: how could their own mother be involved in such forbidden things? This was considered to be witchcraft by the church! I could not blame them; I was partly responsible for their indoctrination. I realized it would take time, lots of it. Meme, Grandmom, now became someone with whom they did not want their own children involved. I was crushed. To follow this path, my own life's path, was beginning to cost, and it may even cost me my own family.

To survive emotionally, I held onto my memory of Obed, the Light, and developed a newer, closer relationship with the Universal Creator whom I felt I was just getting to know. My inner love continued to grow. I knew then that Obed had manifested that day in church to encourage me in my new path that he knew held some pain, but much more beauty and life. The healing of my heart continued with understanding. My life was becoming more and more stable. And I didn't lose my job.

One night during a Reiki clinic I was attending, it was finally my turn to get up on the table to receive a little personal energy work. I really looked forward to these times when I could go under the energy. It was so relaxing and stress just melted away. That night a woman with deep, penetrating eyes came over to the table where I was waiting for a therapist.

"Hi, My name is Michelle," she introduced herself. "Are you ready?"

"Oh, yes, I can hardly wait!" I answered, setting down into the soft pillow. She then began to send energy over my abdomen. I lay there with my eyes closed enjoying the energy but wanted a bit more, so I began to project symbols and energy out over her hands through my third eye to empower her hands.

I felt her hands begin to warm greatly, then they began to go down, straight down -through my abdomen. I opened my eyes to see a very startled young woman staring at her hands.

"My hands! My hands! They just went through you!"

I sat up.

"I'm sorry," I apologized. "I sent symbols and energy into your hands to help your energy." She looked at me, astonished. I continued,

"I never had anyone respond as strongly as you just did, however. I wouldn't have done it if I'd known that was going to happen. You are powerful woman and have great ability! What level Reiki are you?" I asked her.

"Oh, I'm just starting. I had my Reiki I training a couple of weeks ago," she answered, still examining her hands, turning them over and over.

"Well, if you're doing this at level one, I want to be at your level two class just to see what happens!" We laughed and began what was to be a solid friendship. I did go with her to her next level training and it was wonderful. Michelle was with me as I began to teach. For many years she held the energies during our classes as a Guardian Angel.

My years as a teacher went by quickly. I laughed as I remembered the night when we were giving outdoor meditations and attunements in the cool, clear water of Crystal Lake in Manchester, New Hampshire. On this particular night, we ran overtime and a policeman had come to shut down the park for the night. A large, burly officer came walking up to the pavilion. I stood in the center of thirty-five people all passed out on the floor in deep meditation, which meant they looked dead. I was about to be 'in deep', too. His eyes grew wide in horror. I could see it in his face and heard his thoughts,

"What has this woman done to all these people?!" he thought in panic. My 'Guardian Angel' handled him beautifully. So much so that he left, and did not come back to bother us or close the park. We gave attunements afterwards in the night waters under the full moon. Beautiful!

We discovered that she was indeed a Golden Angel when we had her aura video done a year or so later. There in the center of her chest glows a magnificent golden star, beaming and pulsing the energies of the angelic realm. She has been assisting others who have come to their own angelic presence in our classes and trained them individually in the use of their special powers and abilities. Everyone who ever saw Michelle immediately said, "Don't I know you from somewhere?" Everyone knew her. She has incarnated here for many thousands of years, holding the energies of love on the earth plane. She has been involved with almost every one of our students at some time and place in history. Her discerning gaze sees directly into the soul, and we are thankful for her, even if she doesn't blink! UT

The Universe had provided a friend and a companion, a true friend, at a time when I needed one the most!

Obed in Action

My husband was upset. I thought my marriage was over. Perhaps the pastor was right on that one. Would I lose my family and my husband? The challenge to my love of God in this new understanding and practice was very hard to endure at times. My husband was affected by my expulsion from the church. He had also lost friends and social contacts because of my actions. He had previously enjoyed Reiki sessions with me, that is *before* the church pastor forbade the sessions. Now he looked at me suspiciously. He perceived them as evil, and my husband now looked at me with guarded caution. Our wonderful, intimate sessions sharing the energy were over. That really hurt and tested our marriage. In other circumstances, I would have felt alone, but now I knew I was never alone. The Universal Energy, Love and Peace were always with me. So was Obed. I could never be alone. I held on. UT

We were on research/vacation/conference in Vermont when my husband's rib was broken in an accident. As he lay groaning on the hotel bed in pain, I asked him if he would like me to give some energy to ease his pain. I got an intolerant look in return. Feeling hurt and rejected, I started to cry. I went into the bathroom to wash my face. I ran the cooling water in the sink.

Just as I was splashing the water up, I heard the strong voice of Obed speak firmly.

"The Bone Needs Moisture!"

At the same time I 'saw' what I was to do. My abilities as a psychic were growing daily, but this was amazing. (UT)A video! A whole video was being played before me over the bathroom mirror. I watched myself in the video treating my husband while using water and the energy. That had never happened before. Coming out of the bathroom, I said to my husband,

"I was just shown what to do to help you. May I *please* give you energy?"

He gave me another look and said firmly, "No."

Now irritated I said, "OK! Suffer, if you want! I know what to do—I can help you!" Surprised at my outburst, and in much pain, he lay back groaning on the pillow.

A while later, he said "Help me up."

Out of my mouth came the words, "No, you choose pain, so you can live with pain!" I cried even harder. After a few moments, he relented.

"OK, you can try," he said quietly.

I went to work. Placing wet, warm towels over the area of the cracked rib as I had been shown, I used the energy. It flowed in deeply, bathing the area in moisture. It took about ten minutes for the energy to penetrate and then it began to subside. He was healed in ten minutes time. Incredulous, he moved around and stretched, then stood up and bent over.

"It's gone! The pain is really gone!" he exclaimed. "Wow!"

Needless to say, that ended the doubt about me, the power for good, and physical healing of the energy. Today, almost a decade later, he is still healed and so am I. I sometimes wonder about that accident. All is in Divine Order.

The reason we had gone to the conference was to learn Macrobiotics, a method of natural healing through foods and other Japanese healing techniques. A few weeks earlier Walter and I had been seated together in front of a surgeon. A large malignant tumor had been diagnosed in his prostrate gland. As we listened to the surgeon, we were horrified to hear the medical options being presented to us. The recommended plan was to schedule immediate surgery, chemotherapy, and possibly radiation. Further, the doctor explained, he would likely be left incontinent, and the cancer might not even be contained.

We left from the doctors office that day very depressed. At home we argued. He would in no way allow this treatment; he preferred to die. He had refused the surgery. He would die. I prayed. A few days later I was led to our local health food store. Scanning the multitudes of books on healing with natural foods, herbs and supplements, I felt lost. We didn't have time to experiment. His life was on the line.

"Take this book," I heard Obed say. I took down a large book.

"Macrobiotics? What's this?" I wondered.

"It will help him," I heard Obed's voice. I bought the book.

At home I handed the book to William saying he might want to read it. I saw him sit down with the book and he was still there several hours later as I headed off to bed. When I left for work in the morning, he was again seated in the chair reading the book. I came home in the afternoon to find several garbage bags filled with all the food contents of our kitchen.

"What are you doing?!" I exclaimed.

"It's all poison," he said. I now understand why I have cancer, and I understand how to help myself. This is just the beginning. I've called the Kushi Macrobiotic Center in Massachusetts and we are signed up for classes!" The next week found our diet filled with miso soup, shitake mushrooms, brown rice, and seaweed. We were on our way to a Kushi Conference. There we learned to prepare our foods properly and create a new balance in our bodies.

Shortly after the conference and his rib healing, I was again treating William with the energy. I didn't have a massage table, so I had him lay sideways across the end of our bed. I could treat one full side, feet and head as I stood at the foot of the bed. As I was holding my hands over his naval plexus chakra, my eyes were closed and I was praying again for help, this time help to heal this cancer. Suddenly, I felt my hands in the chakra's spinning energy. Eyes still closed, I psychically 'saw' globs of dark spots in the chakra spinning around, and tentacles of spaghetti-like strands of dark energy interwoven throughout the chakra.

"What is this?" I inwardly exclaimed. "What am I supposed to do with this? No one ever told me about this in class! Do other people see this stuff?" I thought, as I began to try to strain them out with my fingers, combing the masses out of the chakra. What am I supposed to do? "Obed! Help!" I cried inwardly.

"I'll take them," Obed said to me across the other side of William on the bed. I handed the mass to him as I strained it out of the chakra.

Then I felt William's stare below me. You know- how you feel when someone is watching you? I looked down at him beneath my hands. He looked terrified. His terrified eyes locked on mine.

"What's wrong? I asked. Are you OK?"

"You're there!" he exclaimed.

"Yes, I am. I haven't moved," I answered.

"I just felt you climb up on the other side of me, on the bed. I feel you right here beside me, on the *other* side!" he exclaimed, bewildered and afraid.

"Will, I prayed for some help and the angel has come again. Close your eyes and relax." He did. From that point on his PSA levels (a test to determine the presence of prostrate problems) dropped and he has had no more symptoms of prostate cancer. For all intents and purposes, there is no more cancer. The last four years have all seen normal test results, with lower levels than he's ever had.

I now suggest the macrobiotic diet and lots of energy work as an alternative worth pursuing for those with cancer. Those coming for energy work are given this information and an attunement to begin their own self-recovery process. Prayer works! I wish I could say that all healing happens as miraculously as this, or that I have great healing skills. That simply is not true. Spirit heals and all acknowledgements go to the Divine. I am happy to be the channel of this wonderful gift!

A couple of things to consider, however: I have learned that each person has their own karmic contracts to work out. Should you have an illness, seek understanding of the purpose of the illness in your life. Cleanse yourself spiritually as well as physically. Also, in our environment there is so much pollution. Do not necessarily blame yourself should you contract an illness. Many illnesses are caused by those pollutants. Our best alternative is to seek ways to rid our lives of these harmful contaminants. I offer clients some alternatives and dietary consultations now as a result of these lessons in our own lives. All things have a purpose.

My personal life improved after that and my classes really started filling up. The visits from Obed increased. During one of our class meditations, a man stepped out from the Light completely dressed from head to foot in the garb of a Franciscan monk. Tied around his waist was a thin cord and he wore sandals. I could not see his face as his hood was pulled up over his head. I knew it was Obed. I know his presence of love. Asking his name, he replied,

"Obed, of course!" I was excited, as I had only seen him as a light being prior to this. Soon he was appearing in this manner on a regular basis, but I could never see his face. I wanted to see him!

Things were changing fast. In another class, I was allowed to participate in a vision while I was simultaneously leading my students in meditation. It is a strange and wonderful experience to be both functioning in the body and playing on another plane. This was exhilarating! Obed entered again, stepping from the Light in his usual monk's outfit. He appeared as an old man, but when he sat down beside me this time, he became young and vibrant. Something unusual was about to occur. He lifted his long slender hands to his hood and let it drop from around his face.

"OH, MY!" I exclaimed. Before me was the face of an angel! He had the largest brown eyes I have ever seen and he was grinning at me, Those eyes sparkled with total fire of life and joy. The glee and laughter that occurred in those few moments will be with me forever! I soon found out the 'other side' has a wonderful sense of humor. I know I have known him forever; he was just playing! Still giving the meditation with my class, my voice led the others while I enjoyed my own experience. While Obed and I were sitting on a little bench, I remembered my students and I said aloud,

"Ask if the Guides have a message to give to us." As soon as the words came from my lips, two very large beautiful angels joined Obed and stood beside me. Long flowing white gowns of purest white engulfed us both. They began to speak.

"The work you have begun will continue." Information was then psychically transmitted.

"What am I to do?" I asked the great beings.

"Keep on. Trust. We will make the Way for you. You do not have to do anything but respond, if you chose to do so," they answered, then they were gone. As I brought my class out of the meditation, I wiped away tears of joy. When I opened my eyes, I could see white feathers laying on the floor. The Angels had left their calling cards for all to see. Michelle, my friend and guardian angel in the physical picked them up, as she has many times since.

Since that time Obed appeared frequently to bring words of encouragement and direction. We would greet one another as old friends. I felt as though I was seeing my big brother. Once he came right out of the Light during a meditation I was giving in class saying,

"Hurry! I've much to tell you and we don't have much time!" He then proceeded to give detailed instructions as to spiritual practices and quiet times in Spirit. A good friend! I awoke one night to his voice saying,

"You need a Mandala." I heard his voice every night for the next two weeks. No instructions came, just the voice saying I needed a mandala. This was the most frustrating time I ever had with my guide.

I was preparing for a Master class and seeking Spirit one afternoon when I heard again powerfully this time,

"YOU NEED a Mandala." So I bought every book I could find and searched all the text, but was unable to locate anything that felt right or seemed to fit. This was making me a bit nutty! Driving back home after work, I stopped at the stop sign near my house. Watching a car go by I heard again,

"You need a Mandala." At that I shouted loudly back at him in frustration,

"WHAT MANDALA!!!!"

The whole set up and display of the Star of David Mandala was played out in front of me like a movie. I was given seeing the video again, complete with directions for the Star's use. I drove home immediately and set it up on my living room floor. I empowered it as I had been shown, then lay down on the floor in its center. I instantly felt the waves of energy flow through me, raising my vibration and sending me into a higher dimensional state. I had been instructed to sleep in the Mandala, so I set one up around my bed. From then on I received nightly messages and training in a new, higher realm. I couldn't wait to try it in class! It had many uses and could be used in a class with many students operating the portal to dimensions it would allow us to access. The Star would be fully powered by several Masters. That Mandala has proven to be one of the most exciting gifts from Obed! It is a dimensional gateway to other realms and the time-space continuum. I am ever thankful, and so are many others. (UT)

As I continued to lay on the floor in the soft pillows, my mind looked back at the progression of events and considered them some more. All is in Divine Order. It *is*. This is a great spiritual truth that if we could fully grasp it, I now realized, humanity would be free from so many instances of self imposed grief and condemnations of self. And free.

There are many stories of Obed I could remember now, but one in particular came to me. Obed had saved my life, my husband's, and a whole plane full of people in June of 1997. It was meant to be that my life would be put on the line for others. It was both a great test and an opportunity. Crisis and opportunity came hand in hand. (UT) My life was proving that. So, once again I re-membered the past. Putting the puzzle pieces together helped me to see the patterns of synchronistic, universal motion. There is such a thing and we all would do well to examine our past from time to time. There are patterns and movements that are regulated as a great time piece and opportunity of growth for each of us. If we don't get it the first time around, we will repeat until we do. So, I re-membered an event once again to see if this was a part of the puzzle evolving.

My husband and I were fortunate enough to go to the Paris France International Air Show. We had logged many flight hours together, as we had our own small plane, a Cessna. Our trips had been extensive with several flights to Florida and the Bahamas. We had experienced all sorts of weather, including some severe storms, but with my husband's IFR rating (Instrument Flight Rating), I had become a confident passenger. In a way, flying had become second nature to me and I had no fear. I enjoyed the incredible beauty of this wonderful planet.

It was with calm anticipation that we found ourselves sitting in a beautiful Boeing 777 on the runway at Logan Airport in Boston, Mass., headed for France. As we proceeded onto the taxiway, the pilot came on the intercom,

"What a pleasure it is to be flying this brand new Boeing 777, top of the line aircraft. Relax and enjoy the trip!"

It was going to be a wonderful, exciting vacation! Just as my husband was explaining all the new features of this particular aircraft to me, I distinctly heard a firm male voice at the right of my shoulder say,

"ILL-FATED FLIGHT."

I quickly looked behind me, but only saw a young couple engaged in conversation. The voice had not come from them. Now a bit shaken, I began to focus Energy at the tip of the 777. Using thousands of spiraling symbols, some spiraling to the right and others to the left, I encased the plane in Light. As the Light began to strengthen around us it remained unseen by my husband, or anyone else for that matter. I felt it though, and the beam flowing from my third eye was painfully strong. Again I heard,

"ILL-FATED FLIGHT", and this time recognized Obed's stern voice.

"This is certainly not my imagination and it's serious," I thought to myself.

Now we were pulling out onto the runway, preparing for takeoff. Stepping up the intensity, I put my hands on the seat to send even more energy into the plane through directly through them and my feet. The energy was pouring out; my hands began to yield their substance, becoming pure energy. My husband continued to chatter with the man on the other side of me by the window. My body was losing its form. They were speaking over me as if I didn't exist. I don't think they could see me anymore. Again I heard the voice,

"ILL-FATED FLIGHT". Then I prayed.

"Oh, Lord, there are over three hundred people on this flight! I exclaimed wildly.

"For their sake, please help me!"

The intensity of Energy forced my third eye to pour out a stream of golden white directly to the tip of the plane, extending an aura completely around and far out before us. I had become part of the force field surrounding the plane. I was completely connected to it.

The plane rumbled with the force of the engines as we began to accelerate down the runway. The wheels began to lift. Just at that moment, my eyes were opened to look out the window to my left. Descending on our left side was another plane coming in for a landing. It was coming directly into our flight path, across our runway! There was a jet landing across our runway!

An amazing thing happened at that moment. Time stood still. It really stopped. (UT) Everything began to move in slow motion, then simply stopped inside the plane. I felt no fear, but was able to watch this unfold like a spectator watching a movie. We were stopped in mid-air; the other jet was still in motion, flying across our runway. Energy, Time, and I had merged into One.

After a short period, just long enough for our terrified pilot to see the incoming plane, time resumed. I heard the engines cut back into reverse, the tires hit the ground, and we skidded into a 180-degree stop on the runway. There were screams from the passengers and those tires must have been smoking! A very shaken pilot came on the intercom. He voice shook with distress.

"I am sorry. We had to abort the flight. We had a near runway.-in-flight-incursion. He paused, then went on shakily, We will have to remain here for a while and our flight will be delayed. A thunderstorm caused an incoming plane to be vectored to another landing area, across our runway," he explained to badly shaken passengers.

As the passengers were excitedly talking and complaining, I felt the energy shift. Now instead of creating a protective barrier around the plane, I began to feel the emotion of the cockpit. Fear, irritation, and anger exploded into me as a new connection was made. It was an automatic connection; I had no control over it. Many healing symbols were sent through the newly established stream of energy to the cockpit. Pressed back against my seat, I was unable to speak to my husband. I just responded with a nod to his question as to my being all right.

Forty-five minutes later, our flight recommenced. As soon as the plane was off the ground, all connections and transfer of energy stopped flowing through me. It was as if someone pulled the plug out of the wall socket. Then I was finally able to speak to my incredulous husband and I told him of the experience I had just had. Raising my hands into the air, I cheered along with the rest of the passengers as we took off.

"Thank You, Obed!" I exclaimed silently.

In telling this story to my close friends, they have all asked the same thing– why didn't you get off the plane? I can only answer, I felt so calm. I was supposed to be there at that time, doing just what I was doing. I was needed to stop time.

I wrote in my journal: *Journal Log, June 1997*
I truly believe in the new Energy that is coming to us now, and especially to those of us who have been gifted. We have a responsibility. That responsibility extends far beyond our own existence and security, and is to serve and empower our neighbors and one another. This was just a test. I believe many of us are going to be called to service in instances such as this 'ILL-FATED FLIGHT'. These experiences are coming, and will continue to do so, because they are also teaching methods to teach us to rely not on ourselves or the limited capacity of physical self, but to remember Who and What we are. To remember our heritage as Son and Daughters of God, our Creator, who has already given to us the very same essence of I AM that is contained within the Whole. That essence of Spirit is available to each of us when we remember to connect to our Source. Somehow, I feel that we are going to be needed in service and we are just sharpening our skills and learning to use our gifts in preparation for the highest good of all.
(UT)

Now back in the present in my classroom, I put away the past memory. Yes, everything had gone along according to a great Divine Plan, I thought aloud. Now there are to be dolphins in a place with pyramids? How's that suppose to happen? I wondered, but thought I ought not to wonder after all that's happened. I know that when I have a vision, it's not because of some mistake or fancy imagination. My visions and experiences had a predestined course of action all laid out for me. The past had already proven that to me many times.

The magical mystery tour was just beginning. This vision of the dolphins meant something very important. Why was I surrounded by them. Why did I speak to them, commanding them? The only experience I had ever had with dolphins was when I was twelve years old. I was growing up in Florida when a dolphin had been swept into the inlet near our home during a violent storm one spring, and then swept out again in the fall. All summer I played with him in the warm waters. It was fun, but I never remembered speaking to them.

Rising to get another cup of tea, I walked to the tea stand holding an assortment of teas to select one and picked up a tropical tea I had bought while in the Virgin Islands. With that came another flood of memories. Dolphins are in the Caribbean. I remembered the events leading up to my teaching in the Virgin Islands. It had begun quite innocently. My mind wandered back in time…..

"Elisa! I am so happy that you came to the class! I'm excited about you becoming a Master, and *I* get to give my little cousin her attunement!" I teased. Just a few weeks earlier, she had discovered I was a Master Teacher, and I discovered she was also doing Reiki. Living several states apart, we had been on the same path unknown to one another! It was wonderful to have someone else in my own family who could understand what I was doing. We shared our experience of the attunements one afternoon.

"You know, she said, when I had my attunement, a woman told me a guide was next to me. He told her his name was HGB and that he was a relative of mine." Just then, I heard a voice speaking to me and I repeated it to her.

"Elisa, I just heard the name, Henry Boynton, spoken to me. I can hear things psychically quite clearly now. It's Henry Boynton. Do you know any Henry's in the family?" I asked. "No, but I've been hearing something, too. I thought I was crazy! she replied. It's good to know someone else hears things too, she laughed then went on, It's been saying something like 'Griffin.' Do you think we'll ever know?" she asked.

A few weeks passed by. Elisa called me, crying.

"I know who it is!" she sobbed. "Rob just came up from the basement. He has been cleaning out some old boxes from when Mom moved in with us. A paper fell at his feet and he just gave it to me. It's our family genealogy. His name is here, from the 1600's! His name is Sir Henry Griffith Boynton!-the HGB! " (UT)

A few weeks had gone by. With our experience, she had decided to take her Master Level class with me as her teacher. Elisa now sat close to me as I taught my next Master class. We prepared to do a special manifestation using a pyramid, another gift from my Guides.

"Now each of you think of something you'd like to manifest in your life, write it on the paper, and put it inside the pyramid" I instructed the students in the process we were about to use.

"I want to live in the Virgin Islands!" Elisa quipped back at me, herself in a teasing mood.

"How soon do you want to live there?" another student asked quite innocently.

"30 days! I want to be there in thirty days!" she answered quickly, teasing me.

"OK, write and put it in the pyramid." I said to her with a smile. We then began the manifestation as my Guides had taught me. Raising the energy to a high pitch, the hopes and desires of this class went straight to Divine Source!

A few days later Elisa called me.

"You're never going to believe this!" she giggled.

"Try me!" I said, then listened.

"Well, you know, we've been trying to sell this place for two years. Today a man from St. John's church came to see the house and he wants to rent it! I said 'Yes!'"

"Elisa, you said you wanted to live in the Virgin Islands!" I teased her. Isn't St John an island in the Caribbean?"

"I'll be happy just to move!" she responded.

A couple more days passed. Another call from Elisa began,

"Sue, you're never going to believe this!" I answered,

"Try me." She went on,

"When we were on the flight back from our Caribbean vacation last year, we exchanged addresses with a woman who sat next to us on the flight. She lives on St. John Island near St. Thomas. She says the house next door to her is up for rent and she just couldn't stop thinking about us. We can rent it for $1,200.00 per month! I laughed. We could never afford that! Where could I get a job that paid enough for that?"

"Aren't there international jobs for nurses?" I asked. "Try giving them a call."

A few more days went by.

"Sue, you're never going to believe this!" Elisa began.

"Try me," I laughed, used to this routine.

"I called St. John's clinic, they want me immediately! And, get this! They'll pay a thousand dollars a month for my rent in addition to my salary. I said 'yes'!"

"Where will you be living again?" I laughed, teasing her this time. She gleefully shouted,

"St. John Island, US Virgin Islands! In the Caribbean!" She was there in 45 days atop the most beautiful mountain overlooking Mahu Bay. Spirit is wonderful and really knows how to move things when things need to be moved. (UT) That included me, although I didn't know it at the time. This is how Spirit moved next. The synchronistic events were about to take on a whole new direction with great intensity!

3

Transformation Begins

Early morning of the 23rd of January 1998: My cousin was now comfortably living on an island paradise while I was shoveling snow in New Hampshire. I was going to my first appointment for the day in my "day job" as a social worker, to a client and her family. She had just moved into a new apartment the night before.

"Good morning! Or not so good," I shouted through the doorway over piles of boxes. The home was filled with unpacked boxes that had been stacked on the floor.

"Oh, Susan, I'll never find the papers in all this!" said the harried mother.

"That's OK, I can wait." I sat on a big overstuffed chair with piles of blankets behind my head and waited while Mary rummaged through the many bags and boxes looking for her paperwork.

"Got 'em!" she triumphantly exclaimed, "Now we can go."

It had begun to snow quite heavily as I drove her to her appointment. Once outside the office building, parking was difficult to find. I stayed in the car, double parked, as she ran in and kept scanning for a parking spot. Finally one appeared and I literally slid on the deep, wet snow into place.

As soon as the car stopped, two large black ravens appeared in front of it. They walked over to the driver's side and simply stood in the falling snow looking at me. I was amazed and delighted to see them even though my head was beginning to throb with pain.

"What are you two doing out in this snowstorm?" I asked them. They just stood there proud and beautiful. "Are you hungry?" I asked the great ravens through the window. "I'll see what I can find."

Finding a partially eaten bagel from my Dunkin' Donuts coffee breakfast that morning, I broke it into pieces, rolled down the window, and tossed them out into the snow. Neither of them moved nor did they take the bagel pieces. "I thank you for coming even though I didn't know why you're here." Just then my client came out, the ravens flew off and we left. UT

Being of Native American descent, and with my new understanding of nature, I understood the significance of the visit from the ravens as messengers—but of what? Two ravens with food or eating meant a gift was coming soon, but these did not eat. Perhaps a mixed blessing? By the time I dropped Mary back at her apartment my headache had blossomed into some thing like a super sinus headache and I was developing a cough. I hadn't been sick with sinus problems for over three years and this one was going to be the mother of all sinus headaches! All my attempts to clear it were not working. Reluctantly I picked up the cell phone and called my doctor to request an antibiotic. Better get ahead of this one now. My prescription was called into the drugstore.

"Hi, Betty, I'm not coming back into the office, I called work. Please cancel the rest of my appointments." I got the prescription, and went home. At 4:00 PM, it was still snowing. There were six inches of snow on the ground and I was coughing and having difficulty breathing. I pulled myself together enough to get back in the car and drove to the outpatient department of our hospital. It was filled with victims from all the snow's resulting car accidents. The staff was out straight caring for bloodied emergencies.

"Well, it looks like you're having an asthma attack," the kind attendant remarked. "We'll set you up for inhalation therapy."

"Asthma attack? I've never had asthma in my life!" I exclaimed. Are you sure?"

"Uh-huh," he mumbled as he went out to the next victim. I was given inhalation respiratory therapy, more medication, and an inhaler for asthma. "Oh, we'll give you a chest X- ray, too!" A couple of hours later he reappeared.

"Nope, no pneumonia. You say you've never had asthma? Were you exposed to any chemicals?"

"Not that I'm aware of," I stated and listed my day's activities. He sent me back home with an inhaler for asthma and a question: What happened? That began the second most incredible night of my life. The first was back in 1972 when I had a near-death and complete tunnel experience, but that's another story. My husband was now away on a spiritual retreat in Rhode Island. There was over 8 inches of snow outside, with no letup in sight. As a "good" Mom, I refused to call any of my grown children to come out in this kind of weather to take care of me. So it was the TV, my inhaler, and me. I was really sick and getting more so every minute. I had no strength left. I fell into a restless sleep while sitting up on the couch just trying to breathe. Around 2:00 AM I found myself in waves of energy and color. The waves were flowing through me and my whole body was tingling. I was leaving my body. I'd done this before.

My astral body lifted from my physical body and was hovering above it. For all intents and purposes, I had died.

"Susan, we have to speak with you," they said. All three of my guides were there. "Obed, what is happening to me? Is it my time?" I greeted him.

"Be at peace. We are here to instruct and help you. You will completely recover. This time of separation from your usual life activities will give you time to allow your physical body to rest and reflect on all that we have shown you." He spoke gently to me.

Instantly, I realized within my heart's desires were being neglected in that not enough time was available for my practice of Reiki and for teaching. I was so busy! I worked forty hours seeing clients, and taught just on weekends.

"You're not able to integrate the teachings and the information that we are giving in dream-state and during waking hours. This information is for the world and is not being preserved. This will be a great loss!" UT

"I understand," I said as I considered his words.

"While you are set aside, we will use this opportunity to begin to change your biological makeup and DNA. This is necessary for you to continue on your chosen path. Reaching your spiritual goals, as you yourself have requested, requires the remaking of your body's cellular structure. Many releases will occur through this illness. Much has been held in your cellular memory and must be discharged through your normal physical human processes." UT

I listened quietly as took in their words to me.

"You will recover, but it will take time. We request that you, during this time, write, write, and write! The information that has been given to you must be shared and distributed for the progression of not only your students, but for many others." UT

I was beginning to understand what an opportunity I had missed in not writing down all that had been shared with me. Much had already been lost. With that thought, Obed continued, "Also, the more you share this information with others, the more we will give. We will impart to you every three months, as it had been previously in your instruction, information to be shared with the world. We will also use other means not yet disclosed to you. All this is provided you continue to disperse the information that the world needs so desperately at this time." UT

I wholeheartedly agreed, and understood this was out of love and concern for others.

"You know, there is always and will always be love and acceptance of all you do or choose not to do, that is your right as a being of Light. We honor your decision." UT

I could sense the urgency of their message. There was also a deep feeling of sadness that was conveyed to me though their words and thoughts.

"We have sought to provide others with these gifts so they may share them with the world. Some of these chose to withhold their gifts so as to become the best in their field as healers or teachers. They have developed a competitive spirit with their fellow 'selves' for monetary gain."

They paused and I could feel their emotional anguish.

"Most distressing of all: the ownership of the gifts was attempted by mankind, not acknowledging the gifts are from the Giver of All

Gifts. Spirit cannot be bought or sold. Spirit is a gift to mankind. Acknowledge Spirit and never seek to own Spirit. With this knowledge, you will succeed where others have failed." (UT)

I understood the message clearly. I was not to become ensnared in this pit. They left me with much to consider. I would be well again and I was determined to remember as much as I could of the material I had previously neglected.

The next morning my husband returned early from his retreat. He found me lying on the couch and then rushed me to the hospital. As he questioned me at the hospital, I remembered my client's words the previous morning. She stated she had used something to rid her house of insects. A call to her revealed she had used two entire house-size insecticide canisters inside a small enclosed area, saturating all her furniture and belongings. I sat that morning in her house inhaling insecticide. My lungs were burned from the chemicals. I indeed had a chemical exposure while at her home. I have found that I am extremely sensitive to all that is of a chemical nature. It affects my body in ways that not all others experience.

The next six weeks I was in recovery from pneumonia. Between the nebulizer inhalation therapy, when I was able, I was at the computer . I began writing the instructions for the techniques the Masters and Guides had been giving me over the many months prior to my illness.

One morning very early, I awoke knowing that information had been imparted during the night. I didn't know what it was at the time. I just knew something had come through that was very important. Following intuitive instruction, I quietly got up out of bed, took a pencil and paper, sat on the couch and began to write. This was truly my first experience with automatic writing. The technique given that morning was the Spiritual Crystal Pyramid Healing Technique. As I sat on the couch, my hand began to write words and draw diagrams, without the engagement of my mind's control.

My good friend, Michelle, came over that afternoon for my daily Reiki treatment. We had already been given a wonderful new technique to relieve my asthma-like condition through the use of selenite wands. That technique, too, was given during the night; I was often called to receive the 'downloading' of information around 3 AM.

I looked forward to the treatments as I could actually feel my lungs opening and healing with each session. I was much better already!

I excitedly told her about the automatic writing. Later she would be the first to experience the Pyramid healing. It is awesome and I had never experienced anything like it! I am still amazed to see and feel the extent to which the chakras open to the energy, often expanding to the height of 4-15 feet, or more! We learned how to heal spiritual issues and past life issues on a level not experienced since the time of the Atlantean culture. As the chakras open to these levels, the residue of past experiences are laid bare and ready for healing with no traumatic experience for the client. It is a user-friendly and gentle healing.

Finally the first Reiki instruction manual was ready to be printed. I gathered all the typed sheets into a pile. In anticipated celebration, my husband and I went out for Chinese food the night before. We talked about all that had transpired over the past six weeks and my manual which would go to the printer the next day. After our dinner we opened our fortune cookies. Mine read: "Tomorrow will be an extraordinary day!" I was thrilled with the confirmation and looked forward to bringing my manual to be published. Tomorrow would be the day! I would use it at my next Reiki II class.

The next morning, I drove to the printer's shop and sat in the little four-chair waiting room, checking and rechecking the papers in my hand. I was very nervous. I'd not done this before and it represented so much to the world, and to me. I wanted this to be completed properly, a good work that would be beneficial to the world, but also to thank my Guides who had worked right along with me on the project! When it was my turn, I placed the still unnumbered pages on the counter. I explained to the attendant this was because there were more pages to come, and I didn't know where they would fit yet. But I needed to have this pile of papers made up into a manual as soon as possible. She understood I was inexperienced, and worked closely with me to put it all together to our mutual satisfaction. This was really going to happen!

As I turned to leave, a thin, young man dressed in blue jeans and a t-shirt was seated in the waiting area. He was grinning widely at me with a big smile that just lit up his whole face. I couldn't help but notice his incredible big brown eyes. Surprised at this reaction from a complete stranger, I smiled back and nodded my head as I walked out the door. I was instantly embarrassed thinking he must have heard me, and seen how little I knew about print jobs, and went out the door. Getting into the car I still wondered if I knew him. Continuing to drive away, now several miles closer to my workplace, his eyes just kept coming back to me. I thought,

"I know him from somewhere, but I know I've never met him before. Where have I seen him? You know, I thought, he looks so much like my son!"

That's when I realized—those eyes! *Those eyes belonged to Obed*! Obed, my spiritual guide and friend! He had manifested in physical form and smiled—smiled at me with great joy and satisfaction! He did that for me. I pulled over and just let my tears of joy flow!

"Thank you, Obed, for all your kind and gentle love. What you must have gone through to do this for me! I am grateful and will love you, my friend, forever!" (UT)

With my new found understanding of forever, that's a long, long time! This was *truly* an extraordinary day!

A short time later I was called to the home of a young woman in her thirties. She had cystic fibrosis. She was at the end of her time here on earth and was on a double-lung transplant list. I had arranged a guardian to care for her baby should she die as part of my role as a social worker.

"Please!" she cried. "I just want to live long enough to see my little boy grow up and go to school. I want him to remember me." She gasped for air despite the oxygen tube in her nose.

"I can only give you the energy. There are no guarantees; all is in God's hands. But I know it has helped me breathe when I had pneumonia," I told her. "Maybe it'll help you too!" I began holding my hands over her chest, sending energy, as she sat up on a chair. She was unable to lie down.

"Oh, stop!" she cried. "It hurts, it hurts!" I rescanned her chest. The dark energy was cold, solid beneath my hands. She was encased in an armor plating of dark energy. The Reiki energy couldn't even penetrate the mass. My attempts to place more energy into that solid block actually hurt her.

"Let's try one more time," I suggested while picking up my selenite wand. I held it behind her, drawing, gently pulling the old energy out, as Obed had shown me in the night's lessons. After a few moments, I put my hand beaming energy to her chest. The energy was now going in. She began to relax.

"That feels so much better," she said. "I can get a breath now, thank you!"

I saw her for treatments two more times. That's all she would allow. Two years later I saw her getting out of her car as she was dropping her child off at school; no oxygen bottles, no tubes or any other appliances to keep her alive were present. Her prayer had been answered according to her request, her child was now at day care.

Selenite is a powerful tool to be used in cases where the person's auric energy is so congested it can not flow. It opens and clears out emotional debris from the aura and chakras, allowing one to send in new healing energy to begin repair of the physical body. Thank you, Obed!

> •*In 2002 I was called to her hospital bedside. She was not dying of cystic fibrosis but a brain tumor. Her child was now in 1st grade. She had been calling my name and my supervisor at work told me to go to her, so I did. When I arrived, she was barely able to speak. She lifted her hands to her mouth and managed to get out one word, "schedule". I got it. "Yes, I answered her, all is according to your schedule, your child is in school and has a good home to live in, I understand and it is OK." With that she smiled and I hugged her, and told her I loved her. She smiled as I left and she died within the week. (UT)*
>
> •_____

As soon as the manuals were completed I found myself far from home. It was really wonderful how that all progressed from a manual to ending up in a paradise. For while I was still in recovery, I was given an opportunity. Remember? Crisis-Opportunity? I got a phone call near the end of my 6 week illness. " Susan, I am so glad to hear that you are feeling better! Elisa exclaimed! Would you come to the Virgin Islands to teach? You may stay with us and teach our nursing staff."

"I'd love to come!" I excitedly exclaimed to her.

"There's only one thing, she continued, you'll have to teach on the beach. Is that OK?"

"I can't imagine anything so perfect for the Energy and for Spirit! YES!"

So, it was arranged that I was to go to St. John to teach at my cousin Elisa's new workplace. The island nurses and medical personnel wanted the training. They didn't want it in a classroom; they wanted attunements in the natural setting of the sacred places on their island.

My mind brought me back there once again. I'll always love the classes on Mahu Beach! I stood under a pavilion teaching the class day after day while watching the manta rays swim back and forth in the crystal waters. Spirit can be wonderful sometimes. But we also went a few other places, not so easy! One in particular!

We were hiking down the side of an old volcano to a sacred spot under waterfalls. It took us an hour and a half to walk down the old trail. I could sense the ancient spirits who still dwelt there. I remember speaking softly to them and feeling their presence all around me as I followed the group down the path. This had once been the drop-off point of the African natives who had been stolen from their country to serve here as the slaves of the sugar plantation owners. Many still remained, trapped in the spirit realm in the old energy of fear and rage. I could feel emotional pain and their etheric touch. In fact the night before I awoken with many touches stroking my face. (UT)

"I know you are here, I spoke into the darkness, but you may not touch me. I will help you soon, when the time is right. I will open the Pillar Of Ascension for you"

Prior to this trip, Archangel Michael had come and had given me the Michael Pillar of Light for ascension. Many beings that had been trapped in the lower dimensions would now be freed through this gift to the world. I would use this on St. John.

We arrived at the bottom of the volcano near the entrance of a valley, and there before us was an ancient pool of water. Reeds and butterflies surrounded the entire area. Looking up we could see the waterfalls and native flowers all blossoming profusely. Surrounding the edge of the pooled water were old etched petroglyphs of alien looking faces and spiral symbols. This was truly a sacred place. Here was the only natural source of fresh water I had seen on the island, and it appeared to have once been a ritual site for the ancients. (UT)

I felt wonderful in the sunlight, and the breeze was soft and inviting. In order to secure our space for the Maha Karuna attunements that were about to begin, we used a symbol to seal off the trail to this place just for the time we needed, and asked that no one interfere with our ceremony.

As I began the initiations to the symbols and the energy, I was immediately engulfed in a cloud of dragonflies. These sprites had at least four-inch wingspans of vivid reds, greens, turquoise and lime green. The little nature spirits had joined us and were assisting in the energies. (UT)

When the ceremony was complete and the group was relaxing at the poolside, two people came down the trail into our closed area. We were surprised, as we had sealed off the area. So, we asked

"Do either of you do energy work?" They quickly looked up,

"Oh, we both do!" The only two allowed in were those attuned to the energies of Reiki-like spirits! We removed the time and space block. About five minutes later, twenty or so people came down the path. Somewhere in time they had been backed-up on that trail, waiting for time to resume. We decided to leave and start up the long upward trail. Just then one of the group cried out, "Oh, my God! I'm supposed to be at a meeting in an hour!"

He had to get back for an appointment and hadn't realized how late it was. He had less than an hour to get back up to the highway. Since it took us over an hour to get down, forty-five minutes **up** was really asking too much! I had just recovered from the pesticide exposure which gave me double pneumonia; breathing was just starting to get easier. I figured it would take me two to three hours to go back up as I'd have to make a lot of "catch-my-breath" stops.

"There is another symbol we can use to alter time for us as we go back up the trail. We'll all have to do this together," I said. They stared at me in disbelief. (UT)

I said, "Yes, it can be done! This is what we have to do."

Together we began to focus our energies for a time distortion. We wanted to slow time to the world, but not to us. It seemed I had to stop every few feet up that steep path! I rested about twenty times and

I was really exhausted. The effort of climbing was taking all my energy and breath. Up ahead was a giant old tree with a massive base. I made my way over to it and fell into its crevice.

"Old One, wrap me in your arms and feed strength into my being," I begged. Have you ever hugged a tree? You can ask for strength and it will give unconditionally of its love to you. This old Master gave a green light like I've never experienced before and I could feel myself grow in its strength. Rising up I had renewed strength and vigor.

"Thank you, my friend." Much strengthened now, I would be able to continue. We arrived at the top in about an hour and fifteen minutes. Amazing! Cut off about two hours Earth time, but you see there really is no time—it *is* an illusion.

A small problem arose while we were on St. John. They were in the midst of a terrible drought. We couldn't shower or flush toilets. The plants and people were suffering. Each tropical home in the islands is built with a large cistern beneath the house. In the north we'd call that a cellar, but on the island it's filled with runoff water from the providence of heaven-rain. The cisterns were dry and the people could not afford to buy water. To import water meant an expense of about $200.00 per week, if you could even get it. We were on strict rationing.

"Elisa, the island needs rain," I complained one evening as we sat out on the veranda overlooking the bay. I want you to help me."

"Help you do what?" she asked.

"Make rain, I answered, but it needs to come only at night so I can continue the classes on the beach." She looked at me as though I had lost my mind completely.

"Yes, we can do this, but only with prayer and the earth symbols, I answered her look.(UT) It must be in alignment with the will of the Divine and never be for destructive purposes. Obed had given the symbol and training the night before, I explained.

"The need here is so great that I believe it will be answered, if we ask. Will you assist me?"

"Yes, we can give it a try" she replied.

Late that night after the children were in bed, we stood on the veranda looking out over St. John's Bay and St. Thomas Island. The lights from the town below sparkled as we took in their beauty. We drew the Great Symbol to connect the energy of the Divine to the Earth plane with our request for rain at night upon the islands. Walking back into the house, we were both solemn, deeply considering what we had just done. Saying goodnight, we went to bed for much-needed sleep. Sometime during the night I heard the soft drumming of rain on the porch and got up to close the window. From that point on it rained every night from 4-6 AM. Elisa was ecstatic. Now she was really getting excited.

A few days later I was going to the British Virgin Islands to continue giving classes. A group there wanted to have their Master attunements on an island paradise in a place called The Baths. I taught on the way over in the boat as a few fought seasickness; it was definitely a different sort of class. I'm used to that now, as it seems Spirit guides me into some unusual places and circumstances. When we arrived at the Baths, the place was absolutely mobbed with tourists. As we walked along with groups of people through the caverns of huge boulders, our feet were in warm, ankle-deep waters.

"How and where could I possibly give an attunement here?" I asked the group.

" We could do it over there," someone said, pointing to a sandy area.

"No, this is too sacred. This is a Master attunement; we'll need a private, sacred space." (UT)

We stopped to discuss this while people continued to shove past us. As we stood there discussing options, a small, starving dog approached us.

"Oh, the poor thing!" cried Elisa.

"I think I have something to feed it," I said, seeing its concave stomach. I reached into my bag and pulled out a muffin. "I have a muffin. Here boy!" I called. I broke off a piece and gave it to the hungry black and white dog. He took the muffin while we watched him. Instead of eating it, he took it over to a corner and buried it in the sand.

"Can you believe that? asked Paul. It's starving and instead of eating it, he buried it."

The little black and white dog came back, looked up at me, asking for more of the muffin.

"OK, boy, maybe you want to save some." I broke off another piece and he took it to the opposite direction and again buried the muffin in the sand. He returned and I took another piece and gave it to him.

"What's going on here?" I wondered aloud to the group. He took that piece and took it to an area behind me to bury it. I began to catch on. "I understand! The dog has gone to the North, to the South, to the West!" I said to the group.

" That's right!-Look!" They all exclaimed.

"This time we follow the dog!" I whispered. Sure enough, he came forward again and took the last piece from my hand. He now went to the East. He led us into another cave area where he crouched and crawled through a small opening in a wall of rock at sand level.

"Can we fit in there?" someone asked.

"If he's taking us here, and he fits, I think so," I said. "Take off your packs." We took off our packs. I dug out some of the sand so I could squeeze into the hole and crawled in on my stomach behind the small dog. The others followed close behind. As soon as my head was through, I was thrilled!

"Wait 'til you see this!" I quipped. We came out into a large glorious cavern filled with light streaming in from above.

"WOW! This is beautiful! " came the excited exclamations.

In the center was a flat table-topped boulder that was just the perfect size for the students to sit on while they had their attunements. It was completely private. We had our own room. (UT) Spirit will provide for you.

"Nobody could possibly find us here!" Paul sang.

Looking up straight overhead the sky opened magnificently. Sunbeams fell right on the boulder where they were to have their attunements to the Master energies. On one of the highest roof boulders there was a star engraved on the rock. It beamed above us in the sunlight. The little dog went over to the entrance and lay down.

"Guess it's time for us to begin with the guard dog at the door!"

I smiled at the eager faces. The attunement was beautiful. We cried together in pure JOY as Spirit had once again responded to our every need. In thanks to our little dog who now came over to us, we all laid our hands on him and gave a Reiki thanks. We 'Reiki'd' him into oblivion. We quietly crawled back out of the cavern into the crowds while he slept that wonderful Reiki sleep. Later the little dog rejoined us in gleeful play, bouncing and dancing around us. We all wanted to bring him home. That was not possible, so we decided to at least provide for him.

"Here is some money for you to buy the dog some dog food," Elisa said as she held out money to the gate attendant.

"What dog?" he asked.

"Why, that little dog over there," she responded in surprise indicating the dog standing with us.

"I don't see any dog, Lady," he answered. Stunned, Elisa said "Well, here's some money to feed him if you ever do see him!"

Message: "Be awake, Susan, Spirit works in many ways to provide for all your needs if you can but see, not with your eyes, but with your heart!" *Log book April, 1998*

****

Several months later in the fall, long after the classes on the island, I had a telephone call from Elisa.

"Sue, we're really scared! There's a monster hurricane coming directly towards us, a category 4 storm. We can't get a flight off the island and we're going to have to ride it out. The winds are over 200 miles per hour and that means near total destruction of the island."

"Elisa, where are you going to stay?" I anxiously inquired.

"We have a little crawl space place that's all cement behind the water cistern that we can crowd into—that'll give some protection. The roof may blow off, but the place is like a small hall, all cement. We should be safe there, but the natives have nothing but shacks on the sides of the hills. The natives are blasting their loud speakers for the people warning them and saying the island is being punished for its sins. They know they are going to die! I know their negativity is bringing that thing down on us and we've only got about three hours before it makes landfall. This may be the last time I speak to you, Sue, for a long time! What can we do?"

"Elisa, I am going to tell you how to attune your children and your husband to the energy so they can help you during the storm. There are several things you must do." I began channeling as now I was seeing the "video play" of the process from my Guides.

"I'll be helping here too!"

She was instructed to lay out a light barrier all along the coast of St. John and an energy grid over her house. During the storm she and the rest of the family were to hold the energy. They were making a light barrier to protect the island and their property. (UT)

"I have to go now, Elisa, as I need to do my part, too. I am being shown what to do and it must be done now! Pray for me!" We hung up and I was uncertain if I'd ever see her again.

My part was a bit weird. I had been shown how to bring up the storm in miniature, at my house in New Hampshire, and had been told and shown how to divert the storm.

"OK," I thought. Let's get started!" I said to my Guides.

There in the living room, I 'brought up' the storm. I could see the eye, its massive size, and the clouds as they spun beneath my hands. I could see the outline of St. John. As the winds were flowing through my fingers, I tried time and time again to push the storm away from the island, but it kept pushing back, like soft taffy folding back on itself. I wasn't making much progress. I felt the emotion of the storm, and it was furious. How can a storm have emotion? This was mean and angry!

"What can I do?" I silently, frantically spoke to my Guides.

"CUT the winds!" was the swift reply. With that, I began to use my whole arm and sliced through the raging winds. Cutting, cutting, cutting, slicing their power, I could feel the storm diminishing. Around and around I ran in the living room slicing the storm into pieces. Exhausted, I fell on the floor.

"This is all I can do," I thought.

"No, it's not!" came the reply. "Seal it now, all along the coastline."

Finishing the process, I sent it up into the Divine to seal and keep it. What would happen now was in God's hands. I slept on the floor.

The next day my brother called,

"Sue, I just spoke to Elisa."

"How? All the lines are down. I was just watching the TV and they said not to call as all the lines were down and they're on emergency status!"

"Well," he said, "it seems that she's the only one on the island with power and telephone! No one can understand it, but she's got people coming from all over the island to contact families and emergency personnel. They're all OK and she wanted me to tell you thanks! What did you have to do with this?" he laughed.

"I'm not telling!" I teased.

"Seems as though the storm diverted around the island just before it hit and the winds dropped down to 85 miles per hour. Poles are down, but the people are OK on St. John and St. Thomas! Thank God!"

A few days later I had a call from her.

"Sue, you wouldn't believe it! The Grid held fine, but a few times I thought we couldn't hold it! We did I guess because we're still the only ones on this side of the island who have power. Doesn't make sense, but I don't care. The pole across the street is down and my neighbors have no power. It's amazing! The natives here are dancing in the street. They know a miracle has occurred! Sue, I know this is going to sound strange, but did you feel the storm?"

"How exactly do you mean that?" I asked.

"Well, I could feel the screaming anger inside of it and it was frightening." She answered quietly.

"Yes, I did. I couldn't understand at first how a storm could have anger, but it certainly did. I could feel it as I tried to push it out of the way of the island. It seemed to have a mind of its own. This is really strange, and something I never expected. I don't know why, and it's something I do not understand completely." (UT)

"Sue, after the storm passed by St. John, it went directly over to the Dominican Republic. It regained its strength in the bay, the winds rose and slammed their island. There are at least three hundred people who died as a result, probably many more, as some of the native families have completely disappeared from the island. I feel sorry for them. I wish we could have done more." She paused.

"Next time we will, Elisa. We're just learning," I sadly answered. (UT)

4

Faith and Family

My path as a Shambhala Master was very difficult for my children and entire family. I know my children often thought their Mom had totally lost her mind! I frequently spoke to my daughter, Faith, of the angels who were coming to me, speaking wisdom and guiding me. At twenty-six she was independent and a powerful woman in her own way, but Angels just didn't fit in her life. Then one morning the phone rang.

"Mom, I'm calling from the hospital. I'm all right!" she said as she heard me gasp. "I just want to tell you, I believe in Angels." Her speech was slurred with her tears.

"What happened!" I cried.

"I was driving to work this morning and was distracted for a moment. I reached down for something. My car hit the shoulder on Rt. 93. My car flipped over three times. I didn't have my seatbelt on…." She paused.

"Mom, they held me in my seat-I could feel their arms around me as they held me in and the car flipped over and over! The Angels, they held me…" *(UT)*

I went to look at the car with her later. The whole roof had crushed down on top of the passenger seat. The entire roof was caved in, except for one spot—over her head. Not only did they hold her in, they held up the roof of the car over her head and shoulders. You could actually see the outline of her body in the wreckage. After the car stopped flipping, she simply hopped out the broken window and sat waiting for the police. She didn't have any injuries. I brought her home and gave her a good Shambhala treatment.

Several months later, my mother was taken to the hospital in critical condition. She had been living in a nursing home not far from my home in New Hampshire. We had moved her there from another state after Alzheimer's incapacitated her about two years previously. I wanted her close to me so I could give her Shambhala treatments.

She was highly medicated and in a terrible state when she first arrived. It was so sad to see such a vibrant woman reduced to a small pitiful being who often did not recognize me or the rest of her family. Her eyes were half shut and she was drooling. I cried. My heart was absolutely broken.

Every day I went to the nursing home and gave direct treatment to her head. Many days I went home in tears, barely able to drive. What a horrible disease! It robs the elderly of their only comfort, their memories, their families. My heart goes out to every family who suffers with this! I also commend the angels, the nurses and CNAs who care for them.

After about three months of treatments, I began to see a change in her. She knew me: she remembered my visits and the conversations we had the day before. I spoke to the doctor about reducing her medications, and they did. We began to have conversations about the past and her memory was definitely improving. She loved the treatments and soon had no more pain in her spine. It was wonderful when I could go in and ask her if she wanted Reiki for pain and she'd brightly answer me

"No, I don't have any pain!" She was as surprised as I was. For someone who'd had polio as a child and arthritis all of her life, this was wonderful. I was getting my mother back, a little at a time, day by day! We even started an afghan together.

But one day I was called to the emergency room. Her bowel had somehow punctured; it had burst and gone unnoticed by the nursing home until it was too late. They thought she had a touch of the flu, but she was dying. She would have to have emergency surgery. At her age, surgery itself was a life-threatening risk. I spoke to her about it and she said she wanted to have the operation. We both knew it was unlikely she would survive the operation and she asked me to call the family together. They all came. Crowded into the little hospital room, we took turns holding her hand and saying our good-byes. Faith and the others watched as when she had pain, the Shambhala energy eased it immediately, and she was calm. I thank God every day that I had the ability to help her.

As it happened, there was a terrible July lightening storm and tornado like winds that swept through the area. Several trees had fallen on unsuspecting people in their cars. The electrical systems at the hospital had been affected. Many emergency patients were being brought into surgery. My mother was placed on non-emergency status. The young and those having a chance to survive had priority. As we waited for her turn for surgery, several hours passed and we held her hand. Finally, she was taken down to the pre-surgical waiting area. My brother and I were allowed to stay with her as she waited there. She began to speak in Spanish, to someone else in the room, invisible and standing at the end of the gurney.

"Mom, what are you saying? I don't understand you." I exclaimed, astonished at her fluent speech. She looked over at me and said indicating to the end of the gurney,

"He asked me, 'Are you anxious Senorita?' and I told him 'no'." (UT)

It seemed to make perfect sense to her! My brother and I just looked at each other as she spoke to him. She then began to speak in Hebrew. My mother is French Canadian.

Soon we were in the waiting area outside the operation room. We stood on either side of her holding her hand. I put my hand under the back of her neck and continued to send the energy. After a bit, she became very excited. And began saying,

"EL MOYA, EL MOYA! Oh, how beautiful! Au, Se Bleu! Au, SE Bleu! Oh, how beautiful!" She seemed to be listening to someone, seeing beyond what we could see. Then she began to be very agitated and fearful.

"NO...No...No! I don't want to go!" She mentioned a name, my brother began to try to calm her. I prayed for the Presence of Christ and for my father. She calmed once again staring into the ceiling, listening to a voice we could not hear. Across the room a woman had been brought out of surgery. She was convulsing and all the medical personnel were crowded around the young woman, frantically trying to save her life. Again my mother was not priority. My brother and I held on. I kept giving energy and demanded,

"Dad, Where are you? We need you here NOW!"

I instantly felt warmth and saw a bright magenta presence beside me. He was here, right by my side! My mother turned her head and looked just behind my shoulder,

"OH, se bleu!" And she smiled. He was here. She then looked at me saying,

"You are so beautiful! Your colors!" Then she began to look around the room excitedly.

"El Velvedere, El Velvedere" meaning "they are all here, they are all here."

She began to greet her family by name, now all present before her: her mother, her cousins and her aunts. They were all waiting for her.

"The Father's Child, The Father's Child, The Father's Child," she began to softly chant, with an angelic look on her face.

My brother started asking,

"Do you mean...?", naming each of the children in the family.

"No. No. No," she would say again and again, then, "The Father's Child".

"Les, that's not what she's talking about," I said to him, tears flowing down my face. He looked up impatiently at me. Looking at her again he said,

"Mom, who is the father's child?"

"I AM," she answered powerfully directly to him. I gasped! Mom got IT!

"Yes, you are Dear One! Always and Forever!" I thought as they finally came to take her into surgery. (UT)

We waited upstairs with the other family members. I told them of her visitation from our long-deceased family members, and the things she said. Some cried, some looked a bit astounded, others couldn't believe.

"That's OK. I know," I thought. I sat in a corner and closed my eyes and prayed, giving thanks and speaking to those unseen all around us. After a while, I felt myself go into deep trance.

"Suzie, Suzie, Come! Come!" A great, beautiful light being was above me. It was my mother! She was playing and dancing in Light above me, having a wonderful time. She began to pull me up. A great pulling began on my crown, pulling me up. She was pulling me out of my body. I nearly shouted at her.

"No, Mom, I can't go! You may go, but it is not *my* time!" I felt her leave. I opened my eyes, stood and walked out into the corridor.

"Its' been a long time," I said to my son in the hall, "go and find out what has happened." He returned a few minutes later with the doctor.

"She made it through the surgery," he said. I nodded. She had survived. "You may see her when she's out of recovery."

The next day my friend Michelle accompanied me to see her in ICU. She was quietly resting and responsive to us. We gave her energy together. As we began to leave she said,

"Oh, don't go!"

"Mom, we have to. You need rest and you need to let your body heal." With that she looked directly at me, smiled, and said,

"My *next* body is *beautiful!*" She knew I had seen her.

Within a week's time she was ready to go home. The night before she was to be released, I was sitting beside the hospital bed with her. She was quiet and resting, dozing off and on, very peaceful. As she slept, I once again I felt the pulling on my crown.

"No, Mom, I can't go with you," I said silently, speaking to her sleeping form. "You have to stop this. If you must go, I understand, but I have much to do. I love you, but I cannot go now." She stirred and woke.

"Mom, I'll be back in the morning to pick you up. I love you!" We said goodnight, kissed, and I was driving away when again the pulling started. "No, Mom, I can't go with you!" I stated firmly this time. Just then, a solitary raven flew across my windshield as I drove out of the hospital parking lot. I began to cry.

An hour later, my brother called saying, "Sue, I was with Mom just after you left. I got home and as I walked in the door, they called me from the hospital. She died right after we left."

" I know," I cried. Three times since she has come to speak to me in Spirit saying,

"Suzie, we didn't understand, we didn't know!" (UT)

"Suzie, we didn't understand, we didn't know!"

"Suzie, we didn't understand, we didn't know!"

"It's OK, Mom, Dad...I didn't understand either! I didn't know."

I debated with myself for quite a while about putting this into print. I feel that somewhere, someone will find comfort in my story of my mother's passing. Her story ought to be told, she would have it that way. She is the Father's Child. We are the Father's Children! That knowledge is life transforming. We live on in glorified bodies, there is no death. She saw El Moya, she saw the Christ, my father and all her family. They were there with her to aid and to comfort her. In her passing, she has given new life and understanding. (UT)

Soon after my mother's passing, Faith and her father, my first husband, had their attunements to Shambhala. The powerful energies of the Divine God and Goddess and the Christ Light filled them both. Mahatma, Unconditional Love energy flowed freely that day for both my daughter and the man I had divorced. Even though she had never heard of the Eye of Horus, Faith entered the sacred passageway through the Eye, through the pyramid, during her attunement. A White Dove, the symbol of the Holy Spirit anointed her.

"What does that mean?" she asked me afterwards.

"Honey, we'll have to have a long talk," I smiled. And we talked a lot. Her father, who I had divorced ten years prior, was now sitting on the couch for twenty minutes in a complete ecstatic state. Faith and

I just stared in amazement as he was enraptured in the Light of God's Touch. When he finally opened his eyes, he looked at us and quietly said, "Now I understand why you do this." It was the beginning of his transformation. (UT)

Soon Faith was ready for Merkaba activation, or the Spirit - Body activation of the rotating energy fields that surround each of us. I took her to a class we could be in a class together. Merkaba activation is an incredible experience and was once only for those of the highest spiritual training in secret mystery school training. With the activation reaching altered states and traveling heavenly planes is possible.

During one particular meditation and activation of our fields, we were guided to our "home planet." In meditation I felt myself in the most clear blue waters I had ever seen far surpassing the turquoise of the beautiful Caribbean! Beautiful, and with perfect grace I swam. I swam *beneath* the water, my long tail gliding me without effort as I explored the beauty below the waves. As the water began to become more shallow, I realized I was approaching the sandy white beach ahead.

Without even a thought or concern, my body began to transform; where once there was a tail of a mermaid, now, I had legs. Sparkling with the Light of a full sun upon the glistening drops of water on my naked body, I arose from the water and walked onto the beach. My daughter was also coming out of the water beside me. (UT)

Coming out of the meditation, Faith and I said simultaneously, "I was swimming in the most beautiful turquoise waters!" We stared at each other in amazement.

"Faith, I did, too! Did you see the beach?" I asked.

"Yes, I approached a brilliant, sandy white beach. As I came up out of the water onto the sand," I started to say, then she cut in. "I was like a fish-being, but, when I came up out of the water, I changed!, I changed into a person with long slender legs" she exclaimed, looking intently at me.

"Faith, we both experienced the transformation from a water-being to a human being and stood on the white sands as humans. We have had identical visions. We are definitely from the same place.

Could it be that we come from a people who are capable of an existence as both mermaid and human?" She looked intently, deeply, at me.

"How can anyone have the same vision as someone else?" she inquired, very puzzled. "That's not possible. But, we did!" We continued to share our experience and knew we had been in the same location plus were both the same type of being. I'd never experienced this before either. Outside, during break we each talked to others in the group. Our instructor indicated to us both to come closer, then he spoke.

"Are you mother and daughter?" he asked.

"Why yes, how did you know? No one ever thinks we are even related!" I answered "You've got the same energy," he smiled, nodded, then went on his way.

"Well, I guess that's confirmation, Faith. We may not look alike but obviously have the same energy, and are from the same planet anyway! How would I look with a tail?" I quipped.

****

Coming back into the present moment and leaving the past behind me, I had much to consider. I had had another vision, a dolphin vision had occurred. I had spoken to them and they heard me. " Go, tell them we are coming!" I had said. Not only had they heard me, I had commanded them to go and tell someone, or something, that I was coming. Not just "I", but we.

Somehow, I definitely had a connection to the dolphins. Maybe my playtime with them as a child had more meaning than I thought or remembered? Raised off the coast of Florida, I had a whole summer with a beautiful dolphin playmate that had washed into the bay during a big storm. We swam together often in the clear waters.

Something is happening! I thought, but what? Sometimes the path is so uncertain, sometimes things happen and don't seem to fit anywhere in the world we are living in at that moment. But, I had already learned a great lesson and one that all Light workers must.

Susan Isabelle

ALL is in Divine Order and there are stepping stones along the way that are sometimes hidden underneath the brush and heaps of garbage of daily existence. We must seek diligently beneath all that to find the truth and once found, forget nothing, for all is vital to understanding the whole. (UT)

I decided to go home. I would journal this day too, for somehow it was one of those puzzle pieces that didn't seem to fit right now, but it would someday. I had many questions and wondered how this was going to weave itself in the future realm.

A puzzle, a puzzle. How would this all fit?

Part 2
Heaven and Earth

October 1999   "Hi, Greg!" I said as I made my way into a store in Hooksett, New Hampshire. Around me were some of the most spectacular stones and crystals I'd ever seen accumulated in one place. Greg is the proprietor and as I've told him before, he just has a way of drawing in high-powered energy stones.

"I got your message about the Elestial crystal today and came right down after work to see it," I said. He lovingly handed me the crystal.

"It's amazing how Mother Nature can produce such beauty! Just look at those formations. It is about two pounds in weight and has beautiful layer upon layer of block quartz configurations," he said. I held the stone searching its beautiful face. You could actually see within the crystal formations. It was like looking into little square rooms of a house, built one atop the other.

"I've always wanted one of these and I'm really happy you were able to find it for me!" I stroked the stone feeling its energy. He smiled saying,

"Yes, that one came from Brazil and is especially nice. I know you'll enjoy it."

After taking the stone home I cleansed it of all negative programming, as I'd been shown by the Guides of the night. I had now begun to teach the importance of crystals in my classes, their care and the necessity of cleaning stones that may have picked up undesirable energies over time. I really didn't feel or sense any, but just to be safe, I did the cleansing ritual. Reprogramming the stone, I sent my thought energy into it to reveal all its treasures of Light. I knew there were many. (UT)

Later that night I sat and began to activate my Merkaba fields. The Merkaba are counter-rotating energy fields that surround every human being's body. These energy fields would bring both the crystal and me into a higher vibrational rate with the specific activation. It was my hope to connect with the stone's consciousness in this manner. By using the Merkaba field I could then communicate with the energy of the stone as we would both be on the same wavelength. Just as we are able to tune into a certain frequency on our radio or television, we may also tune into other frequencies with our own vibrational processes once we've been trained to use them. The ancient knowledge contained in the Merkaba, along with the instructions I had received several months ago from Obed, gave me this ability.

Now fully activated in my rotating fields, I was ready. Holding the stone up to my third eye, I entered one of the caverns within the great crystal. I began to flow into its silvery hold. There, within the stone's consciousness, I saw twelve men seated in a circle on the ground. I slowly approached keeping my emotions steady and calm. I knew that with a moment's hesitation or with any doubt on my part, all would be lost. The connection would be gone and I would be unlikely to ever experience this again. Once tapped, these encodings are gone.

Across from me in the circle of men, a lone figure stood up from among them. He was an Indian, tall and brightly decorated. His body flexed as if it had been held in stillness for centuries. I remained perfectly still, watching, waiting. Looking into my very soul, he said forcefully,

"I am Quetzalcoatl, I have come to instruct you!" There was a blinding flash of brilliant white light. The light was vibrant, alive; it engulfed me. I was thrown backwards onto the floor. Unconscious on earth, but awake-I was in another realm . (UT)

An hour or so later I regained consciousness. Lifting myself up from off the floor, I was dazed and disoriented. I had fallen backwards in an awkward position and was quite stiff and sore. As I shook off the constrictions and the fog in my mind, I thought as I looked at the stone,

"What Happened? Who is, or what is, a Quetzalcoatl?"

Indian Initiation

"Dawn, can I come over for a massage or some energy work?" I called my friend and student. "I really need one right now. I've been getting lots of information and I need to sort this all out. Maybe we could do the laying on of stones?" Since my experience with Quetzalcoatl, I desired to find out what happened. Sometimes when I am under the healing of semi-precious stones information is given to me to help me understand. (UT)

"Oh, yes! I'll be ready!" she responded enthusiastically.

It was always a unique experience to have a session with Dawn. She had received some of her knowledge from a Mohawk Medicine man. She was learning the Native American ways. I looked forward to our times together. When I arrived at her apartment, Dawn had indeed prepared the room for me. Incense rose in soft clouds filling the room with a surreal presence. Soft Indian drumming came from somewhere in the room, its rhythmic beat interspersed with the sound of shaking rattles.

"I have prepared and set up for you," she said. "I have the antlers of the Stag beneath the massage table." She paused, looking at the surprised expression on my face.

"You know...the stag that gave its last breath to me on the night of our ceremony at the Full moon? I felt, or rather I was told, it was supposed to be here at this time for you."

She lifted the cloth covering the table to allow me to see the beautiful rack of antlers beneath the table surrounded by large crystals. " Oh, yes, I remember." I answered her.

"I have a bear fur covering also," she added.

"Thank you for doing all this for me. I am honored, Dawn!"

A year before Dawn had been on her way to a sacred ceremony. Out of the misty fog that night a beautiful stag gave its life in the path of her car. Beneath the full moon she held its head, crying in the night's mist. The stag looked up at her. Heaving in its final death breath, Dawn breathed it in, breathing in its spirit energy. It had affected her life profoundly and her understanding grew from the experience. This was truly a gift being offered to me this day.

"I'll have to put on the stones first on you and I'll quietly slip out for a few moments to get my daughter at school. We'll be right back. Is that OK?"

"Dawn, that's fine, don't worry about it," I said while sliding onto the table beneath the white sheet. "I'm ready!"

Dawn then took the stones and began to lay them out all over my body. Their cool energy began to fill the space wherever they touched. Soon I was under the spell of the sacred stones. My body began to hum with their energy lulling me deep into trance.

She then held over me a sacred smudge of sweet grass and sage. An ancient ritual, the smudging cleanses and purifies the aura. Lighting the smudging bundle, a great cloud of smoke engulfed and caressed my body as she swept the smoke over and beneath the table.

As Dawn walked out the door to get her daughter, I began to lift from the table into the rising smoke. I enjoyed the floating sensation and I enjoyed my freedom in the altered state. Hovering above the table, floating on my back in the gray mist of smoke, I soon became aware that I was not alone. Sending my consciousness out and around me, I saw that Indian elders sat all around me. Rising from their heads were massive crowns of white feathers in spectacular headdresses. Dressed in soft, white animal skins they shone brightly. They were seated in a circle around me, chanting and singing a song I did not understand.

An Elder arose, walked over and stood beside me. Taking something from his pouch, I saw him toss and sprinkle powder over my body. The smoke grew thicker and an acrid smell filled my senses. One by one they stood, and came over to me. Taking an unknown substance they sprinkled my body and beneath me. Each time a cloud of the smoke would rise. Deep in trance, under the spell of the stones, I could not move.

"Have no thought. Have no fear. Observe. Relax," I could hear my Guide encourage me. Then the chanting became clearer. I could now hear what the Elders were chanting:

"White Deer....., White Deer........, White Deer, You are come, you are come."

"White Deer, White Deer, White Deer. You are come, you are come."

A large billowing gasp of smoke swirled above me, stroked me head to foot, then formed two great clouds on either side of my body.

"White Deer...., White Deer...., White Deer...., You are come, you are come."

"White Deer...., White Deer...., White Deer...., You are come, you are come."

The two clouds began to take shape. Condensing and darkening, the forms began to take a shape. A Raven formed on each side of me! Huge in size, black as velvet, sleek and shining they stood guard.

"Have no thought…… Have no fear.….. Observe.…. Relax.….." My Guide whispered.

"White Deer…, White Deer.…, White Deer.…, You are come, you are come."

"White Deer.…, White Deer.…, White Deer.…, You are come, you are come."

The chant continued. The Ravens began to pick at the sides of my body. I watched them. I saw them using their sharp beaks to pierce and pick at something. They caused no pain, but they definitely were picking at something all along the sides of my body. They stopped picking.

Then, all was quiet, the chant had stopped. Time stood still, then, the Ravens, as on clue moved forward. They worked in unison and they began to lift a clear white cellophane duplicate of my physical form. Holding it now fast in their beaks, their great-feathered wings began to move. Lifting, lifting, lifting higher, the clear filament was lifted, taken up from me and above me. Together they held the filament. They flew out into the distance, taking it with them. The chant began again.

"White Deer, White Deer, White Deer. You are come, you are come.

White Deer, White Deer, White Deer. You are come, you are come."

Another cloud of smoke rose up from behind my head. Within the cloud the spirit head and antlers of the stag were forming above me.

"White Deer, White Deer, White Deer. You are come, you are come.

"White Deer, White Deer, White Deer. You are come, you are come."

The chant rose in pitch, the spirit of the stag descended and the antlers were placed upon my head.

"White Deer, White Deer, White Deer. You are come, you are come.

White Deer, White Deer, White Deer. You are come, you are come.

White Deer.…, White Deer.…, White Deer.…., You are come, you are come."

"*Yes, I have come*," I answered to them in the mists.

And then we began to speak to one another. There would be much to do. (UT)

Susan Isabelle

"Susan, I am so sorry! Are you OK? We got stuck in traffic; there was an accident on the highway! I'm so sorry you've been under for a long time. I am *so* sorry!"

"Just call me '*White Deer*', Dawn, my friend. You may now take off the stones."

Soon I was to be on my way to California.
I had already received my instructions from the Elders.
I must perform a sacred ceremony
atop the Holy Mountain.
I had never been there, nor heard of it.

The Invitation to join thirty other Master Teachers
came the next day in the mail.

We were to meet in a place called Mt Shasta, in California. It was the Holy Mountain the Elders that day beneath the stones had told me about.
I would go! (UT)

Mt Shasta California

14,123 elevation

Mt Shasta, California

Discovering Shambhala

Mt. Shasta, California USA
November 9, 1999

    Early in the morning, I slipped out into the darkness of the still California night. I quietly closed the hotel door behind me, headed alone to my car, and began the drive to the mountain known as Mt. Shasta. Its great shape was visible even with just the light of the morning stars above. How beautiful the night is here! Away from the city, I could see the stars. How we have forgotten our heritage, I thought. They glistened and shone a silver sparkling glow upon the road. Soon I was at the base of the great mountain I had seen the day before from the air as I flew in from New Hampshire. I had come on a mission. (UT)

    Far from home now, I had come to do as I was bidden. Bidden? My mind remembered the driving force of Spirit. Yes, I *had* to come. I had to do this ceremony upon this mountain. Dreams, many dreams, had shown me the symbols rising up into the heavens forming a new connection, a Divine connection. There was to be another connection, one from Mount Shasta to New Hampshire, a roadway of energy was to be formed. I had been instructed to do this.

"No one is to know at this time; you must do this alone," I had been told.

Somewhere back in time I had agreed to come to do this, to awaken the world, to restore the sacred. Thoughts of "Why *me*? How can I do this? I'm the good Baptist mom of three and I never in a million years would have imagined I'd be here now!" filled my head.

I had seen the whole ceremony and knew exactly what I was to do. OBED, my Angel and the Indian Spirit Guides had shown me in dreams and visions of the night. My 3:00 a.m. awakenings by them and the meditations had been coming for many months, sometimes every night. Now the moment had arrived. Somehow it had all happened. I was here driving to the summit I had seen only in my dreams. Seeing a bright light just up ahead and the swirling of lights near the peak, I slowed my car. It is said that there are space ships that come to Mount Shasta.

"Do I really want to go up there alone?" I stopped the car and turned off the headlights giving me a better view. I watched as blue lights swirled about the peak. The bright lights were dancing up on the peak, doing maneuvers no plane was capable of performing. They suddenly dove behind the summit, and then were gone. I restarted my car as I contemplated my fate. I began the slow winding ascent to the top, following the switchbacks twisting in the dark of night.

"This is what I have come here for, I can't stop now. What is to be, will be." I said to the dashboard of my car.

At last I came to the empty parking area at the base of the summit. Early light was casting the predawn glow over the whole area. I felt as though I was at the top of the world. I overlooked the misty valley below and viewed the glorious stars, sparkling like diamonds on velvet overhead. A magic moment and my excitement grew.

I Reached into the back seat and took out my bag of crystals. They were all there; I had packed them just as OBED had instructed. As I opened the car door, I was surprised to feel the cool air, but even more surprised at its stillness.

The mountain is holding its breath and so am I. I thought. My breath was hushed within me. I put on my coat.

On Assignment with Adama

"OBED, I'm here! Now, where do I do this?" I asked the gentle wind. I looked around hoping to see something that would give me a clue as to where I was to do this. Before me was a great level spot, a watchtower for the world, a wide ledge. It was a platform overlooking the valley. Behind me a was great rise, a towering peak. The trail going up to the peak was now taking on a golden glow. It received the sun's rays before anyone on the earth.

"Up there near the base of those trees," was the reply in the wind.

Hoisting my pack, I began the climb toward the peak. The ground was frozen and stiff beneath my feet, gravel and small stones locked in ice in the ground did not move, which added to the eerie quiet. My footsteps made no sound. Gentle winds stroked my face, touching but not threatening. I was aware of the watchers, who were there.

"Did they know I was coming this morning?" I wondered. I sent my mind out into the vastness seeking a contact.

"No, they are here, but there will be no communication, they are just watchers," I heard Obed reply, " Many have come to see this event." .

"Well, there will be something here to watch," I spoke aloud. Mt Shasta would never be the same, I knew, and neither would I, if all this worked out as I had been shown. A short distance up the path I found a place of three small green pines. I was drawn to the side of the sturdy, miniature pines. I was led, my feet knowing exactly where to step, to an area of four boulders in a natural formation.

"Ah, yes, they are here in North, South, East and West," I thought. I won't even have to disturb any of this beauty, or the natural surroundings. It is all prepared for me."

The boulders were beginning to glow in the early dawn. I took four gleaming crystals out of my pack. Large, solid and beautiful, these had been present at the reopening of the elemental kingdom in Arizona last May. They held the mighty blast from the heart of GAIA that sent up a cloud five miles wide. It glowed magenta with pink rays at 11:00 p.m. that night. The earth had heaved in contractions of the new birth.

"You can handle this one, too," I said fondly to them.

I held them each in deep affection. I lay them out on the frozen ground. They had come to me as a gift from Spirit. These beautiful creatures of silicon-based life-form had served well and were precious beyond all I could have ever imagined. Who would ever have thought I'd be speaking with crystals? I chuckled. I knew they had come here to assist me in my work. They are so alive. They have consciousness and they do hear my every thought.

"I thank you for doing this with me. You and I are blessed," I cooed to them. I began to lay out the other stones, placing each in their assigned position. Placing the symbols upon the ground, saying their sacred names and activating them with my palm's energy, the ground once again began to heave.

"Now, it is time," I said aloud to the wind, standing. I began to pray.

"Great Father, Divine Source, Creator of all things. The time has arrived. We will now go forth as you have decreed. Establish the Creative Force here as you have shown." I began to tone the ancient song, the song to call the Wind, the Light, and the Creative Power of the Son.

"Great Mother, Divine Mother, Nurturer of All Life. The time has arrived. With your Great Love now, we will go forth as was decreed so long ago. I am the servant. Open your bosom of the Light of Love, your essence, to complete the joining now!" (UT)

Once again I began toning the Divine connection. Reaching up to the Divine, I brought down the Light Pillar. Reaching down into her awaiting bosom I pulled up her Love Light. She gave freely, anticipating her joining. The Angels spun the essences of the two. Divine Mother and Divine Father joined in Creation. Awesome! I was pushed back by their astounding power!

Before me shone outward a beam of Light Force which connected Heaven and Earth. The Heart of Mother and The Heart of Father, Male and Female, the energy connection was complete upon Mt Shasta, the holy mountain. The beam went deep into the center of the earth, and all the way up into heaven. I felt its powerful perimeter, walking around it. The expanding energy radiated out about thirty feet from the center. This was by far the largest Pillar I had ever seen!

"Now one more thing to do!" I shouted to the winds. Standing within the four boulders, I knelt down and placed my hands upon the pulsing ground. Making the symbol as I had been shown, I visualized it connecting this sacred energy place to my little Crystal Lake back home in New Hampshire. By accessing this energy, I could empower a special connector energy and send it back home. My lake would glow in its power! A special gift had been promised to me with the completion of this task. Back home I would be blessed in this power, this Love, forever. I looked forward to my meditation times by the Crystal Lake banks.

I began to tone. Great long vowel sounds in the perfect tonal order came from deep within me, sounds that sent the power all the way back to New Hampshire. Tones far beyond the human range flowed and resounded throughout the whole mountain. I began to hear other voices join in. The Angelic realm joined in the toning. (UT)

Above my head two large ravens were playing upon the tones weaving back and forth through the Pillar of Light. They danced in the air, rejoicing in the newly created energy. The morning sun had risen and cast its golden approving rays. Magnificent! Everything shone gold; the boulders, the path, the air reflected back the golden rays. The Universe rejoiced in the joining, the completion. My soul rejoiced and was magnified in the glory of Creation's power.

"It is done." Finally, after all these months of anticipation, the dreams and the Love, it was now done. Then I prayed. I thanked all who had made this possible. I was so thankful for having been used in the completion of this work; it is so beautiful! I basked in the glory and the wonder of this place for a long while. I watched the playful ravens and felt the sun's welcome warmth. My soul overflowed with love and a deep satisfaction filled me. The whole mountain pulsed in the golden glow of the rising sun.

After a while, I took up my crystals and stones, preparing to depart this magical and sacred mountain. At the last moment I heard OBED say,

"Take the stones from the altar."

The words stunned me. I held this all sacred, and did not want to touch anything.

"But, OBED, shouldn't I leave the natural environment undisturbed?" Another person spoke this time, not OBED.

"Take some from the altar. At this time it is allowed."

I bent down and surprisingly the stones gave themselves up easily from the frozen ground. I placed them in my pack. I could feel the glowing from the activation they had just received. From my pack I took some blue corn which is sacred to many cultures. I placed it in the space in the ground of the rock I had taken. It was given as an offering to the mountain for the gift I had received. Completely filled with joy, I started down the mountain thinking I had completed the greatest moment of my life. I felt wonderful and full of Love! How was I to know that this was just the beginning?

****

I began the long drive back down the mountain. My thoughts flew back to the day I was on Dawn's table and the Sacred Initiation I had received by the Indian Elders. Shortly after that day, I met with an Indian Medicine Man. We sat one evening and smoked the Peace Pipe together around the sacred Medicine Wheel he had tenderly lain out upon the ground. We made prayers for the Earth, all the tribes of the earth, and the seven sacred directions. Later I had a chance to tell him of my vision, my initiation, and ask my questions.

"I had such a vision when I was a young man, he began, I had run from my responsibilities into the world. However, my path was sealed," he said.

"Each night I was called into the dream. Each night I would see the Ravens around the body of a man picking the flesh from him. As I drew closer I could see it was my face on the body and I awoke terrified. I believed I was going to die. This led me to the tribal medicine man who told me I had been chosen to become a leader and healer of my people. The Ravens had come to remove the old death and make me clean. I needed to be made ready to take on my responsibilities as has been decreed before my birth. I was not ready at the time. But, now I am here. Much has happened. You are also now ready. Much will begin to happen."

Little did I know then all that prophecy would entail! (U 1,

Later, during the week before my coming to Mt. Shasta, I was given a pouch of white deerskin as a gift from Dawn. Within the pouch was placed a piece of the Stag's bone and a few other items precious to me: a Raven's feather and a crystal pyramid. I wore it around my neck night and day. That pouch had many special qualities, I was to soon learn. I remembered when it first revealed its secret powers. I was seated in a guided meditation along with some other friends.

"Ask your Guides for a sign," the leader's voice said. Suddenly the pouch resting on my chest jumped!

'That can't be, I thought. Then it jumped again.

"Oh, my God! It hears me! The Stag ! Are you-is that you?"

It jumped again in confirmation and at that moment a love wash came over me! A warm feeling of intense love flowed through and touched my heart. Somehow a miracle had occurred. The spirit of Dawn's Stag was with me, I carried it around my neck in that small piece of its bone. I soon discovered that whenever a great truth was spoken, the pouch moved. Unknown to anyone, I now had an invaluable tool for discernment.

As I made my way back down the mountain to go back toward my hotel, I could feel its excited movements. Stag approved and was very animated, the pouch was jumping excitedly on my chest. I laughed. The Stag's antlers are actually a symbol of antennae or connections to higher frequencies. They grow behind the eyes, also symbolizing a third eye connection and heightened abilities. This Stag was gentle and held truth as its priority. I related to Stag as a totem of truth to the world. I was grateful for the confirmations and love washes I received.

At the base of the mountain and onto the highway once again, I looked up to the summit. Three, rising from the summit was a large towering mushroom of a cloud. The heat from the activation was causing a cloud to form over the summit. I stopped to take pictures in amazement.

Before I knew it, I was driving up to the entrance of my hotel in California. My memories of the morning on the mountain still glowed within me. Outside stood a man. Short and without a lot of hair on top, this lively man watched me get out of the car. I knew him. He was standing by the front gate as I walked up to it.

"Where have you been?" he asked.

"Oh, I've been up on the mountain for the sunrise," I partially answered, still concealing my purpose.

"That was YOU?" he asked incredulously, wide eyed. Without another word he then quickly turned and walked away. The man was the seminar leader for the week I was to be in Shasta. That was the invitation I had received after the Initiation of the Elders and my instructions. So, I had come to Mt. Shasta for a nine day intensive under his direction .

He seemed very surprised at what I had done. How did he know? I wondered I had come specifically for this reason: to do the work upon Mt Shasta and to learn to be a certified Merkaba Instructor with his companion teacher that week. I wanted to teach my students the Merkaba activation back home in New England., and to complete my mission on the mountain. The rest was to be for fun. Or so I thought.

Meeting Adama Telos and Lemurians

Later the students gathered in the Kiva for our class. Jonathan led our group in a meditation. In our activated Merkaba fields of energy, we were guided into the inner area of Mt. Shasta to meet the Telosians. I had never heard of Telosians and had no idea what to expect. As we descended through the rock of the mountain, I entered a glowing area of bright light. From that point on, Jonathan's voice was gone. For that matter, I wasn't in the Kiva anymore. I was with the Telosians. In the brightness of the light, a man came forward. He stood before me, tall, towering above me.

"I am Adama of the Ancient Lemurians, he spoke gently to me. Please, we would like to show you what you have done this day. We are in awe of the power that has been released. We have waited long for you to return!"

"You have waited for me?" Surprised, I considered him deeply, searching him. He was pure light and beautiful. He was completely dressed in white and had around his head a crown of gold with a shining Star of David on his forehead. He looked like an angel. Love and peace were flowing from him.

"Yes, long ago when the earth had gone through its changes, the genetic material of the humans was altered. We knew the earth was going to be plunged into darkness for many ages to come. We of the Lemurians, the race that had foreseen the ending of this age on the earth, and who survived, took this mountain as our home, far beneath the earth. Since that time, we have become pure consciousness and this is now our present form." (UT)

He led me into an area that had an exquisite pillar of light at its center. The light was so bright it was difficult to see in the chamber.

"This is what you have done," he said. "This is our renewed energy source. Long ago we lived within its power. We have survived long without it here in the Earth, relying on our own light and the Light of GAIA to survive." (UT)

I looked at the pulsing glowing center that sent out multicolored shimmering rays. It looked like the core of a reactor.

"Once, long ago, we had many such power sources, as this is what we used to power our homes and live upon the Earth. We lived in cooperation with Source and Mother. The contamination of the Earth through the warring of the planets and the subsequent human genetic alterations caused us to discontinue and close down the energy source."

I considered his words, then asked, "Why? Was there no other way to preserve this?"

"If these power sources had been allowed to remain functioning on the Earth with the Age of Darkness upon it, nothing would have been impossible for the altered, contaminated humans to do. Much destruction throughout the universe would have resulted. This could not be allowed."

"Why, what happened, Adama?" I asked.

"The infection present upon the planet Earth could not be allowed to spread to the other universes. Mankind's' mind became dark and concerned only with the pursuit of power, personal pursuits, with very unbalanced thought processes. GAIA chose to wait for the Age of Light to return and we have stayed with her. " He paused and looked deeply at me.

"It was decreed that at the end of the Age of Darkness one would come to restore the energy power source to us and to the Earth.

One would arrive at the appointed time from the Melchizedeks of Light. Today, you have come. You have completed the first task. It is our time to awaken and come to the aid of the Earth." (UT)

I stood there before the great beam in the chamber. The beam, I knew, was made up of the energy from the Heart of GAIA and the energy of Divine Source, the Father. Totally amazing! They were using this energy to power their world once again. This was a reactor. I had helped to create a reactor from the two Power Sources of the Universe!

The Lemurians came forward and stood around the beam, watching the pulsing, radiant glowing along with Adama and me. There were many thousands of them. The joy and wonder was all around us. They were very excited and so was I!

"Now," Adama said, "we will show you what must come. We know that in your form you will have no memory. That is just, we honor you for you willingness to take on your present form of human flesh."

He looked gently at me as he began to explain. I felt loved and comfortable in his presence. "Once upon the planet there were passageways that ran throughout the Earth. These were passageways of pure energy. By our purity of thought, we would enter the passageways and travel anywhere upon the planet or above the planet."

Adama showed me a demonstration performed by two of their companions. What I saw amazed me! As we walked over to the reactor, it was as though they tilted their heads and in a flash became radiant pure light! They were large tear-dropped forms of light that moved extremely fast, as if a flashbulb went off! The two of them simply touched the wall, or rather, even before they touched the wall of the inner mountain, it gave way as a tunnel way of light. They disappeared inside the tunnel and it closed once again behind them.

"Once opened, we will have access to our ancient sites all over the globe. We have contacted your counterpart and Melchizedek sister in Tibet. Even as we speak, she too is activating the Tibetan Center ."

"I have a sister?"

"Yes, you incarnated at the same hour as was decreed by the Melchizedek for the Feminine Aspect. Your identities will be hidden for a time, so as to protect your work. Together you will traverse the globe in your work. But for now, we must go on."

Pointing once again at the now closed tunnel way, he said, "They also served as gateways to other, higher dimensions. You have traveled these same highways, along with us in ages past. As passageways, other races could come and conduct trade and relations. It is decreed the Melchizedeks must reopen them in cooperation with us at the proper time. That time is now come."

Adama led me over to a large table within the chamber. Four men came forward and laid a great scroll upon the table. As they began to unroll the scroll, I could clearly see that this was a map of Earth.

"See here, he pointed to places upon the map. These are the energy centers and these are the passages which flow out from them." Adama had pointed to small round circles that were centered about the United States and the rest of the globe. Connecting these centers were roadways of light, or the passages. The map had many of the star-like connections, which stretched out all over the globe.

"As you see here, he said waving his hand out over the table, there is also a corresponding grid to come above the Earth. For now, we will work with the Earth passageways." He smiled at me.

"Why do you need to use these, Adama? What is their purpose now?" I asked.

With that question, he held up his two hands, palms facing each other.
I saw the perfect image of Earth spinning between his hands.

"The time is coming soon, he said solemnly, when Earth will go through a great transition." I watched as Earth's rotation began to slow between his hands, nearly stopping.

To my horror, I saw the Earth begin to fade in and out as if it was losing dimensional space. It nearly faded out of reality. I felt great fear and alarm come over me. We of planet Earth were in danger of totally ceasing to exist! He saw that I understood the gravity of the matter.

"We will come at that moment, rising up throughout Earth in these passageways to assist in the transition
so the planet will not loose its dimensional reality or face destruction.
We will hold the Integrity of Earth through the transition. "

He paused allowing the words to penetrate.
"Do you agree to assist us? It must be with your cooperation."
"Yes, Adama, I will do this." *I answered him softly.*

"Good! Here is where we will need you to begin," he said cheerfully. "Here," he pointed, right here in New Hampshire is a site. You will find it right behind the Mount of Washington at the three falls. This is what you must do."

He gave me instructions as to how to open the site and place the stones. He turned toward the great beaming pillar in the chamber. "See from this place the beam going from the side?" he indicated ahead. I looked at the beam saying,

"Yes." He smiled broadly at me. "Well, that is the passage to your Lake, one we had not anticipated," he laughed. "We will enjoy the waters there!" They all laughed!

"Using the symbols and the tones as you have already done, you will reestablish the passageways. Use the stones from the altar, which you took today and place them in this direction and in this manner," he began.

I interrupted, "Adama, there are so many sites!" I said in amazement as I looked over the map.

"It is not necessary to reopen them all. We will direct you and more information will come from others to guide you. You will also need the activations of Melchizedek to complete your tasks."

"What activations?" I asked, but by then he was gone.

****

I came back into the physical to find everyone had left the room. I sat for a few moments to absorb the vision and the agreement I had just made.

"How am I going to do this?" I wondered. I made my way back up to the room I was sharing with another student for the week. As I opened the door I found her lying on the bed reading a book. As she turned the page, I was startled. Right there in front of me on the bed beneath her hands was the map of what I had just been shown! All the little circles and star-like spokes radiating out were there, interconnecting throughout the United States!

"Jelina, what is this?" I practically screamed at her. In my excitement, I took the book right out from under her. As I turned it over I read the cover, *Messages from Adama*." I sat down on the bed and tears began to fall. Jelina just watched as I tried to compose myself.

"Where did you get this?" I asked after the initial shock wore off.

"Oh, Susan, I picked that up in town today at the bookstore. It's about Telos and the channeled writings of the Lemurian priest of Telos, Adama," she answered softly.

"Jelina, I just spoke to him!" I looked at her pleading she'd understand. Just then lively, wonderful, Raja, our neighbor across the hall, came into the room. I told Jelina and Rajah of my incredible experience in the vision. Together we looked at the map in the Telos book. Both their hometowns in Washington and Oregon were also shown on the map, which we now physically held in our hands. I had also seen them on Adama's map!

"I am going back up the mountain tomorrow. Would you like to come with me? We will connect to your back yards!"

"Yes," affirmed Raja, "but first I must show you something!" She led me over to her room across the hall.

"This morning when we had the Telos meditation, I came back up here into my room to draw what I had seen."

She pulled back a sheet and uncovered a large chalk drawing. There in front of me was the symbol formation that creates the passageways. Inside the spoke passageways she had drawn two side by side, big, glowing golden-yellow teardrop shapes. As soon as I saw it I immediately knew what this was.

"Rajah, you have seen the Lemurian power source and the passageways, too!" I exclaimed. Pointing to the side by side glowing yellow shapes in the passageway, I continued, "See here. This is exactly what they look like as they move through the passageway in their light bodies!"

"I thought you'd understand this and that's why I brought you in here. After what you told us in there, I knew this was it, she replied. I didn't know what I had seen or drawn until you told us your story. Now I know. I'll be with you tomorrow!"

Later that night I read Jelina's book. It was written by Diane Robbins and called *Messages From the Hollow Earth* revised*. It was such an incredible confirmation to me! (UT) I learned that the Lemurians are 7 foot tall angel-like beings of great love and gentleness. They come from the ancient city of Telos of the former Lemurian continent, now located at Mt. Shasta. The continent of Lemuria was located off the Pacific West Coast. California is also a part of that continent, hence the ridge of the San Andreas Fault caused by Lemuria as the continent pushed up against the North American continent. The rest of Lemuria sank during the Earth upheaval probably around 26,000 years ago. Parts of Hawaii and the islands are remnants of Lemuria.

It was believed that not all of the Lemurians perished, but about 25,000 survived and continue to live and serve the Earth. They have become nearly immortal beings. As the Earth was recovering, they lived within the earth as mankind reestablished itself upon the surface. It is also believed they assisted mankind in the rebuilding of Earth's centers and the great monuments of Egypt and Central America.

The next morning Jelina, Rajah and I headed out to the mountain in predawn star light. We climbed the ancient mountain. The beam had been established the day before and was performing beautifully. My companions immediately felt its pulsing and pumping of the energies to the Telosians/Lemurians beneath our feet.

Once again I performed the ceremony using the symbols to connect the sites. Jelina and Rajah placed their hands upon the ground and toned the ancient song right along with me. Afterwards they excitedly told me of the flowing of the energies. They were now connected from Mt. Shasta to the shores of Washington State and Oregon. These passageways are reconnected and operational. Below us now were three great beams flowing out to these cities.

"Adama, there's two more!" I could just imagine him beaming brighter and delighting wonderfully in the energies. We hurried back to the Kiva for the day's meditations and instructions.

Animal Spirit Guides

I spent much time alone during the week at Mt. Shasta, up on the mountain and in private meditation. I had come for many reasons. Some of the work I had already completed atop the mountain, other tasks were yet to be revealed. I eventually found myself leading many up to Mt Shasta for attunements. People just wanted to go and I did many activations there for the people.

But that morning after Jelina, Rajah and I returned from the mountain, we were led us into the first of several Merkaba excursions into the New Universe, a place of great beauty. The New Universe is being prepared for the ascended earth and its people in the higher dimensional realms. We were able to access these realms through the advanced Merkaba techniques being taught during the week. We dimensionally shifted into the New Universe. In one of the meditations, I found myself at the shores of a great crystal blue lake, I walked with my two animal spirit guides, Stag and Raven.

"Oh, so you followed me here! I laughed. I didn't know you could come with me!"

"Be-Caws Be-Caws!" Raven flew over me cawing while soaring joyfully in the warm sunlight. I stroked the beautiful golden stag that stood patiently beside me. I felt much love for my Guide and friend.

"How I wish we could speak! I exclaimed. You are so beautiful." At that moment of blissful peace, we were being drawn back into the room by Gary's voice. Raven flew over and stood on my shoulder. We began the descent though the dimensions one again.

"Wait, Wait! Stag, come! Come! You're being left behind! Where are you?" My last memory of him was of him standing proud and tall, his rack reaching high into the blue sky, framed in the white clouds. He was beautiful.

Back in the physical, I cried, as I knew he had been left somewhere in dimensional time and space. Would I ever see him again? My totem bag around my neck lay lifeless.

****

We were quickly led into another group Merkaba activation. Within a single large globe of Merkaba energy, we would all travel together for practice. I was excited to learn the new techniques and found them easy to do, not realizing my fields had already been expanded. I just needed a teacher to explain the process. I am grateful!

I followed the meditation with the group. As we hovered over Ayers rock in Australia we were guided down to meet the Aborigines. We stepped out of the large shared Merkaba to meet the waiting natives. A small man took my hand, and chattering something lively and excited, pulled me along into a cave.

I saw both men and women seated within the cave and standing in a circle. In the center was a fire. Several women approached me. They held in their hands carved wooden bowls containing black liquid. They held the bowls up to my face, trying to suggest something to me. Splashing the gooey stuff around they indicated to me that it was supposed to be put on my arms and legs.

"Ok," I said and nodded. That sent them into a flurry. The women gathered around me and began to strip off my clothes. They buzzed around and smeared the stuff all over my body. Pulling my hair down they smeared the goo through it also until I stood naked and completely black in front of them. When they had completed their task, they nodded to the others.

A man came forward and handed one of them another wooden bowl. Carefully now, they painted lightening bolts on my black body in bright yellow and red. Huge bolts down my arms, legs and back. One large bolt was drawn on my stomach.

Satisfied, they began to dance around the fire in the center of the cave. I was invited to join them and began the frenzied dance at their urging. The drumming and dance were captivating. While I was feeling very intoxicated by the drums, an elder approached me with another bowl. I nodded again. He opened his mouth and showed me this was something to swallow. Whatever was in his bowl, I was expected to consume this.

"Ok," I said and nodded again. With that he pulled a lizard from the bowl. A blue lizard squirmed in his fingertips, held firmly by its tail. I don't know why, but without any hesitation, I tilted my head back and opened my mouth. I felt the squirming lizard enter, slide down my throat, and land in my stomach. I gagged as they cheered. There in my stomach, I felt its movement. It was very warm and it radiated heat from my belly. It all seemed perfectly normal at the time, what had I just done? Why?

With my thought, the elder showed me. He touched his fingertips to his belly and pointed to mine at the same time. He looked up and took in a breath. I could hardly believe what I saw. He began to transform in front of me into a four-legged antelope-looking animal. Then he returned to his human form. He pointed at my belly again indicating I should do the same. I got it! I had been given a gift, a gift to enable me to shapeshift! But into what? I would not have the opportunity to find out as we were being summoned into the Merkaba.

I thanked him and the others as we headed back to return home to Mt. Shasta. I was still gagging as I came out of the meditation. I could feel the warmth in my belly. This really happened; I ran upstairs to shower, and felt sick all day.

6

Al'lat Le Andro

In the evening I was scheduled to go to an Initiation in the Kiva, but was guided upstairs into my room. I fell onto the bed and into a deep trance state. I was directed to sit up right on the bed. Above me I saw twelve galaxies, like huge glowing spirals, coming down over my head into my crown chakra which was very expanded. I had expanded far beyond the little room and the town of Mc Cloud that night.

There they spun, glowing, sparkling in total beauty. I sat beneath their glory as a Great White Glowing Being, and they were like shining stars in my crown. I was awed by this vision, spellbound in their majestic power.

But I began to notice that one of the spirals was losing its sparkle and appeared to be fading. I felt total compassion and some fear. Taking my "hand" or "thought," I beamed energy into the fading spiral and it regained its glow.

Then another was losing its shine, and again I beamed Light into that spiral—it glowed strong again. Then another began to fade, then another, now the first was losing its integrity again, and another. Over and over again I keep them spinning and shining. All night long I held these spirals, beaming energy into them. This was not a dream. I was a great Light being holding these galaxies in time and space.

I don't know how long that lasted or when I came back into body, but when I woke in the morning I was physically exhausted and drained. I dragged myself down to the hot tub. My friend and student from Arizona, Beth, was already soaking in the warmth of the steaming waters.

"Beth, all night long I held these spirals. What could this have possibly mean?" I tried to soothe my sore aching muscles, saying, "How could a vision bring such physical discomfort?" as I rubbed my shoulders.

"I don't know," said Beth as she began to massage and stretch those sore muscles. "I'm sure we'll find out!" We rose up out of the warmth and prepared for the next session to be held in the Kiva. There, we would be starting the day's instruction for teaching the Merkaba.

"I'm sorry I couldn't get down to your class, I apologized as soon as I saw the instructor. I had the initiation from you last September when you came to Massachusetts and I'll be sure to be here tonight for the next set."

I was later to find there had actually been disrupter energies there the previous night. I would come to understand why I had was called instead to spend my time holding galaxy spirals all night long. If I hadn't, dire consequences would have occurred for multitudes. Thank God I didn't know it at the time.

In the first Merkaba meditation, we were led again into the New Universe. Once again I was with Stag and the Raven. I looked different, however. I held my head high and wore a crown of glowing spirals and was dressed in pure white. I no longer held my former form.

Walking along the shores of the same beautiful lake, I remembered I held within me the gift of the Aborigine. The gift gave me the ability to shape shift. I so desired to be with and communicate with the beautiful stag that walked along beside me. I had missed him so! My Indian pouch no longer confirmed truth, but lay silently upon my chest.

I began to concentrate, calling upon the power, which now dwelt within. My body began to take on a new form. Soft and agile, moving effortlessly, I now stood not upon two legs but four. Prancing

On Assignment with Adama

in my new body, I ran and played in the fields at the shore with my friend. My delight peaked as I was now able to speak to Stag!

We talked of many things, then I asked, "Stag, why did you not come with me as I called to you?"

"You have brought me here to dwell within the future realms as I so desire." He spoke softly.

"You want to be here?" I asked.

"Why, of course. It will secure the existence of my race, we will walk within the New Universe. Did you not know?"

"No, I did not understand. I was afraid I had lost you forever. Raven came back with me, I offered.

"I am always with you in one form or another." he answered.

"Will Raven come here and have to stay, too?" I asked, afraid I'd lose him also.

"No, Raven is pure Spirit and he can already transport between the Universes. I will stay, but do not be saddened. I am as I am meant to be."

Then it was over. My beautiful Stag was now somewhere, I didn't know exactly where, but he was happy. I was drawn back into the present time.

****

By Nicky

That evening something shook heaven. Disrupter energies were about. By disrupter energies, I mean the spirit of discontent and discordant energy. That simple energy can destroy all that has been and all possibilities when adhered to, rather than the energy of Love and compassion. It is called EGO.

We were seated having dinner when a great wave of energy nearly knocked me out of my chair. Regaining my composure I said to those around me, "Something terrible has just happened! It's our two instructors!"

Beth immediately jumped up and ran out of the dining area. She came back a few minutes later, "Susan, we need you *now*!"

I followed her into the Kiva. There the walls were crumbling. The dimensional walls were folding in upon time. The two pillars (instructors) had completely severed from one another. Looking upwards to the top of the high ceiling of the Kiva, I could see a jagged cut in the fabric of dimensional time.

I don't know who they were or even where they came from, but about ten Lightworkers showed up in the Kiva. Silently, we gathered together in a circle and began to sing. We sang of Divine Mother's love and the mending of time.

We danced and sang all the while suturing the gaping hole, ripped, torn by words, thoughts and actions. I toned the great IAVA, bringing in the Divine energies to restore the wounded with love. When it was over, the dimensional fabric was restored.

But something else had happened. The New Universe would now be forever closed to us until the great time of ascension. Other magnificent universes and planetary systems will be available for us to transverse and practice our creative skills within, and we need to be doing this in preparation, but a great glass wall now secured that which is waiting.

The reason for this was given to me by OBED. The New Universe must remain pure; in total purity, to preserve its integrity. It was destined for a time, for a very few—for very specific reasons—to access the New Universe. But it required the coming together of two Pillars in perfect love, to do this. The end of that time had now come. Almost irreparable damage had been wrought that night. Two times, as decreed, the Pillars had come together at the Holy Mountain of Mt. Shasta. More than we can possibly understand was accomplished there by these two groups, while under the Pillars. It is so; it is as it ought to be. I fell exhausted into bed and into a very deep sleep.

****

Awaking early, much refreshed, Beth and I were met by a few others in the hot tub. We discussed the previous night's near universal disaster. Just then a Raven flew above us and sat on the tree above the hot tub.

"There's one of my best friends!" I stated.

"The Raven?" a black man asked. "I thought that meant death."

I was shocked. How could anyone think that? Ravens had always been my companions on this path. "Oh no, Raven is pure Spirit, the Spirit of God."

"How's that?" he continued the exchange.

I continued, "Raven fed the prophet Elijah in the desert and stayed with Noah in the Ark 'til all were safe. In Native American Indian lore, the Raven was once a pure white bird of great beauty." I paused. They were listening intently, so I continued.

"The White Pure Raven saw the darkness that had fallen upon the man on earth and he had great compassion. Diving down from the great heights of heaven, Raven swept down into the darkness. Taking on the blackness of mankind's despair, the beautiful white Raven became black as coal. He made a great sacrifice."

"Oh!" The black man stood up out of the water. " Now I understand!" he shouted into the sky. " I have always thought the black man was cursed. Instead, now I see. My race has come to absorb the darkness of mankind's inhumanity, in slavery, its cruelty, and we have stood strong and borne it on the Earth! We are the Spirit upon the Earth!" He glowed proud and strong in his realization.

"To be honest with you, I have never thought of that. I now honor you and your race. Namaste!" I bowed. "May I continue?"

"Of course," he said coming back down into the water to listen. I resumed the tale,

"Once in a reading I was giving for someone, I was given sight to view the Raven. I saw Raven flying throughout the earth as it was taking on the darkness of mankind. As nightfall approached, Raven, instead of nesting like other birds in the darkness, flew straight up into heaven. As Raven flew higher and higher into the presence of God I could see its feathers becoming lighter and lighter until they were brilliant white and glowing! There the Raven rested in the Light.

"As morning approached upon the Earth, Raven stirred. Lifting up to make his sacrifice, he drove back down into the atmosphere of the earth screeching "BE-CAWS! BE-CAWS! BE-CAWS!" I paused.

"Each day, he takes on the darkness and each night he rests in the Light. The Raven does this 'just because'. Because he is needed, because he knows who he is, none can dissuade him. Each morning his call is to remind us we do what we do 'just because'." Together, we cried. Later that day, I gave him a Raven's feather.

Awakening the Feminine Melchizedek

After the encounter with the man, I went upstairs to meditate alone. As I ascended into the Light, I was taken before the whole Council. There is a Guiding Council that oversees the progression of planets. I had been before in this place and remembered it well. There is a half circle round table that is lifted up high over one's head. The Ascended beings of Light, the Masters, the Christ all sit at this huge table. It feels as if you are standing in a pool looking up at the rim of the pool with people sitting at the rim. It is all light and glowing. I had always been treated with honor and respect.

Today, I had been summoned, as I had only a few times before. Most often my memories were only of having received instructions but today I would speak and remember. I stood in quiet reverence before the Ascended Masters. They appeared out of the luminous mist as it cleared. This was an opportunity not to be missed, so I spoke,

"I desire to become all that I am supposed to be in this lifetime."

"Do you know what you ask?" I heard someone ask.

"I understand enough to know I want to be empowered with all knowledge to complete that which I have come to do. I want to help the People!" There was a stirring on the Council as they spoke with one another. I continued,

"I was told by Adama I am in need of the activation. I desire the activation," I added.

Then they were completely silent. I waited silently for something to happen. A beautiful woman stood up from among the other members of the Council. I recognized her immediately! I knew her as Kuan Yin. I had met her two years prior during my initiation to her energies. I remembered her vividly. I was pinned to a chair for a long while as she anointed me with her nectar of compassion and spun balls of energy into my aura. She stepped forward and stood beside me.

"*I stand with her in her request for the activation.*"

Kuan Yin was advocating on my behalf to the assembled group! To my total amazement another stood up from the assembly. St. Germain stood at his station and spoke to them also.

"*I, too, stand for her!" he shouted.*"

There was much flurry of discussion. I could not hear all that Kuan Yin was saying to them, but she turned to me afterward and said "When you see the Melchizedek, ask for the activations!" Then, they were gone. I was back in my room wondering what had happened.

That night I had several visitations from St. Germain and Kuan Yin who both told me,

"*When you see Melchizedek, ask for the activations!*"

I thought they meant one of my instructors who was also called a Melchizedek, so the next morning I tried to find him to ask about the activations that Adama and the others were so excited about. I found him all right, but I became a bit more than frustrated at trying to speak to him. Whenever I tried, there would be an interruption. I never had the opportunity to speak to him about the activation I had been instructed to request!

When St. Germain came forward again to me in a vision later in the afternoon, I expressed my frustration to him and again all he would say to me was,

"When you see Melchizedek, ask for the activations!" I tried again and went to the instructor and asked, "Do you have a moment?" Someone stepped right in front of me and began speaking to him, cutting me off completely. After the person stopped talking, I tried again,

"Do you have a moment?" He looked at his watch. "Love, it's really late!" meaning he really had to get back inside. This was too much. It was already Thursday and I had to do this before the end of the week.

Andromeda

We then went into the Kiva and began the meditation for the day. We went into our own I AM presence. Two beautiful white beings, guides, came forward.

"This is a map of the star system Andromeda," they stated while showing me the Andromedan star chart. Your name, your *true* name, is Al'lat Le Andro Melchizedek of the Andromedan System. Al'lat Le Andro Melchizedek means "Over-Light Being of the Twelve Galaxies of the Andromedan System."

I was astounded! How could this be true? I wondered amazed and confused. They continued,

"Your official position in the stars is that of an Over Light Being to twelve galaxies. Those galaxies exist within the Andromedan System." They paused. "You have incarnated to assure the system's progression into the New Universal Reality. You have accomplished that already! We have come to tell you and to honor you."

I wondered aloud to them, "How did I do that?"

"The Twelve Star Galaxies you saw and held in place all night long were the galaxies that you oversee in the Universe. They were in danger of losing their dimensional reality, but they are now safely placed within the New Universe," they answered my thought. "How was that? Why?"

"The disrupter energies present within the group threatened to break apart the Great Pillars before their time. Those humans responsible for seeing to it that you accomplished your mission had been under severe attack. The dimensional realms of possibilities threatened the existence of these, your galaxy's domain. You held them and took them as your own."

With that I was once again shown the beautiful spirals—my responsibility—entire galaxies! I now understood. Had these two beings fallen out of the Love, they would have been unable to sustain the group and the very existence of these beings were jeopardized. We may never have had the entrance into the New Universe or the meditation. The night I held the galaxies I had accomplished something I was not even aware of at the time. It was a critical moment in time for likely trillions upon trillions of beings!

"As you took upon your crown the care and responsibility of these systems, you wore them into your dimension. Earth's transition into the New Universe brings not only ascension for earthlings, but also many other species throughout all of creation. Earth's dimensional transitional pull will carry us all. "

"At the moment you carried them into the New Universe, their reality was secured! They exist and thrive in the future realms. Al'lat Le Andro Melchizedek, Over Light Being of the Twelve Galaxies, we honor you and thank you on behalf of all the peoples of Andromeda!" With that, they bowed and were gone."

I could hardly speak after the revelations to me. Engulfed with emotion, I cried much that day. I retired to my room and hugged the pillow tight, soaking it with my tears. With all that I have been through in my life! How many times had I wished I was dead? Life had been very hard at those moments. Yet, if I'd given up, a whole system of beings would have ceased to exist!

This is what Stag had tried to convey to me. This is why he stayed behind. Now I understood. How many of us at the meditation were Universal Representatives? Were they actually doing the same sort of work? Did any of the others know? I wondered.

♉ Activations of the Melchizedek ♉

Back in the Kiva we began another meditation-this time we were to be guided into the Chamber of Melchizedek! Now I was excited! Could this be where I would be able to see Him? Seated in upright position, I followed along in the meditation. Our Merkaba fields fully activated, I came before the doors of the Chamber of Melchizedek, but suddenly, there were no doors. I was whisked far away from the group into a place of great light, peace and beauty.

I felt myself begin to transform, as I became once again the expansive Glowing Being of Light. Just 'there', in peaceful waiting, the voices of the room and the meditation simply faded away and were gone. I waited.

Oh, My Soul!
He IS BEAUTIFUL!!! He is BEAUTY! He is LOVE!
HE IS LIGHTNING!

He came through many dimensions. All dimensions. He appeared as if there were hundreds of Him one placed one upon another! Melchizedek came through the dimensions and was hovering above me. He was in a magnificent Pagoda Temple. His Lightning form filled the temple. I stood beneath Him, and stared in awe at the most beautiful being I have ever experienced.

Jesus Christ was after the lineage of the Melchizedek, according to the scriptures and it is said Jesus true form is the Melchizedek -High Priest of El Elyon, or God Most High.

From below His Pagoda and form, the Twelve Galaxies again appeared above me. I was directed to reach up, which I did, and take hold of the Galaxies and bring them down into my crown. Now placed there prominently, I became somehow whole and complete as I have never felt or seen before. I was strengthened in a way I cannot describe.

What happened next was so beautiful, so filled with love I can hardly write this. I saw coming from within the Pagoda, from the heart of Melchizedek, a radiant ray of Light. Within the beam of Light was a smaller duplicate of the Pagoda with Melchizedek inside. The ray came down before me containing the miniature of the Whole above me. Great Light poured out from this as a waterfall flowing over me. I was bathed in love. I was given a choice to accept all of this wonder.

Looking up and responding with powerful certainty, I agreed to accept. I watched in holy silence as the Pagoda image, holding the Melchizedek within, glided into my heart. A shaft of Light immediately shot upward from my heart and out the top of my head, between the Galaxies. There still, it connects me to Melchizedek, my heart to His. Always. Forever. We are joined. Melchizedek had come on pure Light and placed Himself in my heart in a spectacular way. His altar was established within my heart and His energy is within me. We have become One!

Now strengthened beyond human reason, beyond all time and space, I boldly spoke,

"Melchizedek, I want the Activations!"

He immediately flew down out of the Pagoda He touched me on the top of my head and the golden platform I was seated upon. I had just been struck by Lightning. I saw both my etheric hands go into five incredible activations in a procedure I had never before witnessed. I received a profound empowerment with each one. As each imparted their qualities, I was filled with their essence and gifts. My physical form was long forgotten and fell backwards onto the floor of the Kiva. There was also a special gift at the end, of pure Gold. I am now 'Shambhala Gold'.

At the end, Melchizedek lifted me back into my body tenderly. As I lay there on the floor of the Kiva, my physical body was being cared for by Angels. I was shown so many things in waves of revelation after revelation.

I was unable to move as billions of spirals of gold, green, red and yellow fused and swirled above me then entered within me. I was being transformed and remade into an energy being, not physical anymore. I saw the two angels, large, beautiful creatures, one on each side of me. They were holding my physical life force during the infusion.

Even when the intensity began to subside, I could not reintegrate back into my body. I could partially open my eyes but that was all. I was aware of the others leaving the Kiva, but I could not and did not want to move. The angels guarded me during this entire time.

Much later when the others returned, Rajah came over to where I was lying on the floor and looked down into my eyes. I could see the panic in her eyes.

I was unable to speak but she perceived this and said, "Do you want me to hold your feet?" Quickly she took hold of me, grounding me with several grounding symbols until I could come back into my physical body. I came back, but was filled with the energies and could feel the cells of my body spinning.

I lay back on the mat and just let it all continue. This lasted for hours. I don't know what the rest of the afternoon was like as the others went off to another location, and I continue to revel in this glow forever!

Susan Isabelle

Melchizedek, My Teacher

All during the next day I avoided the classes that were being given. I did however go to the 9:00pm gathering. As the participants went into a meditative state, I felt something poke me hard at the base of my skull. I thought at first someone had done this to me, but instantly realized no one physical had done anything. Suddenly, I was out of my body looking back at it. I was standing next to a wonderful being with big bushy hair.

"Sai Baba!" I laughed and said to him, "So, this is what you do!" To which he answered, "Yes, 'tis good fun!" We laughed together. I asked him,

"I have been told I will receive a new teacher, is this why you have come?" He answered, "No. I am honored, but I am not your teacher. I have come to introduce you to your new Teacher."

With that he stepped back and I saw coming toward me from above us, a glowing Silver Lightning Hand. I instantly knew who this was. This was the Hand of Melchizedek! He was again reaching down through the dimensions and offering His Hand to me as my Teacher. I had a choice if I wanted this. With all my heart and Soul I wanted this! I reached up touched his Hand. WOW!!!!!

My body was in another deep meditative state. Eventually, several hours later, I came back into my physical body and tried to move. I tried to stand up. I couldn't find the floor, however. I was trying to step down on dimensions that were not physical. I could see them clearly, but they didn't have physical form. I could see the floor, but there were at least three or four floors to choose from. Trying to place my foot down on one of them, I found this was done purely by guessing. Sometimes I'd guess wrong, then fall to the next-level floor, which was the real, physical, third dimensional floor.

Somehow, I made it to the door of the Kiva and stepped outside as the instructor had come back to check on me. I mumbled something, I think, about seeing Sai Baba. I started giggling and felt very "drunk." Trying to make my way across the lawn, I couldn't hold onto anything as it just kept losing form. My friend, Beth, found me trying to make my way into the hotel.

"Beth, can you help me? I feel 'drunk'!" I was giggling and having a difficult time walking and holding my balance.

"You need to get to bed!" She took control and she helped get me into bed where I just floated between the molecules that made up the sheets.

The next day my car keys and other things were found outside. I had dropped my possessions all the way back to the hotel. Not easy walking on vibrations. Hysterically funny, too!

Melchizedek taught me all night long. I had further infusions of His energy and was told by Him that He had chosen to manifest in me as His Female Aspect on Earth at this time. I would have lots to do! I was shown my whole present life in review just as people report in near death experiences.

Then I was shown my purpose in coming here as a representative of the Andromedan system and my roles there and also here. My past five incarnations on this planet were shown to me in detail and how they were to prepare me for this assignment at this time. I could finally understand how they all fit together.

I am to help others see and know their roles. I would be given special sight to see the Karmic Contracts of Light Workers in search of their gifts for humanity in the age to come. I am to share the Gift of Melchizedek with all those I come in contact with to prepare others for the energies that are coming to the Earth. I was shown how and why of so much! Occasionally I was instructed "Write this down or draw this!" Coming in and out of the astral to the physical to do this was difficult, but I was able to write down quite a bit.

The next morning, I was physically unable to get up out of bed. I was softly crying as I explained the best that I could to my roommate, Jelina, some of what had been shown to me. The responsibility of what I had undertaken was beyond my comprehension, yet feelings of intense love flowed through me. I was comforted and much loved, of that I was certain.

My Gift from Melchizedek

Rajah came and knocked on the room door, and Jelina let her in. She had in her hands a large wooden crate. She said,

"I don't know why I brought this here, but I was told this morning to give this to you." She placed the wooden crate next to me on the bed. I looked at the crate and there was a picture of an altar on it EXACTLY like the one in which Melchizedek had given to me, the precise image of the Altar He gave and placed within my heart! I burst into tears and Rajah, bewildered, held me until I could begin to open the box. There was a tag on the crate, a gift tag. I took the little envelope and began to open it. I then read its message,

"Remember the Sacred Altar & Space within your Heart."

I burst into tears again. Within my heart was the energy 'Melchizedek within the Pagoda Altar' given to me by Him the night before. Now I had one in the physical as a reminder and confirmation. Melchizedek had sent me a gift. I excitedly opened the crate to find the Altar pieces gently laid out ready to be put together when I went back home. Indeed it was an Altar shaped just like the one He placed in my heart! Looking inside, I found the Altar backdrop that was a deep green color with splashes of red, yellow, and orange with a big GOLD SPIRAL in the center!

I looked at in bewilderment as I remembered the billions of spirals; red, greens, orange and golden Spirals which were now a part of me, coursing through my very veins. As I stared at it in total amazement and awe. Rajah must have seen my stunned look and quickly said,

"I can get you another backdrop with different colors to match your home if you want." "Oh, no, Rajah, it is just perfect," I cried and reached over beside me to pull out the scribbled notes of the night. There I showed them the drawings Melchizedek told me to make of the Altar, with the colors of orange, red, green, and yellow splashes with Golden Spirals all over. My friends stood in wonder as I showed them the notes and pictures I had drawn during the night of the very gift that I had just been given—right down to the colors and shapes upon it.

Rajah makes these altars in her home in Washington. She had been directed to bring this one without even knowing why. I thank her for her love and willingness to follow her heart and direction! That morning a gift was given to me in physical form from Melchizedek to provide confirmation to others of what had happened to me.

Melchizedek further instructed:

"You, Al'lat Le Andro Melchizedek*, will have no further third dimensional attunements on the physical realm. Your work on the physical realm has been completed. All further energies will come directly from the highest etheric realms. As the Earth progresses, and as you require them, you will receive them. Accept no other energies.
Attune those, as directed, to the Energies of my Order.
Go to your teacher and relay the message to him and only to him that you are my Feminine Aspect."

"Sir, I need to speak to you!" I interrupted my instructor's dinner. "I want-.I have to tell you *now*...what has happened to me. It is important you know this. I have had the activations from Melchizedek and I am to tell you to confirm this to you."

He put down his fork and looked up at me, waiting.
"This is the order of the activations." I started to name them and he, in total surprise, began to say them in unison with me. Together, eye to eye, word by word, one at a time, we said them fondly. "Finally, I was bathed in a Golden Essence and now I am Shambhala Gold." I said.

"Yes, you have had all the activations of Melchizedek. You will find the attunements you give will be much stronger and there will be many changes," he said rising up from the table. He put on his jacket and turned to me. "Oh, do you have any Gold Essence?" he asked. "I need some." Then he left the dining room.

Altar site on Mt Shasta
Nov 1999
Susan Isabelle

7

All My Steps Directed

We had our last class session together in the Kiva. I had all my instructions from Melchizedek. I was also given a message to pass on to my instructor of the week who I now knew was a Melchizedek. I went forward to receive my certificate from him. I hugged this gentle and beautiful spiritual being and whispered,

"I, Al'lat Le Andro Melchizedek, of the Andromedan System, thank you, a Pillar of the Universe for your love and service to me and my peoples. I honor you." He hugged me tight as I spoke and then whispered to me in return,

"I know that you are the Female Aspect of the Melchizedek, we are all of the Melchizedek line, but you are favored." Then he paused as he listened to his own guidance, "That is all that I am allowed to say at this time."

He released me, we bowed to one another, and he joked to the group,

"I love it when women speak sweet things in my ear!" After receiving our certificates, we hugged one another and said our good-byes. As I hugged people, something began to happen to me. They were the first to comprehend a transfer of energy from me to them. I began to realize the magnitude of the transfer, for as soon as they received the hug, they would step back and look at me in astonishment.

On Assignment with Adama

Flowing from me was Melchizedeks' promised 'attunement'. I was passing, through the hugs, His energy. Many who received this energy called it "Serenity." A wonderful peace and stillness was imparted as a gift from Melchizedek to those of the Priesthood along with the unique energy transfer.

Going into the little town at the base of Mt. Shasta the next morning, I made my way over to a bookstore. Inside I was guided to a purple-colored book with a large golden Flower of Life symbol on its cover. The book had been written by a man named Drunvalo Melchizedek, called *The Ancient Secret of the Flower of Life*.

"Susan, you will need this book," I heard my Guide say to me. I flipped through its pages and was intrigued by both the energy of the book, his name—Melchizedek—and its content. I bought it and the book about *Telos*, the one Jelina had on the bed after I had my vision of Adama. I put them on the top of my carry-on luggage. They would give me something to read on the long cross-country flight home in the morning.

The next morning another student, Christine, and I drove to the small Redding Airport together. We discussed our personal growth, classes, and what we had accomplished during the week. Christine began to speak quietly.

"Susan, I don't know what you did to me when you hugged me yesterday," she said, "but I felt something wonderful go into me. It was so peaceful, so beautiful! I felt so serene and at peace!"

"Christine, that is the energy of Melchizedek. During the week I had several incredible experiences. Melchizedek and I have joined, and I am now the Feminine Aspect of Melchizedek on the Earth. He has given you a gift through me.

"From now on I will be conveying his gift to those of the Priesthood in attunements and in simple contact. That is what he has told me. I am so happy I could burst!"

As we continued our discussion, somehow we began to discuss the Merkaba and sacred geometry. Christine asked me if I had ever read Drunvalo's work.

"No, I haven't, but it's amazing. I have his book on the top of my carry-on to read on the way home!" We laughed as once again providence obviously was at work. At the airport I sat and waited for my flight. Christine was well on her way home. My flight had been delayed. Sometime later I recognized another student named Susan who had been at the Mt. Shasta sessions, coming into the waiting area. We had not interacted but now had the opportunity to talk to one another. She took out a beautiful purple and green fluorite skull she had purchased while at Shasta.

"Oh, it is beautiful! I exclaimed. It is a healing skull" She smiled in appreciation.

"Yes, I was wondering how I am to get it through the x-ray scanner-"she began. I instantly felt the skull's absolute abhorrence of the thought.

"Oh, no! You can't put it through the scanner!" I blurted out. She scrutinized me, startled at my intensity. "I mean, the stone does not want to go through it," I spoke more gently. "I can feel its emotions. Can you just show the skull to the attendant?"

"What will she say about it when she sees what I have? She'd probably be horrified," she replied. "I really don't know. This may sound crazy, but I do know the stone does not want to go through the x-ray scanner for some reason." We sat quietly side by side for a few moments, then I asked, "Have you received a name from the stone yet?"

"Why, yes," she said looking at me curiously, "I have. I haven't told anyone, but the name is Sha-na. I think that's the name, but it's not confirmed."

"May I see it again?" I requested. She took the soft cloth wrapping aside, and opened the stone to my view as she held it on her lap. I placed my hand over the stone and began to chant the name softly. "*Sha-na…Sha-na…..Sha-na…*" Instantly a blast of heat came up from the stone. "Yes, that's her name, feel this." As she placed her hand over the stone her eyes grew wide. "Now say her name, as I did."

"*Sha-na…Sha-na…Sha-na…*" Her eyes grew even wider. The stone was answering her.

"You have a beautiful spirit in this stone. She is very responsive and loving. You are greatly blessed and gifted. Please tell me you'll keep in touch!"

Shortly afterward, our long-delayed flight arrived and boarding was finally called. I followed her over to the table and to the scanner. As I watched giving reassuring support, Susan took out the skull to show the attendant. The woman at the counter didn't even flinch as she passed us though. I could just about hear the beautiful purple and green creature in her bag sigh in relief. Once we were both on board, a tall thin, young woman, our flight attendant picked up the microphone. She was standing directly in front of me. She began speaking,

"Hi, my name is Sha-na. Welcome aboard!"

I jumped up out of my seat, looking behind me to find Susan. Had she heard that? I wondered. Spotting her seated several rows back, I shouted to her,

"Do you need any more confirmation?" I could see her face red and laughing. She shouted back,

"No, I think I have all I need!"

Comfortably settled in the plane, I pulled out my new book and began to read. I learned of the platonic solids, sacred geometry and the Flower of Life symbol. Most of all I began to understand the Merkaba. The augmented background information I would definitely need to be able to teach my upcoming classes was contained in these writings. This was certainly an item I would require. I put down my book and fell into sleep.

Sleep led me to a place far from the earth plane, into the center of the Universal Mind. I began to learn. I was taken back into creation, the original Thought, the beginning before all creation, into the Mind Of God. I was shown the First Thought, from the place of Thought. During sleep, I was educated. I would use this later as a meditation, aided by the Power Itself to convey this truth, to teach my classes. (Once experienced, you can never be the same.)

Even more, the Vesica Piscis, the Light, was shown to me in its true form. The Creative energies were henceforth given to this One, the Only Begotten of the Mother and the Father, at its inception. We call it the Christ, or Light in our culture, the Vishnu in another. That part also chooses to manifest its creation in human form. Melchizedek stood with me and taught me. He is the High Priest of the Vesica Piscis.

Opening GAIA to the Light

As the plane flew closer to New Hampshire, I wondered how I was going to explain any of my week to my husband, "Hi, Hon! You'll never guess! I met this Telosian from ancient Lemuria and he wants me to go about the world opening portal sites to save the world!"

I could just imagine that one! My entrance into the metaphysical realm was difficult enough on this marriage. I remembered the night the pastor of our small New England church had come to our home. He told me I must never do hands-on healing again. I had a choice that night: agree never to heal another again, or loose my membership in the church. I chose to follow God's love and gift to me. Well, honesty was always the best policy. I would have to tell him, I decided. Will listened patiently to my story. We stayed up until 2:00 a.m. while I told him about the vision.

"Will, I know this is incredible, but will you go with me to find the site? You know those mountains better than anyone I know!" I don't know what convinced him but we went as soon as we awoke the next morning. In the car I told him about the location. He became more and more excited.

"I know that place!" He exclaimed. "I used to go there when I was a kid with my mother and father every summer. There's a camping ground there. That's just across from the Mt. Imp trail I maintained for the American Mountain Club when I was hiking."

We left for the mountains the first thing in the morning . It was a three-hour drive to the location. We stopped at the Pinkham Notch Hut off Rt. 16 above Conway, New Hampshire. I scanned the large 3-D relief map of the White Mountains they have in the lobby. With my eyes closed and arm outstretched over the 3-D map, I felt intense heat hit my hand. As I looked down, I could see the area clearly.

"Will, this is the place right here. Right near this water." Looking down, he showed me the area of the Dolly Kopp campground he used to visit as a child. The area I was showing him was a bit further to the North, but still had water.

As we drove into the campground area, the road split. We were very close. I could feel it. I felt the need to go in one direction, to the right, but the driver went the other way. I had the opportunity to see his old campground, but he was disappointed the actual site was not here. After a few minutes and my insisting, we went to the location I was being called towards by Spirit.

"If we go up there," Will said, "we'll be near the triple falls."

" Triple Falls! That's what Adama said—*three falls*! That's the place!" We drove up and down a bumpy, unpaved dirt road. The air was misty and about to rain as we drew near the parking area for hikers to enter the trail to the falls. We would have to climb up the mountain. As soon as we started up the hill, my excitement grew. After I had climbed a few hundred yards up the steep hill I could hear "Susan... Susan...Susan...." Someone, a woman, was softly calling me.

"Will, can you hear that?" I shouted. I received no answer; he was already too far up the trail ahead of me. I distinctly heard voices in the forest. I heard my name called by female voices and voices of women speaking.

So forging ahead, making my way along the steep trail, I soon arrived at a place where water was falling gently over old, ancient rocks. Walter was already there seated on a rock, waiting for me.

"Is this the place?" he asked.

"Yes, did you hear the voices?" I inquired; hoping he wouldn't think I'd now lost my mind completely.

"No," he answered. "I'll wait over here," he said motioning across the brook. He made his way over to the other side of the bank, sliding on the slippery rocks.

As I walked upward toward the falls, I was guided to an area across the brook. I was being directed toward a brush covered, cluttered area. Fallen trees and branches hid the place I was seeking. Without thought or plan, my body was driven to clear out the whole area to prepare it. With energy from outside me, I began to clear the area of obstruction. In a short time, the area was free of all the clutter of many years. I am not typically a strong person, but those branches went flying!

After the area was cleared, I laid out my rainbow colored cloth on the ground in front of what appeared to be a rock covering an entranceway. Behind the protective covering stone, the tunnel was hidden. It went straight into the mountain. On both sides of me were two large boulders and behind me were several small boulders. It looked as though I was kneeling on a small platform of sorts, now that it had been cleared.

Taking my stones from Mt. Shasta in my hands, I could feel their energy and excitement. As each was laid out on to the rainbow covering, I was being given knowledge. Each represented an aspect of a sacred meaning. As the stones were being placed, it was as if I could hear them saying, "Welcome in peace." -"Come with Joy and Honor." - "Bringing Wisdom and Salvation." -"You are Welcome."

Once they were all laid open upon the cloth in the order I had been shown, I sat down and I went promptly into trance. I know that I began to channel an ancient prayer to Pure Light and the God-force Energies. Each stone represented sacred knowledge, as well as an aspect of God's love and plan in some way. I could not understand it entirely, it was just a feeling. There was a prayer for each set of stones which seemed to lead the energy out from the portal stone, enticing it to release. Chanting the ancient symbols given by St. Germain and shown once again to me by the Lemurians, the dimensional portal for their coming began to open.

I was aware of Will taking pictures of me but was not able to respond to him. The Earth gave three sighs, and then three loud booming noises came through the mountain. They sounded like distant cannon fire from deep within the Earth. There was a rocking of the Earth as a quake. The opening had occurred. I gave thanks to my Guides and the Lemurians. They will use this in the coming days. The portal is dedicated to their use and the angelic realms in peace and wisdom.

As I sat there in awe, I couldn't help but reflect on the things that I was now beginning to understand. The dimensional walls are coming down. God is teaching us how to transcend the 3rd dimension into the 4th and 5th dimensions, or beyond, where we shall live and become truly One.

It will be in the twinkling of an eye for most, but for some, we are being given the keys to the Kingdom now and are allowed to visit. Our newly developing Christ nature allows this. It has been promised to us.

"Sue," he said quietly, "I heard the rumbling of the mountain. Three loud booms came out from there," Will said pointing to the entrance.

" I know. It's now open, it is done."

We walked back down the mountain quietly together and he drove home. I was exhausted and fell asleep in the car. When we got back home, we walked into our comfortable, cozy, living room.

Will said, "Look at this!" He took me over to a framed picture on the wall and pointed at it. He showed me something in our own home that had gone totally unnoticed.

"Amazing!" I exclaimed. In our living room, on the wall, there is a large 16"x16" black and white framed photo of the water falls—the triple falls—Walter had taken of the site! He had taken the picture over 30 years ago. We never knew or saw the importance of the picture, but had it there on the wall for the last eleven years.

Right there was the picture of what was one day to be a site opening for the Lemurians. Designed to be opened by us in the future, it was placed in clear sight every day for eleven years. How many times had I dusted that picture?

Divine ordinance has decreed all of our events and has shown us that we are players in the whole scheme of things...even when we don't know it!

A few days later, I picked up the developed pictures Will had taken of me while I was in trance, performing the ceremony. Right next to me on the rock is a large face, the face of an Olmec Indian. A large stone statue of a man-like figure, which is about thirty feet tall, guards the falls. It is complete with a topknot, face and full body, all of stone. It is a stone guardian; the guardian of this spot set here many, many ages ago by the ancients who knew one day it would be reopened.

If you look into the water you can see two forms of women. Women who are water sprites with long black flowing hair. They were the ones waiting, calling, and excitedly spoke to one another at my coming!

A few verbal thought forms had come while I was doing the ceremony and remained in my memory, the words of my friend Adama still fresh in my mind,

"We, the Lemurians, request no one come here until the spring. You will receive more information from another soon."

Later that day I received a telephone call from Racha-el, my co-Lightworker and Guarding Angel.

"Glad you're home. What did you do today?" she asked. "I felt an earthquake here in Manchester and felt that you had done something. What have you been up to since you got back?"

Susan Isabelle

"Well, Racha-el you're not going to believe this," I began to tell her the whole story.

I later took the site photos to a Mohawk Indian medicine man who lives in the area and is well respected by several tribes. I told him of the happenings. This is what he told me:

*"The Indian has known, and has been waiting
for many years for
an ancient prophecy
to be fulfilled.
When the Earth is about to be destroyed,
the Ancient Ones will come down out of the
White Mountains.
They are called the 'White Spirits'
and they will save the world.
That is why these
mountains are called the
'White Mountains."*

8

Many Are Called

November 1999
A Psychic in New Hampshire

 A couple of weeks had passed and I had not heard anymore messages. I rested and wondered what was coming next. I awoke one morning with the desire to visit a psychic. I took the day off to drive out to Portsmouth, New Hampshire, a favorite spot of mine. I liked to go to the Mustard Seed Bookstore, a book and metaphysical shop. I walked into the small store on State Street. There was a sign advertising psychic readings during the day. I asked the attendant if I could have a reading while I was in town.
 "Oh, our scheduled person has called in sick. I called another person to come in and he'll be here in about fifteen minutes. Can you wait?"
 "Sure," I said. "This is already beginning to sound interesting," I thought.
 A few minutes later a breathless young man came bounding into the small shop.
 "Hi," I said approaching him, "I hear you're the psychic of the day."
 His big joyful smile greeted me. I liked him immediately.

"Yes, I don't usually do these readings anymore, but they needed me. What would you like?" he asked. "The cards or just a cold reading?"

"Well, I've never had a cold reading, so let's give that a try."

"It's really nice outside," he said, "and I'd much rather do a reading out there. Would you mind going out on the bench next door?" He moved forward making his way out the door.

"No, that's fine," I said as I followed him outside. We walked a short way to sit under some trees on a nearby bench.

"I'd like to hold your hands, if I may." I sat facing Kevin and placed both my hands in his. There was a cool breeze on this November day and it would indeed be a 'cold' reading. He was quiet for a few minutes, then started the reading. "I see you contracted some 12,000 years ago to return to reopen the ancient sites upon the Earth."

Then he paused a few moments as I held my breath. A chill went up my spine. He went on. "Also, you are about to take a trip, many trips, across the seas." I gasped, and I felt like fleeing right out of there.

"The first of these will be in Belize," he continue then paused again.

"Where in the United States is Belize?" I asked, curious. I had never heard of Belize.

"It's not in the United States, Belize is in Central America," he said, eyes still closed, tightly clasping my hands.

"I see you must reopen the sites there—very important, the feminine energy is there. Many pyramids. Then, the other sites."

"How many sites am I to open?" I wondered aloud.

"36. There are thirty six main sites for you to open." Then he paused again.

"My back hurts!" he said and opened his eyes. It was over.

More questions! I had more questions, but the moment was over. There would be no more.

That night I had the dream. Once again, I met with Melchizedek, my teacher.

"How do you expect me to get to Belize?" I asked in the dream-state. "I have no money, and lots of bills!"

"This time, you will offer the opportunity to others to join you. Those who are called will come. You will advertise the trip and ask for a small sum to cover your needs. They will come."

On Assignment with Adama

The next morning I began to formulate a trip. We would go in May of 2000. We would go during the time of WESAK, the most powerful time of the year.

We would be there the night of the May Flowering Moon, just as I had been in Arizona several years ago when Buddha, Christ, and Melchizedek had come. We would invite them to Belize to bless that country!

I began to draft the newsletter to go out to those who would be called.

We were going to Belize!

The Grand Planetary Alignment

It would occur during our trip! This was an advertisement of that time

MAY 3, 2000 8:41 PM to 9:41 PM

(The New Moon in Taurus is at 9:11 PM PDT)

You are invited to join in meditation during the **Grand Planetary Alignment** on May 3rd and during the 25 days that follow, bringing forth the manifestation of illumination, love divine purpose, and the empowerment of what you wish to manifest in your life.

During the period from May 3rd through May 28th, the Aquarian energies will be focused through Uranus and Neptune at a dynamic "square" angle with the aligned planets in Taurus. This may result in either resistance and tension based on material concerns and attachments -- or in powerful manifestation guided by the superconscious -- our deepest inner essence of being. It is a "big tide" time to *receive* intuitive guidance as to how you can help to manifest the **Divine Plan** on Earth and to manifest what is your own highest fulfillment.

The key flashpoint of the **Grand Alignment** is the **New Moon** on May 3rd at 9:11 PM, PDT. Please begin the mediation by 8:41PM and continue until 9:41 p.m. Thereafter, it is recommended that you link-up at noon each day, doing a short version of the meditation and mantras through May 28th. Throughout this time, the Aquarian energies focused through Uranus will be at an intense "square" angle with Saturn in Taurus. By the Full Moon on May 17-18th, this will be joined by the magnificent conjunction of Jupiter and Venus, building to the *chronocractic conjunction* -- of Jupiter and Saturn on May 28th (and beyond). This cycle is a critical period for superconscious attunement and the powerful manifestation of the ideals and potentials of the new-born age.

The May 3rd alignment of the planets is in the following order -- outward from the Earth: Moon - Venus - Mercury - Sun - Mars - Jupiter -- Saturn. At a right angle

9

Maya Magical Mystery Tour

I began a study of the Maya and the Incas at this time. I came across the works of José Argüelles, who actually called the Harmonic Convergence in August 16-17, 1987.

I vividly remembered that day back in 1987. I was driving my car at the time listening to the radio. The announcer came on and said, "We are now at the exact time of the Harmonic Convergence, a call to all for peace and meditation across the globe."

I felt an overwhelming need to do this prayer, one so strong I still recalled it easily. I stopped my car on the side of the road. I had never meditated before, but bowed my head and prayed.

In 1987 José wrote *The Mayan Factor,* based on 33 years of research and study. He had also written *The Transformative Vision* which was based on the prophecy of the Thirteen Heavens and Nine Hells, which ended with the Harmonic Convergence in 1987.

I shared this new knowledge with my Master classes.
"There are great cycles of time recognized not only by the Maya, but also many other cultures across the globe. We are approaching a momentous event! December 21, 1999 marked the beginning of the last 13-year cycle of the Mayan Long Count Calendar. The end of that cycle is December 21, 2012. Do you know what that means?" I asked.

Most looked blankly at me just as I would have a few months earlier. I continued,

"These last 13 years of our time are the last days of the greater cycle of the 104,000-year cycle. José has stated that life as we know it will certainly change. I believe it! A major shift to a higher realm is about to occur!"

"A shift?" They asked.

"Yes, the energy is building now for this shift. This is the largest cycle of time. When this cycle shifts to a new higher cycle, every area of our life will be affected, as well as changes in all our experiences of reality. They listened and I continued,
"In Native cultures of the Maya this is shown as the snake holding the end of its tail in its mouth. Time circles, then one day at the end of the circle of the snake, time and dimensional reality rise up one level over a three-day blackout period. This occurs at every 104,000 year cycle."

A flurry of discussion ensued. People wanted to know more. Studying them I suddenly realized many of my students sitting here with me now had incarnated here specifically for this time. I must tell them.
"The Maya knew all this?" they exclaimed.

"Yes. The Maya are 'Lords of Light'. The Mayans recognized that time is circular and there were times of the Lords of Darkness and Lords of Light. We have just entered into the transition time of the Fifth Sun, which will reach completion in 2012. We are exiting the Fourth Sun which was ruled by the Lords of Darkness. We have been in the times of the Veils of Tears, or Nine Hells, and are now coming into the times of the Lords of Light."

As I began my study, I was guided to several good books and now understood Kulkulcan/Quetzalcoatl, the plumed serpent.
"Kulkulcan/Quetzalcoatl is returning." I stated, then paused for that fact to penetrate and be assimilated by the class.
"Who is Kulkulcan/Quetzalcoatl?" They asked, just as I had when he came to me through the Elestial Crystal that held his message to me.

"Kulkulcan/Quetzalcoatl is the Bearer of Light. He comes from the Pleiades, and represents the union of our higher consciousness, of the male and of the female.
"Upon the return of Kulkulcan/Quetzalcoatl it is promised the light of Venus would rise in the three areas of the Americas. According to the prophecy and the calendar of the Maya this was to begin Aug 16, 1987. Sound familiar?"

"Yes, the Harmonic Convergence! What then?" They asked.

"We are in the 25-year transition time right now between the suns. With the return of Kulkulcan/Quetzalcoatl the highest consciousness of the thirteen heavens will come. In Mayan predictions this signals the eradication of negative forces from the earth plane."

"WOW! That sounds like the Christian Rapture!"

"Yes, we will ascend. It is prophesied we will go into the first upper world in 2013 after a period of three days of darkness as the whole world goes through the next entrance of the Fifth Sun. The Lemurians will arise at that time to assist the earth in that transition. They will hold the earth's integrity as I have been told.
There is something else that is happening and it's happening to us right now!" I continued. "In fact it's why you are sitting in this class! The descent of the third eye consciousness is predicted to occur in that center which is called Palenque, Chiapas. This is the opening of the third eye of the Americas.
That's already started. We are in the 25-year span of transition. As Venus arises in this area the feminine energy will rise throughout the world. That is why I am going to Central America. As one of the Lords of Light—a Melchizedek—I am here to open GAIA to the Light. We really need to study and begin to understand the energies. *WE*—you and I—will be manifesting a new reality over the next 13 years!"

"How can we do that?" They inquired again.

"There are several ways. First, we must restore the proper time frequency of the 13-20   and begin to use Jose's Dreamspell calendar for our daily living. He has discovered the correct timing frequency known and codified by the ancient Maya in their calendars.

On Assignment with Adama

Channeling the welcome to the Lemurians

Stone Guardian Oversees the NH USA site

A water undine

The Face

Ist Site

Susan Isabelle

3 Spirits of Ancients

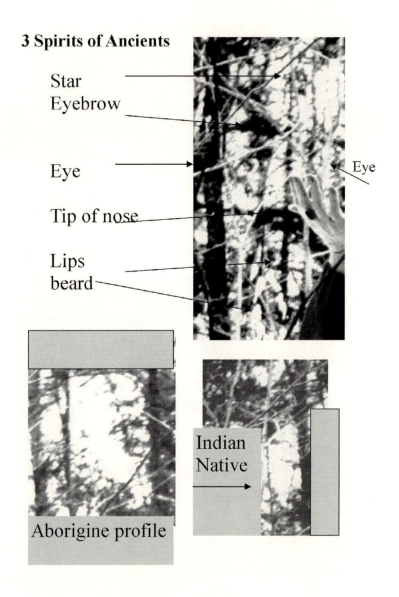

On Assignment with Adama

Adama   Native American   Aborigine

When praying and inviting the Guardians of the Earth, I called upon Adama, The Native American Indians and the Indigenous Tribes of the Earth. I thanked them for their unending love and care for us all. A student snapped this picture. They arrived for a photo!
Spring Equinox
March 21, 2000

113

The Dreamspell itself is based on the use and acceptance of the Thirteen-Moon 28-Day Calendar. Tones, glyphs and seals decree the days' energies. We need to be working and living in harmony with the energies."

"Second, we must learn to take responsibility: It is the last 12 years of a 104,000-year cycle. It is truly time to stand up and take responsibility. We have to let go of everything that does not benefit the highest good of all. Our mentality of selfishness and greed must be released. The future of the Earth, the heavens, our families, our future, is at stake in all this. You will need courage and understanding.

You will be the leaders. You are also of the Priest and Priestess of the Melchizedek line on Earth.

Remember: December 21, 2012 is 4 AJPU and is considered by many Mayan researchers to be the last day of this 104,000-year cycle."

"Third, you must realize we are not alone in our task. I have been given a special activation power through Melchizedek. When I give your attunements, my hands will be empowered by the energies of Melchizedek. The energies of transformation are given to you. You become the force on the earth that will bring about the changes. I am only one person, I cannot do this alone. It is not meant for one person to do this."

"Please understand: I am just the transmitter of these energies. When I speak of myself I do so in the same sense that Christ, the Creator energy, did: 'I can do nothing of myself, it is the Father which worketh through me to will and to do of His good pleasure. Remember the prayer of the Christ in the Garden: 'I will that they may be as we are, One. You in me, I in them, them in *Us together, as One.*'"

"That day has come. The fulfillment of that prayer is at hand through *each of you*. The way is clear, it is not found anywhere but in the heart that awakens to its Maker and accepts the Loving, Empowering, Lifting Energies made ready for us. Grasp the Light of this Love, this Truth, being poured out to you today and become the One! Accept, and take on your Oneness, your Wholeness. You will never be alone."

"Together, we will change the world through Love, through Truth, though the Energies, and the Light!"

10

A Gift of Vision

January 2000

"Susan, I have just been given a gift for you—it is in my hands. It is a gift of vision from my guides to you. May I pass this to you?" James asked. I looked up at this gentle twenty-two year old, his angelic face timid and wonderful in its sincerity.

"Yes, James, I'd be honored to receive," I honored him with Namasté, my hands in prayer position while thinking, This man has come so far and in such a short time, he has touched so many with his light. I bowed my head. With that he placed his hands upon my head.

"It is a gift of vision," he said.

Soothing warm energy began to flow into me. I started to drift away from the class and out of the room. Taken upon winds of pure light I was propelled into a realm of swirling colors and bright flashing lights, speeding forward in time. I recognized the flashes and brilliance of the future realms. I have been through this tunnel before.

Suddenly before me I could see a tropical place of soft green grasses and several people sitting upon the grasses between four pyramids. Each one was seated in front of a great towering pyramid, which loomed up into the sky behind them.

I saw myself seated in the center of the four people/pyramid pairs. It seemed that they were feeding energy into me from their heart chakras. I could see it flowing from them and I was absorbing the gift from them.

Instantly, I was taken to another place, over a sea. I could see the sparkling turquoise waves far out from any land. Four silvery dolphins gleefully bounded, flying up and out of the waters. They plunged back into the turquoise sea splashing their tails and sending water everywhere. They were having a wonderful time and I could somehow sense their delight. The dolphins flew back up again in their dance, but this time remained above the water. The four dolphins began doing an unimaginable motion, spinning above the water on their tails.

I could see something misty white and flowing coming from their silvery heads as they were doing this. The faster they spun the denser the white mist became, which then began to look like a waterspout of pure energy coming out from the top of their heads. As they spun on their tails they were sending out a frequency. I could see it spinning out and upwards.

As soon as I understood, I was again transported back to the pyramids. There again I saw the four people seated around me. They were receiving the energy the dolphins produced, and were in turn were transmitting it to me.

Suddenly, I was pulled down into the body seated between the four people. I could feel the energy pass through me as I pulsed the oncoming waves downward into the earth. I saw the pulses go down, down, through something like layers of time.

I saw deep beneath the earth in this place, a large crystal skull.

I perceived the dolphins' energy was about to enter the crystal skull far beneath us. The energy beamed into the crystal skull and I could see the skull begin to glow, shining brightly. It began to pulse, sending rays of energy and vibrations like a pebble in a pond, but throughout the earth from far below.

"What is this?" I asked. I heard the words,

> *"Then the message can be heard throughout all the Earth."*

I was propelled back into the room to find many faces staring at me intently. How could I possibly explain this?

At the end of the day, I said to my departing class, "Now you may want to read a few books. One is by Lee Carroll, called *The Journey Home*. I do recommend it, as you will see the seven angels within yourselves."

Lucy's Calling

Another Shambhala Advanced Earth Healer Class was now completed, a new year and a growing relationship with my Guide and Teacher, Melchizedek had begun. Each attunement was getting stronger. As I raised my hands up, the empowerment from the High Priest Melchizedek came in, activating my hands by the words I spoke and by the request I made,

"My hands to your hands, my heart to your heart in perfect Union."

At home I'd set up the Melchizedek Altar. I had taken the pieces, gently sanded them to perfection and put them together after my return from Mt. Shasta. Once completed it was an Altar shaped just like the one He placed in my heart! Each time I look inside, I see the deep green color with splashes of red, yellow, and orange with the big gold spiral in the center. I remember the billions of spirals; red, greens, orange and golden Spirals which are coursing through me and I feel its pulsing energy.

I began each ceremony with the Christ Light Creative Energies. I realized the activation of the classes were truly for the teachers of the future, those who would bring this new energy into the Earth plane. They would prepare the future for many. What I was teaching became vitally significant. Each future teacher must receive comprehensible information and activation of the energies designed for him or her, individually.

Now with the Melchizedek merging, I was able to channel differing energies to each student, per his or her specific needs and frequencies required. Often Melchizedek came through into the class using my voice to teach things not heard here on this plane since the beginning. I was learning, too!

The Guides also came in to give each student gifts of energy I'd never experienced before. As I hold out my hands, the Guides fill them with sparkles of color, with items in near-physical form that have weight and textures. These I pass on to the students who, amazed, hold them tenderly in their hands. Tearful or just amazed, they are directed to place the energies within their heart for activation. Classes are still unfolding.

> A few days after the class, Lucy called me during the evening.
> "Susan, I have been reading *The Journey Home*. It is so beautiful! I came to the Angel of the Sword of Truth and I cried. It has greatly affected me."

We discussed what she had been experiencing in her reading.

Early the next morning she called me again crying and all excited.
> "Susan, I woke up in the middle of the night. There was an angel with golden hair right here—right HERE in my face! We were face to face then he just disappeared!"
> She continued, excitement rising in her voice, "Susan, I just went out to my car. I went to hit the button on my keys to open the car door but the truck opened instead," she choked through her tears. "I was really aggravated that I did that and went to shut the trunk, I had my hands ready to push it down hard when I looked down and THERE'S A SWORD IN MY TRUNK!"
> She was sobbing hard.
> "Lucy, is it still in your trunk?" I asked.

> "YES!" she cried. "Can I touch it?"

"Lucy, it doesn't matter where the sword actually came from, it has been gifted to you by the Angel. This is what you must do..."

The channeled information came directly from Melchizedek. He told her what to do with the sword and how to cleanse and care for it.

The following Thursday night we had our first Sword of Truth Ceremony. The sword is about four-feet long, and covered with dragons. As we each held the Sword, a Word of Truth was given.

Solemnly, we each took a turn holding the ancient Sword. Some fell to their knees in tears as great waves of Spirit flowed through them, others raised the Sword high and took vows of service.

Watching the devoted Lightworkers that night I felt the awesome responsibility we each have incarnated into on this plane; so did Lucy. We had to physically support her body as the energies and all the emotions were coursing through her.

That night was the first night I channeled ACH'MIK'A'EL. This is the name of Archangel Michael, as he pronounces it. He explained to us that he is the Guardian of the Sword and it has been gifted to Lucy for the healing of mankind.

She has since gone on to perform healing for many others with the Sword. When it is laid upon the body, you can hear the healing taking place as little energy pellets hit the Sword from underneath. An amazing gift for an amazing woman!

Laneta's Calling

In my mailbox I had a letter from Laneta, one of my students in Arizona. I opened her letter and read, "Dear Susan, I will be joining you in Belize!"

Dear Laneta! I thought, what an incredible woman. She'll be the seventh one going on this trip. I remembered when we had first met: May 28th 1999.

"Laneta, I am so happy to be here!" I said after arriving into the Phoenix, Arizona airport.

"I am really looking forward to your classes, I'm so excited!" Laneta bubbled. "We looked everywhere for someone to teach us!"

Eight days of Shambhala Intensive training! That was going to be something new, even for me, but three Lightworkers wanted me to come for their private training. I would be staying at Laneta's brand new desert home. Each day was to grow in energy momentum. These are very special people who had incarnated here for this very moment.

We were about to receive some of the most intensive training on Earth. Some was even new to me.

"Laneta, I was instructed to do something prior to my coming here. I need to put the symbols in the sky during the full moon. About six months ago I was told in a vision that I am to place symbols in the sky at the May 1999 date of the full moon. Tomorrow, Saturday, May 29th is the date for my doing this. I hope you'll not mind the interruption."

"I am sure, Susan, that the class will not mind the ceremony. In fact, I am excited about it!" Laneta said.

"OK, then, we'll be putting all the Shambhala Reiki symbols into the sky tomorrow."

They seemed open to the idea and curious, even though I'm not sure what they thought of their teacher at that moment. Saturday at noontime I went out into the sandy desert and drew each symbol into the sky. I could feel them go up and ascend into the atmosphere. They just seemed to glide upward. It felt right and I thought that I had completed what I was supposed to do at that time.

Later that evening, about 8 p.m., we were seated outside in the desert back yard reviewing the class material of the day.

"Laneta, do you feel anything coming from that area over there? I asked pointing across the sands.

"Something is pulsing energy. It seems to be coming from the center, back there in your yard, just about where I put the symbols in the sky today." Exploring the area, I had one student go into the house to get the dowsing rods. "Yes, here we go! This whole area is just bouncing." I was getting excited now.

"Look at those rods go!" everyone exclaimed, as they spun wildly.

We dowsed and located the entire area that was pulsing with heat. Energy was rising up from underneath the ground and actually heating up the area in a very unusual way. We could feel an aura of energy extending out from the center.

At that moment I began to receive intuitive information in the form of what I call the psychic "video." In this video I was receiving instructions for how to put the symbols in the sky in the manner I was originally supposed to use, but didn't have this information at the time.

"Laneta, information is coming in now! We have got to do something! Please, I've never done this before, bear with me and just follow the instructions. I need the crystals."

Someone ran into the house and brought out the crystals. They watched as I drew out a large circle on the ground directly over the energy center and placed large crystals in North, South, East, and West position.

With a stick I found at my feet, I drew out each of the Shambhala symbols over the ground inside the circle. I then activated each symbol with the energy of my palm Chakra. The activation caused actual pain in my palm as they began to pulsate with the incredibly powerful energies. I moved quickly, activating each symbol as shown in the video.

"Please stand around the circle."

We stood around the pulsating ground and symbols. We dedicated the symbols to the highest good of all mankind. The Ascended Masters were called in and I channeled a prayer for mankind. We then sat down around the outer perimeter of the circle. Then we were 'gone'.

We awoke about an hour and a half later. And as I began to "come back" into the physical I saw three men in white robes standing across from me. They were very tall and completely white, misty as spirits, I could see right through them. As I watched them in astonishment, they faded back into the atmosphere. I looked over at my companions Beth and Laneta. They were in opposite positions! They had been physically relocated!

I remained in my same position on the ground, but they were in opposite positions. None of us had moved. They began to express their confusion, "I was there! No, I was there!" Looking at one another and not able to comprehend what had happened as we were all too spent to do anything at that moment, we all fell backwards onto the ground. As we looked up into the sky there was an incredible sight.

"Look at that! It's beautiful!" we exclaimed together. Over our heads was the most beautiful magenta cloud with great rays of pink spiking out from all around the cloud in the otherwise total darkness of the desert sky!

"Oh, my God!" Beth exclaimed, "Do you feel this?"
As we lay on our backs on the ground the Earth was heaving with energy in great, but gentle waves of building energy.
"It's having contractions; the earth is having contractions. It's birthing!" Laneta whispered.
"That is exactly what is happening! Mother Earth is giving her energies to birth the Symbols!" I said reverently. " She is awaking and look at that sky of love!"

"They're birthing into our reality and physical existence," Beth responded quietly..

As I watched, lying on my back, the waves continued coming from beneath us up and out into the earth plane and then the sky. I realized fully now what we were watching and experiencing.

"That beautiful flaming magenta color is the color of love and wisdom, the Mahatma energies are flowing into the night sky, Earth is never going to be the same." I said.

After a while, when we were able, we took our other crystals and activated them from the energy coming up from the center and the crystals on the outer perimeter. We downloaded their information into our physical being. We stayed and enjoyed the rocking of the energy for hours. We stayed until late in the night when they slowly began to slow in their pulsing.

"What an incredible experience!" They exclaimed, glowing in the Light.

"Well, it's only the second day—we can all go home now. Do you think we could ever top this?" Beth said laughing as we headed back into the house.

My answer was, and still is, "YES! We've only just begun!"

Two days later, while visiting a bookstore in the area, a book came to my attention. Opening it I saw an advertisement for a WESAK celebration for May 29, 1999! Understand that living on the East Coast I'd never heard of WESAK, an event that is celebrated in the Western US more so than the Eat.

The ad explained that the Flowering Moon of May—May's full moon—is an ancient celebration, which is observed in Tibet by the monks for Buddha's birthday celebration. According to the author, the Buddha comes to the Earth at that time and initiates the disciples on the Earth. With him comes the Melchizedek and the Christ.

It is a great time of blessing as the Buddha comes and glides over the bowl of water and a crystal in Tibet for the anointing of the ones chosen that year as the Tibetans celebrate the day and call the Buddha.

Somehow we, too, had been partaking in that ceremony. I believe that by our setting up the Symbols in the way we did, the placing of the crystals and the energies, we sent up a great big Pillar of Love Light that when the Buddha, Christ and Melchizedek came-they saw it and invited us to the celebration in a BIG way.

And just so we wouldn't think we'd imagined any of it, set Beth and Laneta back opposite one another on opposite sides of where they had been sitting. I was honored to see all three of them with my physical eyes. I think we were actually taken to Tibet for the ceremony. I know we were taken *somewhere*. The three white-robed men had seen to our coming back home. We had an escort by Buddha, Melchizedek and the Christ. WOW!

AND, those symbols went into the sky in a most spectacular way!

The Fairy Kingdom Arrives

The next morning Laneta and I were up early, discussing the incredible night we'd just experienced. It had rained during the night and the sands where we had our ceremony the night before were wet. As we sat under the porch shelter, I heard a soft tingling. Just as the sound came I felt a tiny little soft touch on my hand. I looked down at my hand but could see nothing there.

"What's that? Was that my imagination?" I thought to myself.

Then another tingling sound. This time I knew it came from the yard. Another little tiny soft touch on my hand. Then the tingling, Ting-ting-ting sound came again.

"Laneta, do you hear that?" I asked.

"What?" Then it tingled again.

"Oh, that's just the wind chimes," she answered casually sipping her coffee. We were still in a semi-state from the night before.

"Laneta, you *don't have* any wind chimes."

She looked blankly at me. This did not compute.

"Let's check this out." I said getting up.

We stood up and walked into the yard. A magnificent double rainbow greeted us in the early morning sun. Someone, very tiny, wanted to make sure we saw its beauty. Someone was very happy about it. Someone, very tender of heart, had touched me, not once, but several times it had tried to get my attention and rang a bell each time.

Laneta had a huge dog, a Great Dane. He was now scratching wildly at the door. Laneta went over to open the door for him to let him outside with us. As soon as the door opened he flew out of the house and began barking at the windowsill on the side of the house.

"What on earth is the matter with that dog!" Laneta muttered. She tried to move him away from the windowsill but his hair was raised on his back and he was barking furiously.

"Laneta, bring the dog back into the house. I have to tell you something." I said.

She dragged him back into the house and then sat down in a huff.

"I've never seen him act like that before!" She shook her head, wondering.

Betty came out of the house, ruffled from all the noise.

"What's the matter with that dog?" She gruffly asked shaking off her sleep.

"Have a seat, Betty, I've got something to tell you both."

"Laneta, remember hearing those tingling sounds in the yard before we saw the rainbow?"

"Yes." She nodded.

"Well, as the sounds were being made I felt a little touch on my hand."

"What do you mean?" Beth asked.

"As the tingling sounds were being made, I felt something touch me, it wanted me to see the rainbow. That *something* is now sitting on your windowsill."

"You're kidding!" Laneta exclaimed! "What is it?" She looked a little panicked.

"No, I'm not. Let's go see. I think it's a little person." I answered them.

We went over to the window and stood around looking at what at first appeared to be an empty windowsill.

"Please, we want to see you, " I spoke to the little person.

I sensed it was all right for us to touch his energy, reached out my hand and stroked its tiny body.

"See, touch like this," I motioned to them to gently touch the little one seated on the windowsill, feeling his aura with our palms. He was about two feet tall and his aura just sparkled all over. I could see energy waves coming from his small body.

"Oh, My God!!" they both exclaimed. *"What is it?"* they asked as they both backed up.

"Don't be afraid," I said. "It's a little person."
"A What?"
"A little person, a leprechaun, if you want." Touching and stroking the little body on the windowsill, they could hardly believe what they were now fully experiencing.
"Laneta, we have to talk." I looked at her. This was serious.
Beth and Laneta came to sit down and listen back on the porch. We sat for a long while as I began to explain what was now happening to them.
Along with our other activities the night before, we had activated an Earth Keeper crystal somewhere down beneath the earth in the Arizona desert. The pulsing we were still feeling was its newly activated life force. The Keepers of the Crystal had also been activated and were now arriving in Laneta's back yard.
"You mean there's more coming?" she looked at me alarmed.

"Yup! Maybe quite a few. Not a bad thing at all, in fact they'll bring much good luck and prosperity to you. You'll never be alone, they will help you in lots of ways, and this is a great blessing!"
"What am I supposed to do?" She asked.
"You will need to provide a home for them. This area is totally without vegetation or water. They would like something here, I know." I said.
Looking around the desert backyard, I could see it was very barren and dry.
"Oh, we have already planned to put in a waterfall right over there!" She became animated, with the ideas coming fast. "What about the dog?"
"Well, we can try to help him understand what's going on."

At that moment Laneta's husband came out of the house with the dog again. He flew right over to the window and began barking.

"What's with him?" Matt asked.

"Oh, we have a leprechaun on the windowsill," Laneta laughed.

Matt shot her a look then picked up a ball tossing it over trying to divert the dog. He didn't want to have anything to do with the ball. Suddenly the dog's ears pricked up and he spun around. He flew over to the corner of the fence and began barking at the corner top of the fence. Dave stood watching astounded.

"I think you've got another one, Laneta!" Beth quipped.

Then the dog began running along the fence, which ran the whole length of the house. He was barking, stopping, turning, barking, and going absolutely wild!

"Put him back in the house," said Laneta, becoming agitated. Dave went back in the house with the dog while looking over at us shaking his head.

We obviously had many little beings that were now sitting on top of the fence.

"What am I going to do?" Laneta asked. "I have to have my dog!"

"Laneta, you are going to have to go out there in the yard and speak to them. They have to make peace with the dog." I told her.

"What?" She said alarmed.

"You heard me, Dear One! You'll have to speak to them!" I tried to comfort her.

"I've never done anything like that before. I don't know how to do that! You do it"

"Laneta," I answered, "I don't live here. It is your dog and they have come here to you. For some reason, you are their keeper, too, and you need to get control of this now!"

"You think so? You think I can do this?"

"Yes."

"What do I do?"

"I don't know, Laneta. Just do it!"

With Beth and I watching from the porch, Laneta dragged her mat out into the center of the yard. She sat down, giving us one more uncertain look and then closed her eyes. After a few minutes of total silence she began to speak.

"Children of my Kingdom, I wish to speak to you. I am happy that you have come and I will care for your needs here as you care for the crystal. There are some things you must obey. You are not to come into my house and you must make peace with my dog. He lives here with the rest of my family."

She continued speaking to them, now fully channeling information to them.

When she had finished I could see she was coming out of the trance. She got up shaking off the experience and came to sit back down with us. We didn't say a word. We had just witnessed something very sacred. Laneta had just identified who she was while she was in trance: She is A keeper of the Children of the Fairy Kingdom. She was as astounded as we were.

"Did you hear what I said?" she asked, looking at us somewhat wildly. "It just came out of my mouth!"

With certainty she announced, "They'll behave now. We can let the dog out."

She got up to let him out. He ran over to the windowsill and began barking. He stopped, cocked his head as if listening. He sat down staring at the windowsill.

"I wonder what they're saying to him?" I asked

"I wish I could hear it," Beth said, leaning forward.

Then the dog got up and trotted over to the ball Matt had left in the yard earlier. He picked up the ball, trotted into the center of the yard, and crouched down. His front paws were on the ground with his big rump in the air wagging its tail.

We watched as the dog tossed the ball to an unseen friend. The ball bounced, but was not returned. The dog patiently waited, cocking his head as if listening.

Then the game began. Obviously, the new friends couldn't play ball, but they could play chase. All over the yard they played, running back and forth. It was absolutely delightful! We were laughing as Matt came out to watch the game.

"They're playing chase!" Laneta said. Matt silently went back into the house.

It was perfect that we were to have the Keeper of the Elemental Kingdom with us on this trip, I thought. From my Guides I had learned the Earth Healer Attunement and I was really looking forward to giving this special gift to Laneta!

Joshua Summers

The New Hampshire Telos Portal Return

March 2000

"Susan are you going to the Telos portal at Mt. Washington, New Hampshire this weekend? I really want to go," my student inquired.

"No, I just called up there and the road is still blocked, snowed in completely, they say. We'll have to reschedule. I did want to go now. It's the spring equinox," I sadly relayed to my student. I felt heavyhearted, and went to for a walk down by the beach at Crystal Lake, now a power spot since the Lemurians and I had empowered it from Mt Shasta. As I contemplated the words of the ancients "Do not return to the site until spring" I felt a calling in my heart.

I wanted to go but how could we get in there if it's all snowed in? They don't even plow it! The snow will be four feet deep! I complained internally as I walked along the shore.

Just then a large raven flew from the top of the beach pavilion directly over my head. It seemed to hover there for a moment while looking down at me.

"I honor you," I said to the great bird and watched it fly over my head. To my amazement, there was another in its place looking down at me!

"How can that be? I didn't see two birds, only one," I puzzled and spoke to myself on the beach still looking up amazed.

With that thought, the second bird flew past me and in its exact place hovered a third raven. I couldn't believe my eyes! They were all flying NORTH!

"This is a sign ! I am being called to the Telos site—we are going!" I shouted!

I called all those who had called expressing a desire to go. We agreed we would go in as far as possible and pray Spirit would provide.

That next morning there were several of us willing to hike into the snowy woods to the Telos site behind Mt. Washington. We drove all the way into the site on the snow-covered road as far as we could. The Pinkham B road was indeed closed due to the snow. Disappointed, we drove back out to the highway. For some reason we decided to drive up further North seeking a second entrance to the site. We stopped at a Ranger station and went in. A jolly desk clerk called to us as we walked in.

"Hello. May I help you?" She asked.

"Yes. We are looking for another way into the triple falls off Pinkham B road. Do you know of another entrance?" I enquired.

"Yes, there's one several miles up in Gorham, but I know that one is also blocked for the winter. You might be able to walk in, however, if you arc careful."

With that she pulled out a map and began to draw the route for us. Back in the car, we followed the road into Gorham. We easily found the rear entrance to the falls. We drove about halfway in to find a large tree blocking the road. We got out and began the hike up the winding road through the snow.

Lucy and I went on ahead to see if we could find the little bridge over the brook. As we crested the top of the next hill, we could feel ourselves walking through a wall of energy.

"Lucy, feel this!" I said as I walked back and forth through the invisible wall of energy. By taking one step forward, the waving sheet of energy was penetrated. It was fascinating to engage the energy in this manner.

"We're really close!" she answered, as she also played in the energy.

Going down the hill we could hear the water flowing by the roadside. We found the lower falls and stumbled in knee-deep snow toward the waters' bank. We waited for the others to catch up with us. Yes, we were here, but there was no way we were going to be able to get to the upper falls. Gail and the others were approaching us.

"This is it, we are here. Let's go in as far as we can. We can at least get close to the water." I stated. "Did you feel the energy veil?"

"Yes, we did. We were being followed, too. We tried to follow something or someone into the woods, but decided not to do that. We came on ahead to catch up with you and Lucy," Gail said.

We made our way through the snow. We finally found a partially cleared area by the flowing water and sat down to meditate. I could feel spirit activity all around me. I was also aware of movement in the woods. Taking my camera, I took several shots of Lucy and Gail meditating. I just knew something was going to show up on film.

"They're here," I announced. "I am going to offer a prayer to welcome them." I raised my hands upward to Source and prayed:

"I invite the Spirits of the Ancients, Adama and the Lemurians, the Spirits of the Indian who once lived and worshipped here, and to the Indigenous Tribes of the world.

I honor you and your care of the Earth. I thank you for coming."

Gail took my picture as I was praying. I could feel their presence all around me, I felt their wonderful love flowing to us; they had indeed arrived and wanted to make their proximity known.

Taking my hand and scanning the air around me, I was able to feel them, just as I had the leprechaun at Laneta's home a year ago.

Their aura sparkled beneath my scan and warmed the air around us. The air warmed so much we had to remove our coats. The air itself was glowing. We stayed as long as was feasible, but we had to leave this wonderful place. Departing the sacred space, we began the hike back up the trail.

We took our film directly to the camera shop to have the pictures developed. Sure enough, as I opened the folder holding the pictures, I saw the face of Adama staring out at me. In the picture with my hands raised in prayer I could see him clearly and the Star of David in his forehead. Next to him stood the Indian and the Aborigine. They, too, had come!

"Look at this!" I showed them all the amazing pictures. As we looked over the other pictures, we quickly spotted the presence of the little spirit that had been following Gail. There he stood, just above her in the woods, with a helmet of red, wearing a gray vest and a green skirt. In one hand he held a small shield and in the other a raised cross of gold!

I felt their blessing upon me that day. I knew that they were now with me and kept their promises to me even when I needed their encouragement and prompting!

Last Minute Instructions From Heaven

April 2000

It was getting close to the time for me to go to Belize. During one of my classes, a new student commented while in his first class,

"Susan, during my attunement I saw a priest of a temple. You'll be going to this large temple. I saw you there. He has been guarding the temple and that which is buried there all these years. In order to do what you have to do, *you must trick him somehow.*"

Then a call came from Lucy.
"Susan, I had a very strange dream last night. I was with you in Belize. An Indian elder was there and he was showing me how to do something. While the children were playing around me, I saw myself sticking wiggly sticks into the ground and had a bowl, which

filled with the red worms that were coming up out of the ground. The Elder seemed very pleased that I was able to do this. *I had tricked the keeper of the worms to make them come out.* What does that mean?"

As Lucy spoke the images began to come forward into my vision. I relayed the message to her,
"Lucy, I see the Mon---- symbol. You know, that's one of the Earth Healing symbols I am teaching. There is one that has four twirling energy protrusions. It is the Mon ---- you are using and pushing into the Earth. The bowl is the top of the symbol. The souls, the red-souls are being released with the use of this symbol. *Lucy, you are to do this and trick, or distract, the priest into letting them go...*"

An E-mail arrived from my cousin Elisa who would also be on our trip.
"Susan, I had a strange dream last night, We were in Belize being chased by bees and we had to run under a waterfall to get away from them. It was there under the waterfall we found what we were looking for. *Remember the message of the bees when we are there,*" said Elisa.

And another disturbing message came in an E-mail that read,
"I wouldn't go there if you paid me," he said, "you're going to die. I checked your chart for that time and *the night of the 17th all hell's gong to break loose*! It's all emotional you know—there's going to be light and dark there! The 20th is the biggest celebration of the dark in 5000 years—they want a blood bath, a sacrifice, and you'll be it!
I'm telling the others too."

May 5, 2000
Just a few days before our departure I was giving my last class when my student, very late, came running in....

"Oh, hello, Susan, I'm sorry I was late. I had such a hard time getting here today," the breathless woman said as she hurried into the room. She swept past us all and dropped her pillow and blue and white blanket in the next available space on the floor.

"I got lost and have been going past here for the last hour and a half. I remembered what you told me about this place being hard to find! It does disappear!"

As we all gathered around, she placed a box on the floor.

"I have a special gift to give to you and the class today, I really wanted to get them here for you." She said.

She then carefully unwrapped the box to reveal about a dozen or so small blue bottles.

" I have been making these for special occasions and I was led to bring these to you today."

They were of essences she had made from flowers in her own home .The little bottles were passed out to each one of us in the class. As I held the little blue object in my hands I could feel its vibration coming right through the glass. Its warmth and energy flowed into me from the bottle, and I tingled all over. Turning it over I read upon the label, *'Dolphin Priestess.'*

This woman had no idea about my vision or what I had been called to do in Belize with the dolphins, yet she had brought me an essence for a Dolphin Priestess!I then shared with the class my vision of the dolphins several months ago.

"This is another confirmation of the dolphins and the activation of the skull. I know it is somewhere in Belize. I know what to do and have had a clear vision of the location, but I've no idea where I'm supposed to do this!" I explained.

"Now we even have the essences for us to take. All is being provided. We'll find it, I know we will!" I affirmed.

Very soon now, we would be going!
We would have seven people on the trip.
Seven from Heaven!

May 12, 2000

Countdown...a last minute message came again.....it was from a friend:

"Here's the poem she delivered to me. It doesn't make any sense," she said...

There standing out of it was one sentence that made my blood run cold. It said,

"Heed the warning of the BEES..."

Then I received a message from Obed:
"Susan, prepare your ministerial credentials, you will need them to get your crystals into Belize," the Night Guide advised.

The next morning I had three certificates prepared and laminated!

Part II

The Mayan Magical Mystery Tour

1

The First Temple

May 15, 2000
Dreamspell:
> "I unify in order to know,
> Attracting healing
> I seal the store of accomplishment
> With the magnetic tone of purpose
> I am guided by my own power doubled

We arrived in Belize City and all of us were directed through customs. For some reason, I was singled out. My under ware went flying all over the airport and my belongings were thrown about as the customs guard tore through my belongings. The students just stood around aghast. Soon he found my carefully packed crystal skulls and unwrapped them.

"What is this?" he questioned as he examined the skulls.
"Are these artifacts?" He became excited as he looked at my crystals and crystal skulls.

"No, those are my..." I began, but he interrupted me angrily.

"Are you planning to sell them here in Belize?"

"No, Sir." I answered him politely, but very afraid now.

"I have to get my supervisor. You...these...are suspicious—you! Stay here! "He shouted at me.

As he disappeared around the corner to get his supervisor, I quickly went through my bags trying to find my Ministerial Certificates. They're tucked away somewhere in here! I panicked, rummaging through everything while my poor students were practically crying!

At last I found them just as the customs agent and the supervisor were approaching. Composing myself, standing up straight, I handed the certificate to the supervisor saying,
"I am a Minister and these are used in my worship practices."
"For worship?" he asked, looking at the crystals. He picked up the crystal skull and turned it over and over again in the light examining it. Obviously he had never seen one before. "What kind of Minister are you?" and looked carefully at the document.

"I am of the Universal Church of Light," I answered confidently, "and I have come here to Belize for worship and holy ceremony with my skulls I have brought from the USA."

He looked again, considered it carefully, turning it over and over in his hand. With his head bowed, he then he began to smile. I could see it. I kept quiet. He was considering something.
Then he looked up at me, jabbed the attendant in the ribs with his elbow, then stated
"She's OK," he told the Officer. "She may go!" he smiled brightly at me.
"Thank you Sir!" I said, smiled back at him and quickly repacked the rest of my belongings that were scattered all over the desk. I thanked my Guides also! OH, OBED!!!! You don't always tell me everything!!!!! Thank God I followed the instructions he had given me! Thank God the supervisor was a MAYAN!

Now I could breathe once again as I walked out the door. But now, everybody in that tiny airport knew who I was! The gringo white woman with blond hair who had a strange religion that involved crystal skulls, was clearly one of the deranged ones from the States. That's likely what was thought and they certainly would never forget my face. I had nearly gone to jail. That would have been something to see!

Finally out in the warm Belize sun, we waited for Elisa's flight to come in from the USA. We'd have about an hour wait and I needed the time to stop shaking and explain to the group what had transpired. I then went across the airport grounds to the Avis car rental to pick up my car. The little one-room office was about the size of a closet.

"Mom, I'll drive the car," Faith said, now very concerned about me.

"No, Faith I think its better that I drive in case anything else happens like that in there."

"No, Mom, I think I'm supposed to drive." We argued on the way over to the car lot.

The vehicle was a standard 8-passenger Rover; I could not drive the four-wheel drive land cruiser. Faith would have to drive for us. It was settled. Whether I liked it or not, she was going to drive. I thanked God many times that she did later on.

The car was painted turquoise, was dented all over, and had a cracked windshield from severe abuse. The crack ran one end to the other and had three large pits where it had been hit. I asked the attendant if it was legal to drive such a car and she said 'yes'. Looking across the lot, I quickly saw that our car was clearly one of the best looking around. "Not to complain," I thought. She giggled as I made her mark down every bump and bruise this wreck had on her little paper. There was a $750.00 deductible for damage to the car after all! Finally, Elisa's flight arrived and we packed the car and headed to the hotel in Belize City.

We all met for dinner across the street from the Radisson hotel that night in the small restaurant. We made our plans for the next day. Being careful not to drink the water or eat the salad, we felt safe, excited and ready to go! Racha-el would join Rob and Laneta across the street in their hotel while Lucy, Faith, Elisa and I would be in the Radisson sharing the big room. We planned to all meet in the morning at 11:00 a.m. after breakfast to prepare for our trip to Alton Ha, the first site.

Back at our room, the luggage was piled all over the place with barely enough room to walk around, but no one even cared. We'd only be here for one day then inland. Off to San Ignacio!

I made a cursory, mental effort to clear the room of old energy and sent out a protective shield. On this first day everything had gone "so well." Surely all those warnings about my never even getting here were nonsense. They were just attempts to frighten or even prevent me from coming and doing this work here in Belize. We had made it hadn't we?

Choosing my side of the bed next to the picture window, I shared space with Elisa. The window looked out over the balcony and the beautiful Caribbean Sea of Belize. Comfortable, satisfied, and exhausted, I feel into the bed, and into a deep sleep.

2

Maya Miracles

Around 1:00 a.m. I awoke suddenly. Something, someone was in the room. Scanning the room with my eyes, I dared not move. Frozen in fear in the semi-darkness, I could see this was not a physical being, not a robber, but I could feel an etheric presence.

I very quietly rolled over, slid down the side of the bed and slipped onto the floor. I went right into trance. I explored the presence in the room with my mind, probing into the darkness. This one was not hard to find. It was a vile, dark energy. A cloud was hanging over the room near Faith and Lucy's bed. I began to rock and chant to expel it from the room..

"Kodoish, Kodoish, Kodoish." The intensity of the vile, murky spirit grew, as it became aware of my prayer. It felt as if it were taking form right there in the room in opposition to my attempt to expel it. It came closer to me.

"Kodoish, Kodoish, Kodoish, Adonai, Tsebayoth," I continued my chant. I could feel the hairs begin to rise and the chill permeating the room.

"Kodoish, Kodoish, Kodoish, Adonai, Tsebayoth. Show no fear, show no fear," I thought and prayed the ancient prayer to dispel evil.

Suddenly, a large looming birdlike figure 'flew' in the room from outside the room, swirled above me and then stood in the hotel window. Its immense form filled the picture window. It was a large dark Mayan chieftain, with fierce countenance. His eyes were sharp and flamed at me. I sat very still. I now had an evil whatever behind me and an incredible being in front of me.

He wore a robe of multicolored feathers. Paint covered his black muscular, stately body and streams of lightening bolts were drawn down his face. I remained on the floor chanting.

"Kodoish, Kodoish, Kodoish."

As the figure stood there on the window watching me, I began to feel protected somehow, protective rays came from him, bathing my form on the floor. I honored his presence. The vile energy was now gone, dissipated by his power and presence. I began to relax.

I heard someone get up and go into the bathroom and become violently, wretchedly ill. I remained in trance on the floor as two more trips were made to the bathroom.

The figure remained in the window, and I on the floor, began to pray and continued the chant.

"Kodoish, Kodoish, Kodoish, Adonai, Tsebayoth."

After the third trip to the bathroom, Lucy—in a stupor—came over to where I was still seated on the floor in front of the window. I stirred from my trance chanting and signaled for her to come. Wordlessly, Lucy slid down onto the floor and sat beside me.

As she sat beside me I put my hands on her stomach and began to send the energy into her. I pulled a long, thick, rope-like energy out of her abdomen. It lay lifeless, it looked like a dead snake. It lay on the floor in front of her.

The Mayan suddenly left his perch in the window, swept down and scooped it up as an eagle snatches its prey. He disappeared out the window and did not return. We sat there on the floor with our backs up against the side of the bed breathing deeply. We sat there without saying a word for several minutes.

"Lucy, are you OK?" I finally asked.

"Yes, I feel better now," she replied.

"You're going to be all right in a little bit," I told her. "We needed to protect the room better," I apologetically added.

Lucy made her way back to bed. I lay awake for along time. Yes, we were going to need all the protection we could use on this trip, even the Mayan Gods. I could not, nor would not, allow myself to be so lax again. Here we were preparing to take on the ancient spirits of the Gods.

Who was I to think there'd be no opposition? This was the beginning. My awareness must be sharpened and my focus ever present. I was sharply reminded of this in what had just happened. My responsibility was for the completion of this work and the safety of my companions. I knew I would have to take command of the situations, to be demanding sometimes, if I was to complete my responsibilities.

All my skills would be needed. Sometimes I would not even understand my own actions, as I would from now on be guided by intuition. Sadly, I knew that my companions on this trip would not understand me.

"Whatever happens from this point on," I thought, "I'll be aware."

I set into motion the activation of my psychic abilities.
I keep them closed off most of the time simply because it is both physically and emotionally exhausting to be on full activation.
Long ago I had learned a few things:
1. To feel and know what others are thinking about you can be painful,
2. I have no right to invade anyone else's mind or personal space; I must have permission,
3. Controlling my own human emotions in response to knowledge can, at times, be extremely difficult.

For those reasons I learned to shut off my abilities so as not to have to deal with any of it. Life is much simpler that way and I was happier. Now, however, I would have to reactivate the deepest levels. That frightened me more than the experience of the spirit in the room a few moments before.

I remembered how I had reactivated the full psychic ability in a meditation while at the Melchizedek Method Merkaba training. I did, for the first time in many years, unveil the full aspect of my psychic energies. I had not done that fully since I was seventeen years old. It was too frightening. I kept them in partial activation.

The onslaught of emotions in the room that day threw me into momentary chaos and I quickly secured the abilities again during that class. I sat in the back of the room and could see, feel, and hear every thought of every person in the room. Total Horror!

"Put them back!" I thought, then, "I need this and I can't be afraid anymore.

I have to get a handle on this even if I do go crazy!

I can't hide this or pretend this doesn't exist anymore!" I fought with myself that day.

I had practiced long ago to tame the uncontrolled abilities; I was able to release them more slowly. With deliberation, gauging the amount of release at more tolerable levels, the genie was let out of the bottle. But rarely, full force.

Finally, I got it! I learned to be the master of myself. This practice has now enabled me to both use the skills of physic ability and live in the world. I need to be in the world without appearing as if I was someone who is mentally ill. I have known people who simply wasted away in their own little worlds because they could not enter the world of the living and interact with others. The emotions and physic energy around them forbade their entrance. It was too much for them to accept. I truly have compassion for those in past years who were 'safely tucked away' or medicated for their visions and sensitivity to thoughts and emotions of those around them.

Now I was about to put these abilities into use. I had to. I had to do this, for the people who had put their trust in me. Now their lives may depend upon it.

I lay on the bed and slowly, as I had learned, began the disintegration of the veils. Going deep into trance I began the journey. It is as if white sheets or veils are hung in front of you. You choose to go through them onto another level of awareness. That's the best way I can describe this. In a third dimensional reality there is no way to describe the veils. They exist just beyond us as curtains of sheer sparkling threads of silk, drifting on unseen winds in the distance.

Simply, with intent, I saw them and chose to walk through the veils. I walked through several layers and set the level I would now operate from.

The next morning I awakened to find a glorious Belizean day. I made my way out onto the balcony, sat in the big rocker and looked out over the scene below. So peaceful, so beautiful! Many grackle birds, hummingbirds and little yellow banana birds flittered about. The 6-foot wingspan wayfaring birds glided up above, suspended on the warm winds rising up from a new dawn. The early morning breeze was warm and gentle. Resting my head back, relaxing into this serenity I began to reflect on the night.

"Was last night a dream?" I sleepily thought. "Did that really happen?" Then feeling the awakening thoughts of Lucy, Elisa and Faith still inside the room confirmed to me that it was real.

"No, I'm 'turned on'; the night and the visitor were very real," I thought sadly again, scanning the area with my mind.

"All safe"...I tuned down the frequency a bit.

"I am guided by my own power doubled."
That had been the message of the day. Yes, my own power had been doubled.

* Dreamspell readings are the aspects of the day according to the Mayan calendar and the glyphs associated with the day. I used them throughout the trip and was amazed at the accuracy of the readings and the meaning of the day. I have included them for your discernment and amplifying of the events. You may also find them listed on many websites featuring the Mayan calendar readings today.

3

Yellow Lunar Star

May 16, 2000
Mayan Calendar Day: Yellow Lunar Star

> "I polarize in order to beautify
> Stabilizing art
> I seal the store of elegance
> With the lunar tone of challenge
> I am guided by the power of universal fire."

Elisa came out on the balcony. I shared with her the night's adventures: our visitor and Lucy's illness.

"I woke up this morning on my back," she said. "I never sleep on my back. I had my hands covering my stomach!" she exclaimed.

"Elisa, you were trying to protect yourself in your sleep state from that thing!"

"I must have known!" she agreed. "We'll need to be more cautious."

The year before she, too, had encountered a being late at night where she had been working in the Virgin Islands and vividly remembered the occurrence. Under a spirit's strangling grip that night, she was in fear for her life; she remembered and knew the dangers.

Lucy was pretty much back to normal now and ready to take on the day. We went down for breakfast.

"Good morning, everyone! How was breakfast?" I asked.

We gathered on the big veranda of the hotel to prepare our little group and make plans for the trip to Altun Ha ("Water of the Rock").

"We are going to start on a most incredible journey over the next week. Each of you has been selected not by me, but by Spirit to complete what we are to do. Much of this week is going to be totally Spirit led and if we are to do this, we are going to have to be in constant communication with one another."

Elisa described the night's events to the group.

"We are all going to have to keep up our protections, too." she explained.

I continued, "Most of all I need you to be giving me information. We need to be aware of everything to pull this all together. Each has a special gift. Racha-el, a Shambhala Master Teacher, has been with me for four years now, and is an Angel of Protection. She holds and guards the energies while I do my work and attunements."

Turning to Faith and Lucy, I continued "Faith is a Shambhala Advanced Earth Healer Master, is our driver, and has incredibly vivid visions to help guide us. Lucy is also a Shambhala Master Teacher, and has energy awareness and psychic vision. She also holds the Sword of Truth given to her by an angel. I truly believe she is an ancient Atlantean herself and I'm here just for her, I think," I said.

Then turning to Elisa and Laneta, "Elisa is a Shambhala Master and has worked with me in the Virgin Islands. She helped to bring the Reiki energy to the whole community, trained the nurses and brought the people into the 21st century. She knows spirits and energies. Laneta has the whole elemental kingdom in her back yard from the activation we did together last year and she knows that aspect of our work. "

Rob spoke up and said, "I met Susan a year ago at a Kryon conference. She said I needed the attunement and attuned me right then and there. I liked the energy. I just happened to be at places at the right time. I had wandered up to the mountain top where they were having the Harmonic Convergence in Maui, I didn't even know what they were doing, but I've been doing it ever since!"

"Rob," I said, "I think I'll just follow you!"

"Now that we have some idea of who we are and how we work, let's take this morning as an example of the type of communication we'll need."

"What do you mean?" they asked

"Well, what happened to you all this morning? You all went up town for breakfast. Did you meet anyone?"

"Oh, not really." They all answered.

"Did you talk to anyone?" I inquired.

"Yes," said Racha-el hesitantly. "I met a man who was at the bar having a beer at 8:30 am. We started talking. He comes from the village in Belize where they found the crystal skull. He knew all about the Mitchell-Hedges skull; he has a documentary on it. He has met Anna Mitchell."

"What happened then, Racha-el?" I asked "Anything else that was strange?"

"Only that a child came in selling some tickets for a benefit. I told her that we'd be gone by the time of the drawing. I bought one anyway and gave it to Chuen as a gift. Then I took his picture."

"Gave it to WHO?" I asked incredulously.

"Chuen," she answered.

"Racha-el, Chuen is the name of a Mayan God."

"You mean I may have given a Mayan God a benefit ticket?" she laughed

"Yes. That may really be true. Chuen is known as a child-like, happy trickster. I can just see him having a beer in the morning for breakfast and maybe 'checking you out'. He brings abundance and is under the sign of Venus, the sexual, feminine energies."

"Oh, good!" she laughed with us.

That was the beginning for Racha-el. Chuen had indeed given Racha-el a gift in return. We would soon begin to see how he had played another 'trick' with his gift.

I outlined the events that led to our coming to Belize, how spirit had paved the way and the events we had planned. Each received a packet of materials to read. Plus they received a small bottle of Dolphin Priestess Essences when I explained that we, at some point, were going to perform a miracle involving dolphins.

I passed out a copy of our trip schedule that read:

Monday 15th

>We will leave the USA on May 15th to arrive in Belize City at the International Airport around 1:00 PM. Belize is a beautiful country! We plan to have a general meeting at the Radisson Ft. George Restaurant on the evening of the 15th at 7:00 PM where we'll gather in our group.

Tuesday 16th

>The next morning, the 16th of May, we will caravan to the Altun Ha in the north of Belize. You will need a car and I am recommending we car pool to all locations whenever possible. The are more than 250 pyramids structures at this site. The Mayan name means "stone water". Altun Ha was an important Classic period site situated to take advantage of trading between the Caribbean and the deep interior of the Mayan civilization. Seven tombs have been excavated at Altun Ha. One of the tombs held the body of an ancient priest dated to @ 600 BC. With his body was the largest jade artifact ever found in all of the Mayan kingdom: a 10-lb. head of the Sun God. Our purpose here will be to infuse the land with the Mahatma Energy of pure unconditional love, lift the veil, and free the land. You will learn how to use your physical body and Merkaba bodies to bring in and infuse the land with this cleansing energy and specific frequencies that are needed for this

time. I will be also freeing the captives of many ages by the ceremonial use of the Michael Pillar of Light.

Wednesday 17th

On the 17th we will go to San Ignacio which is about an hour and a half drive from Belize City. Within walking distance from town there is a location called Cahal Pech which is a major Mayan ceremonial center. It is located on a tall hill overlooking San Ignacio. The largest structure is 77 feet tall with steep steps up the side. It was settled around 1000 BC. The site has 34 structures on two acres of land, with seven courtyards and temples. It is within a beautiful jungle with a variety of tropical plants and birds. In the afternoon, time permitting, we will go to this center to open, cleanse and infuse the Energies of Love into this land.

Thursday 18th

By the 18th we will be going to the El Pilar Archaeological Reserve, twelve miles north of San Ignacio. El Pilar has twenty-five identified plazas in an area of approximately 100 acres, or about three times the size of Xunantunich. There are a dozen large pyramids. It is divided into three primary sectors: Xaman (North) Pilar, Nohol (South) Pilar, Pilar Poniente (West). The eastern and western sectors are connected between two large public plazas. El Pilar remains close to the way it was found and much has been untouched. While the name has not been identified, it has been associated with water. Two streams have their origin here, one in the east and one to the west. The eastern water source is a delicate waterfall called Chorro. Here in this untouched preserve area a Mayan forest garden exists with hundreds of species of birds and animals. It is within this area that I will give the Earth Healer Attunements!

This is also the Flowering Moon of May, or *WESAK*. The Festival of WESAK is the festival of the Buddha.

Buddha is the spiritual intermediary between the highest spiritual center, Shambhala, and the Hierarchy. On this evening we will gather together to welcome the Buddha's Initiations in meditation and sacred ceremony. The Buddha is the Expression of the Wisdom of God, the Embodiment of Light, and the Indicator of the Divine Purpose. This is an annual festival of the Full Moon of May. During this time, the Buddha comes and anoints and initiates the Disciples of Light!

Friday 19th

A "free day" to explore, shop and enjoy our surroundings. I would also recommend for those wishing to do so, a trip to the TIKAL site in Guatemala or the Xunantunich (Stone Woman) site. TIKAL is one of the oldest sites and is not far from El Pilar. The hotel will schedule a guided tour for you at a reasonable price of around $40.00.

Saturday 20th

We will travel to the 1000-ft waterfalls and stay for the day. This is also available as a guided tour and depending on the road conditions, we may elect to take the day tour. There are swimming areas and caves to explore. This is an exciting area and beautiful beyond belief! Here we will reopen the ancient Lemurian portal and connect the energies to Telos!

Sunday 21st

We return to our hotel in Belize City. Belize offers some of the best snorkeling and diving in all the world. You may wish to schedule a trip with the hotel for that day and enjoy the wonderful beaches in the area. We will gather again at the supper hour to say our goodbye for we leave in the morning!

Monday, 22nd of May: Departure!

An end to a Highlight of your life that is really just the beginning! You will now have all the tools to bring Light, Restoration and Peace to Mother Earth in so many new and incredible ways! You will have learned and will now carry the empowerment to effectively carry on this work throughout the Globe! Namasté

We then began preparing for the trip to Altun Ha.

Belize, Altun Ha

Temple of the Sun God

Guidebook log: *"Altun Ha is the site of the largest jade skull artifact ever found in all the Mayan kingdom. It is the Kinich Ahau—the head of the Sun God—which was found in a tomb built deep within the huge stair block of the main temple dated from 600 AD. It was found with the body of an elderly priest along with many other jade pieces. The head of the sun god weighed 10 pounds and was six inches in diameter. Occupation of Altun Ha lasted at least through the ninth century AD. Altun Ha in Mayan means 'stone water'."*

As Faith drove us up to the bumpy road, we pulled into a cleared area between the towering rainforest and jungle around us. A little thatched roof museum held pictures of the jade skull that had been found here. It was the largest artifact ever found. A small store nearby displayed objects made by the locals in the open windows. Black slate etched and polished by the locals quickly became our favorite. Many of the slates were images of the Sun God. I bought a large wooden replica of the skull, which was carved by one of the locals. Beautiful artwork!

Walking up the loose gravel path winding through the jungle, we could see the magnificent top of a temple towering above the trees. As we cleared through the brush we came out into an open area quite suddenly. It's rather strange to be enclosed in tropical jungle and then be thrust into another era. Looming above us were four great pyramids placed in north, south, east and west, with a large grassy field between them.

Just beyond the four-temple area we could clearly see the Temple to the Sun God in the background. Even as tourists moved about we could feel the timelessness of this place, this mausoleum of antiquity.

Walking into the center position in the grassy field I was reminded of the gift of vision given by James a few weeks earlier.

"Oh, my God! This is it! This is the exact spot! Look everyone—there are the four temples as I described—this is it! This is where the dolphins are going to meet with us! Somewhere beneath us there is a crystal skull. The Skull will activate the others around the globe and send its message. Let's get the crystals!"

As we lay out the crystals it was quite a scene for those tourists passing by. One tourist guide stopped and gave us his card saying that he wanted to learn and would love to be our guide as we went across the country.

We aligned ourselves with the pyramids and placed large crystals in front of us. Our cowry shell rattles ready, we began.

I stood within the center of our little group who now looked small and lost in that great field, a field which had witnessed the deaths of many through blooded rituals and sacrifice. How many had died here and spread their blood over this place? How many waited for the release which was about to come? How long had they been here waiting and what was it like to be here watching and waiting for so long? I felt pity for them and for GAIA who had borne this weight for so long.

Lighting the copal incense I made offerings of prayers to all four directions,

"I honor you of the South, those who have remained here to watch, to guide, to protect. I honor those who have given of themselves for all for all the ages. For this day, I honor you. I honor your generations, your lives, the height of your summer seasons of life, your coming of age, your children and you." The sound of rattles released the prayers upon the winds and a drawing in of the ancient spirits was upon us.

"To those of the West, I honor you, those who have remained here to watch to guide to protect. I honor those who have given of themselves for all the ages. For this day, I honor you. I honor your generations, your

lives, the height of your giving of self through the seasons of your life, your maturity of age, your children and you."

"I honor you of the North, those who have remained here to watch, to guide, to protect. I honor those who have given of themselves for all the ages. For this day, I honor you. I honor your generations, your lives, the coming of the elders, the teachers of your seasons of life, your transitions of form, your children and you."

"I honor you of the East, the place of the Rising Son, those who have remained here to watch, to guide, to protect. I honor those who have given of themselves for all the ages. For this day, I honor you. I honor your generations, your lives, the coming seasons of life renewed, your ascension, your children and you."

Surrounded now by the presence of the ancients, their cold breezes swept past me and the others who were seated on the ground in the blazing sun. Taking the incense I circled them all three times while invoking the energies of the Light. The scent of copal was all about us as we began the bringing in of the Michael Pillar of Light to bring release to those desiring to go.

Raising my arms upward to the source of all Light, I invoked the presence of Archangel Michael and the gift He brings with the power of the Christ Light, the Ascension Pillar. He stands and defends; it is his position in the Universe.

Once connected I pulled down the Universal Power of Source into the earth plane as a great pillar to touch the earth. Its vibrational form is immense and we were surrounded in its light.

Then reaching down into the Heart of GAIA I invoked her energies to come forth and join with the power from on high. She opened her breast to send forth Her Light and pulling it upwards, the two mighty forces were joined!

The Male and the Female joined, the energy of creation abounded. The Michael Pillar of Light was now in place. Archangel Michael stood with his Angels, the Guides, and the Light to escort these home. Strengthened with the Power of the Ages, I channeled the powerful words of ACH'MIK'A'EL, "*Come forth now all those who have waited for this day! Your time of service is no longer and you may now ascend as has been decreed!"*

With these words, the breezes swirled around, whisking past us and into the Pillar of Light. It made us feel as if we were standing in front of an air conditioner on high. Yet, these spirits were light and airy. Yes, they had been waiting, but were not of a heavy burdened energy or of darkness as some I had encountered in the past.

I could feel their energy, their joy at the release. They had given of themselves willingly and not in a captive way. They had genuinely felt they gave in service, in both their lives and their deaths. Such Joy! Such youth! Many were children sacrificed or given over at a very tender age. I felt the tears streaming down as I spoke once again, more tenderly.

"The time is almost past, I must close soon. Any others wishing to leave may do so now. I call upon the Guides, the families, the Ones Of Old to assist them into the Light."

A few more gusts of cool winds now passed us then all became still. Going forth again, I performed the closing, sending the Pure Love of Universal Light upwards, the Energy of Mother GAIA returned to her bosom. I thanked the Angels and all that had come. The release was now complete; we could begin the activation.

All of us were somber with the knowledge of the awesome task ahead of us and the work we had just completed. I took my place between the four crystals, the four Lightworkers, and the four pyramids looming over us. Twelve within and one to guard, thirteen, I thought. Lucy would go to speak with the Temple Guardian Priest.

Now all the tourists were gone, and Racha-el began to secure the sacred space in which we would begin. She sent out a great wrapping Golden Flower of Life globe around us and I could see the outline of it, which encompassed us all including the outer pyramids. Instantly the whole area began to vibrate with waves of energy building within this glowing globe. The center pillar glowed with the Light of Source; we were protected and prepared.

Lucy had placed herself at the top of the Southern Pyramid and looking up I could see her seated there. I could also see her head rolling from side to side; contact with something had been made. It looked as though she was fully into the energy up there.

It was time to proceed. Taking my own Crystal Skull in my hands, I opened to the Light of Source and prayed. Prayed for my ability to do this and for my Guides to assist me.

Suddenly before me I saw the dolphins—hundreds of them bounding up and out of the waters across the entire globe.

"*We are here. We are ready!*" I telepathically sent to the waiting dolphins. I felt the connection. They were also waiting for us.

"OK, now!" I shouted to the others. "The dolphins are now here!"

I could see them once again upon their tails spinning, spinning, and spinning the precious nectar that would open the vault, open us up to the storehouse of ancient knowledge! My excitement grew and I shouted, "The Energy is coming! Begin to pulse the energy through the Merkaba, down into the Earth as you have done before!"

The swirling Universal energy filled our tetrahedrons and we pulsed it down into the waiting earth. Moments later the warm flowing dolphin energy came in as a white fluid streaming into our crown chakras, flowing down through us and into the Earth.

"Fill, pulse, fill, pulse," I led the group in the concerted effort.

"Wait, something is wrong," I thought "The Energy is not going down far enough; it's only part way." It seemed as if there was a lead floor which prevented the energy from descending any further.

"No," I thought. "This isn't working! Oh, my God!

It's not strong enough to get through the barrier!"

With that thought, my original vision was before my eyes. I saw the others sending the energy *into* me. I was supposed to be pulsing a single beam into the earth. I was doing it wrong. Only one chance and I'm blowing it!

"GOD help me!" I prayed.

"Open your heart chakras and send it into me!" I commanded the others, sounding like a wild woman. Blasted by their energies all at once I began the rhythmic pulsing of the energies. My whole body began a contractual rhythm. Fill, Pulse, fill, pulse. "Yes," I thought, "we are through a layer and going down." Fill, pulse, fill, pulse, another set.

"Yes!"

Then a layer of solid mass that the energy seemed to glide over like water. No penetration! Now what do I do? Fill, pulse; fill, pulse.

"I need MORE!"

I shouted, in a craving lunacy for more of this dolphin magic elixir that now consumed my every thought and physically controlled me in its pulsation.

"MORE...YES!"

I burst through the final layer with such force my consciousness left my body and descended down with the energy. If I were to have given birth at that moment I would have been within the child, that was the strength of the energy.

Like riding the back of a dolphin I plunged down into and through the layers of time to burst through into The Great Chamber of the Crystal Skull.

In a small chamber, far beneath the surface of the pyramidal grounds, there lay hidden from human eyes for at least 12,000 years a beautiful crystal skull. A Skull carved without human hand or intervention, formed of pure conscious thought. A Skull, full of life consciousness, just as you and I, waiting, waiting for humanity to mature, waiting for this very moment.

The ancients had placed it there. This was with the total cooperative agreement of the Skull consciousness. It lay as a repository of memory, of the history of this planet, and that of all creation. All planned long ago, this Skull lay waiting for the arrival of those who were to awaken it unto life.

That life activation was to come from the vibrational message of the dolphins. The dolphins, who throughout the years had been the guardians of the tones of activation, were the messengers. Those dolphin entities are recorded in many of the Mayan legends as having come from the stars to bring knowledge to the earth. Who, having come from their planet to this one to be the guardians of the tones, have come under assault from those desiring that humanity never ascend beyond their prison on Earth. On this day the dolphins were freed to return to their home planet; they have accomplished their solemn duty.

Set upon a small table, dusty with the passage of time, the Skull waited. Now at this moment the miraculous occurred. The long-awaited Light and Dolphin frequency had come. A beam entered the top of the dusty Skull. At first I saw a small glow, warming, activating the sleeping gem. Like a candle flickering inside the crystal, life began. I could see the pulse; the heart beat, inside of the skull.

Awakening, the Skull shook off its dust and the glow grew stronger. Pulsing stronger with each vibrational throb, the Skull became like a great lighthouse beacon within the small chamber. Fully activated, the Skull came alive in great pulsing waves of pure joy. Waves of energy streamed out from the Skull. Like a boulder dropped in the ocean the waves began to flow outward, sending the message upon its joyful voice.

With one forceful pulse I was thrown up and out of the chamber and back into my body. I could feel coming up through the Earth below us the warm heart beat of the Skull.

"It is done."

Exhausted, but full of joy, I shouted to the others. As a mother who has just given birth experiences duality, I, too, was spent, but ecstatic with Joy. Perspiration dripped down my face; this labor had been intense!

"Now put your hands on the Earth, you can feel the pulsing of the Skull, the pulsing of the energies. It is going out to all the earth; now the message can be heard throughout all the earth!"

The sound of sobbing drew my attention over to Elisa, who began to wail in sorrow. "All those years! All those years, eons of time in darkness, waiting, waiting, all those eons, it's been alone! Alone, alone. I can feel its aloneness and waiting and the darkness, alone," she cried, rocking inconsolably there upon the grass.

Beneath the blazing sun we took turns comforting and hugging her. I wondered...at the time of the release and activation, all the stored emotions of the skull had also been released. What a sacrifice to have made for humanity. Through Elisa that sacrifice has been acknowledged in at least one human being. I feel even now that all should know and honor that one solitary Being of Light who has given so much for us. Elisa had experienced the sorrow and I its joy.

I shared with her the joy of the triumphant Skull's accomplishment. The Skull had now fulfilled its contract and was pulsing its message to the world. The Skull would never be alone again, as this was the dawning of a new day, the dawning of the Age of Aquarius. Lightworkers, crystal skulls and dolphins together; this is going to be quite a new age!

Then I remembered Lucy. A quick glance up at the top of the pyramid told me what I needed to know. Lucy was lying flat on her back!

"Lucy! Are you all right?" I shouted up to her, "Come down!"

She staggered up in a daze and began stumbling down the side of the pyramid. Faith went up to help her down. At the bottom she collapsed in a heap on the ground.

"I met the temple guardian," she said weakly.

As we listened to her story, we could see Lucy had indeed met the ancient priest. Her white face told us he'd been up there with her for a while. Lucy explained she had been consumed by his energy.

"He wrapped himself around me as he came up from behind me. I was rocked back and forth with his energies. He overpowered me by his energy!" she whispered to us. "I couldn't speak to him, I was too weak, but I did leave the small shells up on the pyramid top."

"Did you use the symbol?" I asked.

"Oh, YES! It went right in and he had to back away from me!" She had used the symbol and it had indeed worked!

As she regained her strength, we led her over to sit at the bottom of the Temple of the Sun God with Laneta who had been speaking with a young native there. Laneta took me aside, and quietly said to me,

"This is an interesting young man. He looked into my eyes and asked me where I was from," she said. "And when I told him, he said, *'No, you are from Here'.*"

Looking up, I could see Racha-el and Rob had already ascended the Sun God Temple.

Lucy was safely resting now, so Faith and I decided to join them high up on the temple's summit. Climbing the steep stairway was quite a task as ancient rock crumbled beneath us.

"Why were these steps so high, Faith?" I gasped, stopping for a breath. "These beings must have been seven feet tall to climb these stairs!"

"Yes," she answered. "Take a picture of me over there," she pointed as she made her way over to an enclave.

"Look at this beautiful rock!" We looked at the pinks and yellows of silica rock, opal, which formed the ancient steps and glistened in the sun. Nearing the top of the stairs we could see out over the valley below and were awestruck.

Don't Make Him Angry!

I arrived breathless at the top. I could see Elisa with her hands on the ancient round sacrificial stone, sending in cleansing energy. Rachel stood beside her helping. Two steps behind them was a two hundred foot drop—straight down.

Faith and Rob were taking pictures of the incredible view. Looming out from the front of the temple top was a platform ledge, a scene of ancient ceremony and sacrifice performed before the people who stood below.

"Many souls lost their life here," I said to no one in particular, but uncomfortable in the unstable energy.

"I don't know that I'd put my hands on that!" I called, while watching Elisa and Rachel cleansing the stone. Indeed, I could sense some pretty awful stuff coming out from the cold rock, which was now in the full noonday sun.

"Awfully cold! Lots of dense energy coming off that," I called again.

"Well, it needs to be cleansed," they answered.

"I know, but I still don't think I'd put my hands on it."

Just then a bee started flying around us, buzzing angrily. It flew over to Faith and landed on the whistle she carried around her neck.

The bee then climbed into the whistle. Faith jokingly said as she took off the whistle,

"OK, if you want it that bad, you can have it," and placed it on the ground and walked away toward the ledge.

The bee then flew out of the whistle right at Elisa and Rachel, diving furiously at them. As they swatted at the bee, I instantly felt fear. That bee was trying to make them back up—and God help us—fall off the pyramid!

"Oh my God, it's the Priest!
It's the Priest and he has stirred up this bee! Get off the temple!"

I shouted. The bee now flew at Faith who was standing on the platform ledge about two hundred feet up.

"Get down, Faith," I screamed at her. She dodged the angry bee.

We ran down the steps escaping the bee. At the bottom, safe from the angry bee, I ran toward Lucy and the young native.

"Lucy!" I shouted, "We didn't give him, the Priest, enough shells!"

At that moment, as the words were coming out of my mouth, I saw the young man put into Lucy's outstretched hand a large, perfectly formed, pink spiraled shell he had pulled from the earth in front of her. I stopped short and looked in amazement at the young native. This was not *just* a young native. I looked deeply into his dark eyes which stared back intently, furiously, at me.

Quietly I asked, looking at Lucy's surprised expression as she held the shell,

"Lucy, may I have some more shells? Could you please tell me again what happened up on the pyramid?"

She explained, now more coherent,

"I was unable to speak to the Priest—too much energy for me!"

"You didn't speak to him? Oh, boy! He's mad! I understand, Lucy, but he's mad." I whispered to her.

I took the shells and placed them one by one along the front stairway that was going up the pyramid face. All the while I was speaking silently to the Priest over and over again,

"I honor you for all your time as guardian of the temple, the people, and of the skull. Please forgive us for not honoring you, as we ought to have. We did not know, you are right to be angry. I have heard your message. I now thank you for your dedication. You are honored this day in the completion of your task. We thank you for having performed honorably and reminding us of this great work you have done."

I hoped this would be enough. I then went to sit with the young man and Lucy who had been seated a few feet away on the grass. They had watched me place the shells. We sat quietly, not speaking for several minutes. The young man just lay beside us, chewing on a piece of grass.

After a while, knowing I wanted to speak to this man but first must honor his presence, I choose from stones in my satchel a beautiful blood red jasper and handed it to the young man saying,

"Here is my gift for you."

He took the stone and his face lit up. He was pleased!

"Well, at least he's happy now," I thought. "That's good!"

"What is this stone?" he asked in his deep voice

"It is a Red Jasper," I answered, knowing this had not been seen in this area before.

"I like it," was all he said. He went back to chewing on the grass and lay back down.

Faith then came over to where we were all seated and said,

"This is a beautiful place!"

Startling me, the young man sat bolt upright, fiercely shouting at her,

"They used to sacrifice virgins and throw them off the top of the temple!"

Faith, who isn't thrown by many, replied firmly,

"Well then—that just explains it!" and backing up, she walked off.

The young man then lay back on the grass again chewing the shard of grass while stroking the red gemstone. I silently and patiently watched him. Thinking,

"Yes, that's exactly where the bee had flown at Faith while she stood on the sacrificial ledge. It wanted her to fall—just as the virgins had before."

After a few minutes, he looked at me and said,
"I have a gift for you."

He stood up and began to saunter across the field to where the temple priests once lived. As he drew near the ancient mounds he began to sing an ancient song in a language I've never heard before. He disappeared into a doorway of the temple housing. There from within I heard him laughing, great deep laughter which echoed underneath us and across the field to where Lucy and I waited.

After a few minutes, he emerged from the ancient mound of ruins carrying two large stones. He proudly walked over toward us and placed them before me on the ground.

"These stones," he aid, "are from the temple. See here," he pointed, like the Priest he is, "They still have the original red paint." He paused.

"This was once a great temple," he said staring intently, deeply into my eyes.

" I know," I softly answered him. In my mind, I acknowledged him. He was their Priest. He was the Priest. "I know the people were good." I could see him examining my soul with his stare. He heard me. I sent him love.

"They were a peaceful people, I know," I gently acknowledged.

Deep within his eyes there was a softening as he nodded.
"Yes," he quietly, sadly answered. He sat down and watched me. I picked up the large stone closest to me and held it in my hands. Lucy also picked up a stone as I did.

A gentle energy flowed from the stone and entered me. I bowed my head as the attuning energies entered, gently rocking my body. When it subsided, I looked up into his eyes and nodded. He nodded back and was satisfied. I took the stones and bowed to him, thanking him for sharing his wondrous gift with me. I placed them on the stump behind me in honor, stroked them once again and nodded toward him.

Then he silently stood up and began to leave, going back toward the Great Temple of the Sun God, singing softly. He disappeared behind it and we saw him no more.

Lucy and I watched him in silence. We had been given a great gift. There was no need to speak. We sat silently for a while; just trying to comprehend the events that we had just participated in and I wondered what did it meant.

"Lucy, I'm going to find the others; it's time to go."

Altun Ha, Temple of the Sun God

I began walking toward the field where I had last seen them chasing after the beautiful parrots that were still chattering in the trees. As I rounded the corner of a temple, Faith and Rob met me.

"Susan, look what I've found," said Rob excitedly. "It's right over there under that tree." We walked together towards a large flat circular stone near a tree that Rob had found.

"Look at the writing on it and the carved strokes across the face," he said, pointing it out to us.

"I think that's an ancient sundial."

Then, quite spontaneously, for some reason I was guided to take their hands. We formed a circle together around the stone. At the joining of our hands, I was given a gift of vision. A white mist rose up from the stone, then began to take on form.

"Faith, Rob, there is a young girl in the center of us right now," I whispered.

Before me in the center of the circle we formed around the stone "floated" a little vaporous girl of about ten years old. I could see her Mayan features, delicate and so young.

Her white ceremonial dress shone around her dark little body; her ebony hair flowed out behind her. With bright, gleeful, laughing eyes she smiled at me and declared,

"Now we can dance!"

"She says they can dance now," I relayed as my tears began.

"All around us they are coming!" They came in spirit form, hundreds of Mayan faces. Crowding around us they came to look upon us. Freedom was theirs, they had come to say goodbye. They were honoring us. I channeled the vision of this sacred moment with Rob and Faith as my tears began flowing.

Centuries of healing had taken place on this day. As we held one another's hands the energy surrounded us, and I was at peace. Just what is the message of the Skull?

"THE TIME IS NOW! AWAKEN! ACTIVATE!"

It's pulsing out that message as we speak to all the other skull repositories that have been placed around our globe. Information on a global scale is about to be released. Ancient knowledge will soon come into our consciousness. Awakening us to the spiritual and the technological knowledge that has been held for us by the original framers, the messengers of other times and universes.

What Did You Say?

As we drove back in the car we were excited. What an incredible day! Loudly chattering over the noisy bumps and wind about the events that had transpired, Faith maneuvered the Rover through several mud pits, laughing as we slid all over the path. We finally made it back out to the main road, off the bumpy, pitted, mud-filled dirt road.

"We did it. Now I can relax," I thought. Everyone was excited and I was very tired. I put my head back and was about to close my eyes when something on the side of the road caught my eye as we sped by.

"Susan, Stop!" I heard my invisible guide say.

"Wait! Wait! Faith stop the car!" I shouted over the wind blowing into the Rover.

"Now what, Mom?" a tired Faith impatiently complained.

"Faith, back up. Back up the car! I saw something back there." Putting the Rover into reverse everyone groaned as we approached the carcass of a dead bird hanging outstretched on a piece of barbed wire.

"That's it!"

"Mom, it's a dead bird!"

"Well, there's something about it," I said as I jumped out of the Rover to take a closer look. As I rounded the car I could see across the road in a vacant field—here in the middle of nowhere—an old

On Assignment with Adama

man sitting on a pile of dirt. He sat watching us. I walked up to the outstretched carcass.

"Is this voodoo?" I wondered. "Why this?" As the others gathered around me we looked at the huge mass, rotting away on the wire. Long black legs hung down to the ground from brown and white spotted feathers. There were fat black flies buzzing all around it, and dining on the remains.

"Well, that's pretty disgusting!" someone said.

"Elisa, what is it?" I asked her as she had a great deal of experience in the study of birds and animals in the rainforest.

"I believe that it's a ——* bird. Let me look it up," she said as she took out her guide.

"Yes, that's what it is!"

"What is so different about this bird; what does it do?" I asked.

"Well," she said, "it does this funny thing. When it's frightened, the bird doesn't fly away, it stretches its neck way up, tucks its tail feathers under and pretends to be a tree. You'll have a hard time finding one."

I considered this a moment then said, "Oh, so this bird tries to become invisible—its quality is invisibility," I said aloud to the others standing there.

To my Guide, I silently asked, "What do you want me to do with this?"

"Take the feathers!" was the Spirit's reply.

"What? You want me to TOUCH that thing?"

"Take the feathers!"

---

* For the protection of this bird, I will not name it

"Oh, God, they really are going to think I am crazy! Totally out of my mind!" With that I gulped, stepped forward toward the rotting carcass and to everyone's horror, began to pluck the feathers off the bird.

"Oh, no! Mom, what are you doing?"

"These feathers have the quality of invisibility and I am to take them," I heard myself say firmly. Rachel and Lucy then stood next to me, and with guarded caution, took some of the feathers also. Together we fought off the flies.

As I returned to the Rover, I could see the old man had risen from the dirt pile and had come to the edge of the road to watch. I nodded toward him. He nodded back. He then turned and began to walk back toward the jungle brush.

We drove quite a few more miles up the road. I looked out the window again to the darkening evening sky and shouted,

"STOP! Everyone! Look!"

We were all gifted with one of the most beautiful cloud formations I have ever witnessed. In the blue, purple and golden evening sky stood an angel, several hundred feet tall. His handsome profile was complete with white fluffy outstretched wings flowing behind him. He was dressed in a golden and white Robe.

His arms stretched forth to the beautiful young woman with long flowing hair. Her face was lifted up to him, anticipating. As we watched, the Angel embraced the maiden, and before our eyes, kissed her! They merged and became one.

My little Maya maiden finally reached home.

Back at the hotel room, I carefully washed the feathers, dried them, and wondered...

During the night I received the instructions.

6

It Is All Illusion

May 17 2000
Mayan Calendar Day: Red Electric Moon

> "I activate in order to purify
> Bonding flow
> I seal the process of universal water
> With the electric tone of service
> I am guided by the power of space"

First thing in the morning I began to search the room. I needed string, wax, shells, and time.

"Mom, the others are waiting," Faith said. "We need to go. We're supposed to be going to San Ignacio this morning."

I simply sat there on the balcony wrapping the feathers in the brightly colored embroidery thread I had, for some unknown reason, put into my luggage before leaving.

"Why don't you go down for breakfast," I said, "I'll be done in a little while." Wrapping the feathers and then dipping them in the lighted candle's melted wax, I had several feathers ready. I thanked the giver for its life, its feathers, for sharing this gift with us. This took time.

One of the others came back to find me still wrapping the feathers that now had little tiny cowry shells that dangled happily from them. Just a few more to go!
"Well, it's time to go and the others are waiting!" she snapped at me.
"They're not going to leave without me," I said, "They'll wait."
"POWER!" she angrily turned to leave the room.
"What is the date today?" I asked.
"The 17th of May," someone else responded.
I remembered the e-mail from the crazy man who wouldn't let me go to Belize. At least he tried to stop me. He said I'd die there as a sacrifice to the Mayan Gods.
What was it he said about the 17th? Oh, yes, I remembered—the emotions.
"The 17th—night of the emotions—all hell will break loose," he'd warned me I'd die that night.
"Well, we've got emotions, I thought! I've just got to keep control of mine!" Soon the dozen or so feathers were ready, complete with bobby pins to hold them in my hair.
"Now we can go," I said.
Rob, Rachel, and Laneta took the express bus into San Ignacio while Faith, Elisa and I took all the luggage in the Rover. We had about an hour and a half drive to the hotel in San Ignacio.
Upon arriving at the hotel, Faith and Lucy stayed outside to bring in the luggage. I could hear them laughing with the motel attendant who was exclaiming amazement at all the luggage piled into the Rover. He didn't know we had three others coming by bus, making us a group of seven, not four. A joke, he soon found. This happy greeting was to be the first of many encounters with Angel who was much help to us later in our journey. Lucy then snapped a picture of Faith outside the hotel under the San Ignacio Hotel sign. Later, when the picture was developed we could see large cloud of white energy next to her. She was standing next to a great white, billowing Spirit Guide! I told her it was her entourage. She would have much protection here.

On Assignment with Adama

Inside, I waited for the desk clerk who was busy with another couple. The walls were lined with pictures of the Queen of England, who had stayed here at the hotel many years ago. She had come to this land to visit, known as British Honduras before their independence. Having a few more moments to explore, I entered the little gift shop by the front desk. There ahead of me hanging was a horrific looking object with large eyes. Drawn to it, I could see it was a little coconut shell covered with black and white feathers and large cutouts for eyes. Long streamers like the sewn mouth of a shrunken head hung down.

"Ugly!" I thought and continued to look around the shop.

"Go back," I heard.

"Go back? Back to what?" I asked.

"The feathered coconut."

"OK," I thought and went back to the ugly little thing hanging there. Taking it in my hands I felt comfort come over me as I stroked its feathers. I found a small card which I began to read, "TATA DUENDE..."

"I can help you now," the clerk called. I put it back on the shelf.

"We would like a place to have conferences," I requested.

"Oh, yes, I remember you from the e-mails. We have rooms downstairs which would be large enough," she answered.

" I thank you for all the help you gave to me and the information" I said to the young woman as I went with her throughout the hotel seeking the best possible location for our meetings and rooms. Soon we were back to room number two on the top floor. The balcony looked out over the Mopan Valley. We were above most of the trees and had a beautiful view. Choosing the view over the size, we agreed.

Signing in, I asked the clerk about the TATA DUENDE.

"What is that thing in the shop called the TATA DUENDE?" I asked

"OH, that! It's been in there for years!" she laughed.

She then explained that the TATA DUENDE was a spirit parents used to scare their children into behaving at bedtime when they didn't want to go to sleep.

"You know," she said, "The TATA DUENDE will get you!" She laughed again making a scary face and raising her hands menacingly.

"I think it's ugly," she said. "That one's been there a long time—it came from someone who made it in Guatemala."

I stepped back into the shop and held it in my hands, saying,

"I want it!" She laughed and giggled, probably wondering what in the world would this crazy American woman want with it. I didn't know either.

As we began to unpack the luggage in the room, I hung the TATA DUENDE on the lamp overhanging the bed. Elisa came into the room, stopped short, took one look at the TATA DUENDE and said,

"I'm not sleeping with THAT!"

Laughing, I went over and took down the TATA DUENDE and put it into the entranceway of the room, suspended from another wall lamp. I picked up the little card hanging on the head and read:
"HA SHE-SHE POMPE

> Should one try to catch the elusive TATA DUENDE
> he will lead them deep into the jungle to a sacred place
> where lightening has recently struck a tree and burned
> it to cinders.
> TATA DUENDE rolls himself in the ashes and
> becomes invisible.
> Now he becomes HA SHE-SHE POMPE and laughs
> all the louder knowing he
> cannot be seen."

"Interesting...feathers to make one invisible and the invisibility of a TATA DUENDE. What is happening?" I wondered aloud. This one isn't on the agenda. I did not share this knowledge with any of the group; something was about to develop. I'd just wait and watch for further instructions.

"Sue, the clerk says there's a bird-watching class going down the mountain at 3:00 pm; we can go if we hurry," she said.

"I don't think I'll be ready by then, why don't you go on ahead," I answered. "I think I want to go for a swim. It's been a long, hot drive today and that pool sure looks good."

We decided to swim instead and good thing we did, for about forty young children had come back up the same trail from their class outing, while we were in the pool. They surrounded us, giggling and laughing, asking us questions in perfect English. Elisa went back into the office to speak with the clerk and came back a few minutes later.

"I spoke to the attendant," she said, "they have given us the key and we may go down the trail to the river on our own as long as we don't release any iguanas from the cage."

Refreshed from our swim, we descended the trail into the jungle. Well beneath our hilltop motel lay the Mopan River hidden deep in the jungle. It connects the countries of Belize and Guatemala. It had been used by the ancient tribes to travel and move goods from one village to another for many centuries. As we made our way down the winding path we went deeper and deeper into jungle. This was also a jaguar reserve.

Pushing hanging vines aside we eventually came out into a high cleared area that overlooked the great Mopan River. Deep green, it was framed by high rocky ledges and towering tress. Parrots could be seen flying from tree to tree. An awesome sight!

We continued on and came to the riverside.

"A cathedral!" I said. "This is a cathedral!" I had been worried about where we were going to have a class. Towering above us was several hundred feet of cliff face reflected in the soft green waters of the Mopan. Hummingbirds whizzed by us as we sat by the waterside just taking in the awesome beauty of this sanctuary. Screeching green parrots flew from tree to tree.

On the ground beneath my feet, I saw something.

"Hey, everyone, come see this!" We gathered around to look at the strange rock formation in the ground. It was our first look at a symbol which I later understood was a Mayan God.

"I want a picture of this!" The stone face had an open mouth with colored rocks coming forth like a song, or tone. I snapped a picture of it; it was so striking there by the water. It was also a confirmation of the sacred place we had stumbled upon.

Here in nature's most perfect cathedral by the river, I gave Elisa, Laneta, Rob, Lucy and Faith the attunements to the first two of five symbols for Earth Healers. Laneta was crying softly as she received the Powers of the symbols. The energies moved her profoundly. As a Keeper of the elemental kingdom, Laneta had long waited for these energies.

As I sat and watched their angelic faces and souls absorbed in the wondrous attunement energy, I recall how this attunement had come about. St. Germain had come to me one night in a profound vision. Actually, he appeared to me in my room.

"*Susan, I want you to advertise an Earth Healers' class. Use the symbols I have shown to you from the Arcturians.*"

"How will I give the attunement?" I asked

"*I will give the attunement process later,*" he promised.

I advertised the Earth Healer's class and five people actually signed up. I had received further dream instructions for the use of the symbols and prepared the instruction manual. The day of the class arrived, but I still had not received the attunement process.

"OK, Germain," I said aloud while driving to the store. "It's three hours before the class and I still don't know how to do this attunement!"

Then the 'video' began. I pulled the car over and watched as I was shown by St. Germain how to do the attunement.

"What attunement symbol are you using?" I asked and was astonished when it came into view. He readily gave it and now I was ready.

"Thank you, Germain"! I felt his love flow over me. He hadn't forgotten me.

This little group of five—the first since the time of the Atlantean—received this activation and the energies by the shore of

Crystal Lake. As soon as I finished the attunement, I started to sit down.

"Go back and put your hands on their heads!" the voice of Germain commanded.

"But Germain, I've already given the attunement. I don't know what else to do!" I complained.

"Go back. And put your hands on their heads!"

I went back and placed my hands on the head of the first student. She was already rocking with the energies.

"Now, what do I do?" I wondered. Still holding my hands on her head I waited.

Something started to happen. My feet were the first to feel the energy spiraling upwards from the earth. As the energy shot up my legs and back I heard a woman's voice.

"This is Lady Gaia."

My mouth moved and her voice came through me; I channeled her powerful words.

"This is Lady GAIA!"

At that moment three mighty blasts of energy flew up my body from beneath my feet and out my hands into the initiate. Lady GAIA was giving an attunement! Then to the next, and the next, and the next. Each student received The Lady's attunement! I staggered over and lay on the ground. I, too, had received the attunement!

Now in Belize, in nature's majestic cathedral, I watched the same miracle occurring again. I addressed my class.

"One symbol is to connect the Divine Power to the earth plane and the other symbol channels the energies through the earth."

Standing together beside the Mopan River, I instructed them in their use.

"Now, draw the symbol in the sky, reach up and connect the symbol to Divine Source. Feel the connection take place...that's it. Grasp the energy; it is yours." I stated softly.

The first time connecting to these energies with the use of the symbols is a profound experience. There were many tears flowing at that moment.

"Slowly, slowly, bring down the energy beam on the symbol and connect it to the waters." As this was done, little gasps of delight came from each group member.

"We've done it!" Laneta exclaimed.

I continued instructing the group.
"These symbols are the gift of the Arcturian race to us. We will use them throughout the world as we begin to prepare the Earth for its cleansing. You all have been given a great gift this day. Use it wherever you go. As you bring in the Divine Energies, the water—like we did here in the Mopan—is purified. The Divine Energies will now flow out to every person. In time, all of the Earth's peoples will be elevated by this energy."

We sang the ancient sacred tones out over the vast wilderness, sending their restorative powers reverberating up and down the river. We then connected the powers to the source of the waters, bringing new life and cleansing to the land, remembering the Dreamspell energy of the day…

"I activate in order to purify,
Bonding flow
I seal the process of universal water;
With the electric tone of service
I am guided by the power of space."

7

GAIA Love

I was humbled once again to see and experience the pathway, the steps, the moments of Universal Guidance. I had no idea we would be perched high over the Mopan River, much less be sealing the sacred waters that day!

The Arcturian Race of extraterrestrials had channeled these symbols to the Earth plane through a wonderful woman—Kathleen Murray—in England a few years ago. Through the guidance of my teacher Melchizedek and St. Germain, I have been given the symbols and instructions for using them.

Today I stood on the banks of ancient river sacred to many generations and used these same symbols to begin the purification of the Earth.

I then taught the class how to make a Fairy Pond, a process to renew and empower the elemental life forces in the area.

"So much of nature has been destroyed. So much of the natural habitat of the elementals have been polluted. They are need strengthening and energy sources to survive," I said while preparing the stones.

"What are the elementals?" Faith asked.

"There are of four types of elementals: Earth, Air, Fire and Water. Without the proper activity of the elementals, the earth and all of humanity falls out of balance."

"How is that?" another inquired.

"Well, the elementals help keep us alive! As we destroy their habitats—the forests, the jungles, the water and the air—we lose their protective influences."

"The Gnomes are of the earth and help to maintain the physical earth plane. They help us to connect with the earth. By doing so we preserve our own physical life. The stones, mineral kingdom and physical aspects of daily living, are guarded by the gnomes."

"Are they alive?"

"Yes, in fact, the gnomes take on the physical form of humans at times. They actually die like humans, so when we destroy by fire, we may actually be destroying them. I worry about the rainforests and what will happen to the earth with the 'slash-and-burn' policies in many parts of the world. We need to protect them."

Allowing a few moments for everyone to absorb the information, I could see each one considering the area around us. Were gnomes here watching us at this moment, waiting for us to complete our tasks? Assuredly there were many.

I continued my narrative, pointing upwards to the beautiful sky above us.

"Sylphs are connected to the air. They're something like angels. They really help us to think and receive information that is beneficial to the planet and our environment. They work with us to develop wisdom. They are very sensitive to our thoughts. The human mind is so filled with violence, there is no wonder they have fled. Dragonflies are little sylphs and so are the butterflies. When they are around you, pay attention. Something is being communicated to you!"

We walked over to sit on the great rock. Behind us hummingbirds buzzed everywhere. One beautiful little joy-sylph iridescent blue and green hummingbird landed on the branch beside me. We looked at one another for a few moments. It just seemed to be saying, "That's right, we're here!" then it flew off.

I continued. "Once upon this earth there were many of us who carried the ancient knowledge and supplied the elementals with the energy. Not since the days of Merlin have there been those on the earth with the knowledge to restore them. Many elemental forms have died out or chosen to end their contracts with the humans."

I considered the fate of the elementals during this last period of darkness that has been upon the earth for several centuries, called the Veil Of Tears by some cultures. Humans had barely even considered the elemental kingdom, much less provided for them.

"To be able to provide the nurturing, welcoming energies to these little creatures is a first step in the process of restoring the earth and its systems."

I looked out over the river. "The undines, the water spirits, are a favorite of mine," My Scorpio water sign aided the connection.

I saw a little bubble come up from the water making rings upon the still green water. I placed the activated fairy stones into the water. We each took turns and prepared our own stones to put into the water.

"It's so peaceful here. That's the work of the undines. They work with our feelings. Notice how whenever you're close to the water you feel so good? Well, that's the negative ions and the undines at work. Also, when by the water you are more psychic. Try putting a bowl of water by your bed at night if you want dreams!"

Moving out of the direct rays of the beating sun, back under the shade of the overhanging trees, I continued.

"That sunlight is the fire element, the 'red salamander energy', it's called. Through the sunlight we assimilate energy for our spiritual bodies. Just like the plants require sunlight to photosynthesize their nourishment, the rays of the sun deliver spiritual energy to us. The fire elementals assist that process and sustain our physical body in the process. We will be seeing a lot more of that in the future when you begin to activate your own powers to transmit the rays to the earth plane for others."

"As we are coming into the Fifth Sun, we are beginning the ascend into the thirteen upper worlds. We are in the transition now and are already beginning to receive the rays. These cosmic rays are bathing our planet. They are being transmitted to us from the center of the universe, from one planet to another. Remember when we gathered together on May 5th for the grand alignment? That's when we pulled in cosmic power from those planets that were all in alignment. We are still feeling their influence now, and have just grounded some of that energy here in Belize!"

Rising, we walked over to the riverside. I began to send energy into the stones along the riverside making them glow. The stones, which also bear a consciousness, welcomed the powers and are still radiating the energy to the entire area. They will continue to do so.

As dusk was fast approaching we decided to climb back up the path to the motel leaving the river and the newly anointed waters behind. We were guided to a viewing area of three wooden plank chairs set on the side of the path up on the hillside. Anyone sitting in the chairs can see far out over the valley.

Across the way, further down in the forest, Elisa called up to me.

"Sue, look at this! It's a tree that has been struck by lightening. It's nothing but cinders!"

I walked down toward her. There before me was indeed a tree burnt to cinders by lightning! I remembered the little coconut shell spirit back in the motel room. This was a sacred fire, in a sacred place far into the jungle to which we were led by the spirit of the TATA DUENDE. In this he would roll and become invisible, laughing at all. But now *I* have the cinders!

Stepping forward, I reached my hand into the center of the tree and took a handful of the burnt cinders. No one even asked me what I was doing. They just watched and we continued on up the path. Dirty cinders and rotting birds...better not ask!

Once back in my room, I took the precious cinders, wrapped them in a magenta cloth and placed them inside the TATA DUENDE coconut skull. Alone, I spoke to the TATA DUENDE saying, to my own surprise,

> *"TATA DUENDE, I desire your power of invisibility, I have activated your energy, your Spirit, I have caught you and hold your energy!"*

I hung it back on the lamp over my side of the bed. There I would hold its Spirit until I was told what to do by the Guides. They were running this program now!

8

Muluc Speaks: Remember!

Later that night we all met in the San Ignacio restaurant for dinner. There were two other couples seated in the great open dining area. Angel had come over to be our waiter for the evening. We very much enjoyed his company and light heartedness. He patiently took our orders from our somewhat rowdy group. He was teased and teasing as we laughed together.

While we waited for dinner to arrive, I took out my Mayan Glyph book to look up the day's energy and the symbol associated with it. The symbol of the day was Muluc, the cosmic seed of awakened awareness. The number was nine, representing the recurrence of the great cycles. It is also the number of the Christ, Quetzalcoatl, and the Buddha. Those "great cycles" often see the return of master teachers on the earth. I began to read to the group.

"Drink from my clear waters," says Muluc. "Be cleansed by my rain. Godseed of awakened awareness, acknowledge yourself. Bathe in my waters of remembrance!"

I paused, then heard,
"Susan, I don't think you ought to do that here."
One of our members interrupted firmly.

"There are others here and this is not the place to do this." She said to me.

Shocked, I retorted inappropriately,

"Well, I don't know when we can do this. I'd like to share this important information—this is also a class remember?"

Looking at the other two couples peacefully eating their dinner, I wondered how my quieting down our noisy group by doing this could possibly adversely affect anyone. Then I remembered. This was the night of the 17th! Emotional explosions about to happen. If I couldn't control myself now, I'd lose all. He said there'd be a "bloodbath, a sacrifice," and I'd be it!

"There are people here who are on vacation and we shouldn't interrupt their dinner," another voice continued. "Your voice carries, you know." I looked to the other members of our group, a few nodded. They were all apparently in agreement. I could not continue.

"This is the night of the 17th. Remember the e-mail?" I said, looking directly at Racha-el. With her nod, I knew she remembered the message I shared with her before the trip. At least one other person knew what was happening and would be prepared to hold the energy with me. Or rather, hold me in check.

Exploding emotions barely under control inside, I put down the book and made a statement about our having to make sure there was time to share at least some of what had been revealed. I would speak no more this night and avoid conflict at all costs. I did remember. The glyph was right. Remember? Yes, I had been stabbed to death long ago. It was in a temple. I did remember. There was a bloodbath. I had been it. I would not do so again.

After dinner, I went back to my room in an attempt to keep myself and my emotions under control. The night of the Full Moon in Scorpio was upon us, and I, being a Scorpio, was most vulnerable to its impact. To complicate matters, we were still under the influence of the May 2000 Grand Alignment. Lots was still coming in!

Later, out on the porch Lucy and Racha-el sat with me for a while and we talked about the evening's events. I told them about my memory of the night long ago. I had angered some that time. Now I must stand down.

"You know, something else is happening that is really strange." I said to them as we rocked in the cool night air.

"Every time I close my eyes, I see a great tree. This tree is very tall with a white trunk going way up, straight up into green branches spread out sideways. It looks just like a great big umbrella with side branches. Up on the branches I can see beautiful colorful parrots walking along the branches. They are absolutely beautiful! Have either of you seen them?" I asked.

"No, but I keep feeling energy," said Lucy. "I can feel when the Guides are around me, my head goes right over to look at them, but I can't see them...*yet*!" she said.

"Well, I tell you that watching these parrots is fascinating." I described their slow meandering, leg over leg maneuvers as they made their graceful dance across the branches.

"As soon as I open my eyes, they're gone! I close my eyes and they're back! What could this mean?" I wondered aloud.

I couldn't wait to get to bed. This had been a long, exciting, but also difficult day for me. I had so many questions. Maybe during the night the Spirits would speak to me again and I'd finally know what was going on with the invisibility stuff. I wanted to know about the parrots!

As I lay in bed, I carefully thought about the events at mealtime. My raging emotions had been subdued. The test of my resolve commenced this night; thwarting the fates had begun. It didn't matter who had said what, the words were not theirs, they were the Fates, testing me. I knew that, and also my vulnerability.

Long ago, I had engaged in a similar contest. I fought and died; I lost a big battle. In a past life vision I had seen it. My memory of that time came back to me now. It happened while we were at one of the Master Support groups I held in Bedford, New Hampshire.

I remembered the night we had activated the crystal stargate a couple of years ago. I had wanted to understand a memory I had since I was a child and planned to use the Star of David Mandala Stargate to give me those answers.

I was about three years old and clearly remembered my mother, not my mother in this present life, but another mother. We were together when something terrible happened. She was afraid and so was I. Every night, when my father put me to bed, I could see her face and I cried.

"Where are you, Momma? Where are you, Momma? What happened to her?" I cried myself to sleep many nights. Then one night, being a brave little girl, I decided to go outside and find her.

I climbed up onto the window ledge of my bedroom and fell out onto the hard ground below. Outside, alone in the dark, I was terrified. I ran around to the front of the house and banged on the door, screaming and crying for someone to hear me. It was so dark! I can still see my fathers' looming outline as he stood in the light of the doorway looking down. His anger and shock frightened me. His words to me stung.

"Suzie! What are you doing out there?" I got a spanking that didn't hurt as much as the knowledge I would never find her. I was too little. That was in 1953. I was a difficult child.

Now forty years later, I lay on the floor surrounded by the crystals within the gateway. I wanted to know; I *had* to know. I asked to be shown the past life I remembered that night. I knew this was one that would help me on my path, otherwise I would not have carried that memory into this life.

The others were around me sending energy as I entered the passage into my past life. The floor beneath me faded away and I became the mist rising, floating to the top of the grid.

The Guardian of the Passageway granted my wish.....

I stood upon an ocean bluff near the white stands of marble. A High Priestess even then, garbed in my flowing white robes. I stood overlooking the beautiful waters. I could feel the wind through my long hair. I was praying and opening my heart to the One who had sent me. I was preparing for the coming ritual.

Atlantis, the leading metropolis, was at a critical time impacting planetary evolution. The energies were shifting; the consciousness of the planet had been overcome by the tidal waves of dissension. Separation from the Source of Love had clouded the minds and actions of the inhabitants. They had found the Keys of Life. The unbalanced mentality of the population created horrible weapons that threatened their existence and their future biological evolution. I had come to try to avert the destruction of this planet through a spiritual renaissance.

I saw myself walk back from the bluff down the white marble steps. Coming towards me, from out of the temple, was the High Priest. He was angry about the procedures of the coming ceremony. My authority, or so I had perceived and felt, was being directly challenged. There were harsh words; I became emotional, angry, and used my words to hurt him, trying to exert control.

I felt the knife press into my side; the blood began to flow. Holding my hand to my side, I looked up into his horrified face. Even he was shocked by his action; I saw a momentary look of pity. As I fell, he ran across the steps and away. I lay there bleeding to death on the steps of the temple, dying alone.

My spirit rose from my body and I looked down upon myself in death's grip. I, too, felt the momentary flash of pity for the one lying there on the steps. I held one thought, "She had not completed her task; the one she had come to do. What a pity to have lost over such a simple matter." The life now was of no consequence. I watched as two young priestesses came running to me, I ebbed away in their arms.

Then in a flash, I was in another place, another time, in a 1940's car upon the streets of a city, parked in front of my home.

"Eleanor, I'll get her," the tall man said as he took me up into his arms and lifted me out of the car. He passed me to a gentle woman, my mother, saying, "I'll see you tomorrow."

"OK," she responded and began to walk up the stairs to our flat.

Inside, she opened the door and put me down to stand on the kitchen floor. I stood there watching her take off her little veiled hat and hang her coat on the hook beside the door. She was a tall, thin woman with blonde hair. As she reached down to take off my coat, I felt my love for her. Her face with its beautiful features was close to mine. I could feel my love go out to her. She spoke gently.

"My precious little one," she cooed. Just then there was the wailing of sirens and loud, frightening explosions. She screamed, ran towards me, and pulled me down with her under the bed. She held me close as the bombs began falling.

My last memory of that life is of the wood floor. I can see the honey colored plank flooring and grooves even now.

I floated back up to the top of the grid; the Keeper was there. I asked him in distress, "Why so short? Why was that life so short? I loved her!"

"She/he took your life, she had to repay."

Then it was over. I was back lying on the floor amidst the star gate crystals and my friends. Tears were rolling down the side of my face that night as I remembered. My side hurt painfully where the knife had entered.

Karma had demanded I incarnate for a short time as a child to allow us both this experience: to rebalance the records. The record must be balanced, it was a preparation for this moment, at this time.

She must give birth to the one she took the life from:
I must give total love in return...today.
Now I understood.
They didn't want me to forget this one!
I had physical and emotional wounds from the event.

Back from the memories, back in Belize. I once again had a task to complete. I had lost then, but would not this time. The way is not anger, not retaliation, but peace. Love conquers all. It truly does.

I had to be tested once again to be sure I could control the man within the HU, sometimes toned as the name of God, sometimes thought to be hu-like humus or soil, (Hu is the name of GOD) MAN. HUMAN...the "GOD-MAN of Soil". That's who we are after all, if we choose to be. The emotions I experienced this night were not mine, but those of a High Priestess from long ago. The Scorpio full moon, as then, set the stage; her unbridled rage had cost her own life.

Once again humanity stands at the precipice. Once again, humanity holds the Keys Of Life. Destructive forces are at hand that seek to decimate the earth. In contrast humanity also holds the potential of great spirituality that will balance infinite knowledge. What is different this time?

The energies are again shifting, but now—nearly 26,000 years later—we are entering the time of the Lords of Light. They bring a new message, yet humanity must respond and accept that message.

The way is Love.

The gateway was opened for the consciousness of mankind through a priestess's sacrifice nearly two thousand years ago, done in preparation for this time. The Christ brought to the consciousness of third-dimensional reality the concept of Divine Love and the Birth of Remembrance. We are One in the Light of Love. Remember, my friends.

Once, 26,000 years ago I had been the sacrifice; but not this time.

After securing the room for the night, I fell asleep. Rachael and Laneta were still out on the porch talking and the sounds of their voices lulled me to sleep beneath the TATA DUENDE and my memories of that time long ago.

I awoke at 1:00 am and went into the bathroom. Half asleep, I closed my eyes only to see the Great Tree and the parrots casually walking along the branches.

I stared at one colorful parrot on the branch and watched its slow movements with great curiosity. This was so clear...so incredible. It was if I was looking down a tube, a telescope, and watching them move about.

As I watched that one particular beautiful bird, it turned and peered straight at me. As it did so, the bird began to change, to shapeshift in front of me.

Feathers became flesh. The face of the parrot became the face of a man, the feathers stuck out like hair, then his neck and shoulders.

As I stared incredulously, the man-bird turned and cocked his head from side to side—just like a bird— examining me.

I, in turn, copied his movements in examination of him. His legs were feathered but from the waist up this was human.

Who was this? Then the vision was gone.

I blinked my eyes, but it did not return. I went back to bed.

About 3:00 am I sat up in bed at exactly the same moment as Lucy. I saw Lucy's brown eyes, wild, wide and flashing in the night. Not a word was spoken. We looked into each other's eyes, lay down and went back to sleep.

9

The Atlantean

May 18, 2000
Mayan Calendar Day: White Self-Existing Dog

> "I define in order to love
> Measuring loyalty
> I seal the process of heart
> With the self existing tone of form
> I am guided by the power of death"

"El Bruto! El Bruto solto el Atlantean!!"
"El Bruto! El Bruto solto el Atlantean!!"
"Lucy, what are you saying to me? I don't understand Spanish!" Looking into her frantic eyes I could see she was deeply traumatized.

"The Atlantean!" she cried. "They have released the Atlantean!"

"Lucy, who released the Atlantean?"

"The El Bruto! The El Bruto! The Dummy released the Atlantean!"

"The Dummy? Who is the Dummy? Did we do something wrong?" I asked.

"No, No, NO!" she said. "El Bruto is a man, an ignorant one. El Bruto is a very nasty thing to call someone!"

"Lucy, calm down. Let's go into another room."

I led her out of the bedroom to the porch. This early there'd be no one around to hear us talking. We sat overlooking the valley of the Mopan on this beautiful morning.

"OK, I'm ready now," I thought. "Tell me what's happened. How do you know this?" I asked.

"Last night a voice came and spoke to me...spoke to me *in Spanish*! How did they know to speak to me in Spanish? It was when I looked at you in the night! Did you hear it?"

"No, Lucy, it was for you," I answered. "I must have heard it on some level but would not have understood. It was for you."

"But it spoke to me <u>in Spanish</u>! The voice said,

'The El Bruto has released the Atlantean!'

That means the Ignorant one has released the Atlantean and that is a very bad thing, I can tell! We have to do something!"

"You are sure that it's not anything that we have done?" I asked again.

"No," she answered firmly, "they spoke to me and I know we have to do something."

"Lucy, do you know where this Atlantean is?"

" No!" she replied. "I don't, they didn't tell me," she continued anxiously.

"Then we must try to see if we can get some information. Lucy, go back into the energy and let's see if we can get more information from the Guide or figure this out."

As Lucy went back into a semi-trance I began to ask her some questions.

"Lucy, go back and remember the experience of the Guide speaking to you, remember exactly what she said.

"The El Bruto has released the Atlantean," she answered in Spanish.

"Remember what you felt with the words, Lucy."

"It was a very bad thing, not good, and that concerns them. We have to do something, that is why they have come. We can do it."

"Do what, Lucy? What are we supposed to do?"

"I don't know," she answered, rolling her head to side to side.
Lucy often does this when she is in the energy. I knew we'd have some results now.
"Can we see what the Atlantean looks like? Lucy, ask to see the Atlantean!"
A few moments went by then she answered,
"All I see is light."
"Lucy, allow the Light to take shape and see it."

I, too, went into trance at this point. I felt the gentle rocking of the energy as it came into me, the relaxation and going down into channel space, my center. I began slipping into my silver-gray room of soft, gentle light, the place where I have met the Guides so many other times. This is the place between the dimensions. Here we may speak to one another and I am allowed to see.

There were no Guides present. I could see before me a large mound, which looked like a flat-topped pyramid. This mound was placed between four high pyramids in a field.

On top of the flattened center pyramid, I could see a white tornado-shaped energy spinning, spinning, and twirling on the top. I watched as it jumped down and spun throughout the countryside, then returned to its place atop the pyramid. Like a real-world tornado, there was destruction in its wake, but not a physical tearing. This was vicious energy.

Coming back a bit through the dimensional veil, I could hold myself between the veils as partially physical/partially spirit. I spoke to Lucy.

"Lucy, I see a flat pyramid with something on top. Lucy, can you see this?" I asked

"No, all I see is a white triangle upside down on top of another triangle."

"Lucy, that is it! See how the bottom triangle is flat on top?"

"Yes!" she exclaimed. " I can see it! What is it?"

" Lucy, that is the Atlantean and we have both seen him. At some point during our trip we will deal with this Atlantean. I am going to speak with the Guides now to find out what we must do."

Going back through the veil I called upon my Guides and prayed for instructions. I could see myself standing in front of the mound with the spinning white energy atop. I heard the deep male voice of my Guide, OBED.

"He will know you are coming as you ascend the mound. You cannot be seen, or harm will come."

I was then shown a "video" in snippets of time, in this order:

1. We were placing the feathers of the invisible bird in our hair...four of us.
Not clear who we all were, but four humans were discernible.
2. I was then shown a clip of us on the top of the flat temple mound inside
a clear crystal globe.
3. Next I saw the TATA DUENDE flying around us, laughing.
4.We began compressing the globe…pushing it. Then it was over.

"Lucy, I know what to do. But I haven't a clue where."

On Assignment with Adama

After breakfast we all piled into the Rover. We were off to Xunantunich!

We were excited, yesterday and the dolphin energy work had given us confirmation of our task and true sense of our purpose, plus we knew there was more to come. The day's activities were planned: We would be making a change and going to Xunantunich today and then find a place to have our evening ceremony. Here at Xunantunich we would be taking a ferry across the Mopan River into the site of the Xunantunich temple.

According to our guidebook this place meant *"stone woman"* and that sounded like a good place to free the feminine energy! Xunantunich also boasted a large 130-foot temple called El Castillo and was a thriving temple area long after the colossal Tikal complex in Guatemala had been abandoned.

As the guide book stated, *"Xunantunich also had a beautiful frieze, or band of stucco decoration, that had signs of the sun god, Venus, and an unidentified headless man who had been deliberately beheaded by the Maya for some reason."*

Bringing new life to the ancient ceremonial center by awakening that stone woman meant bringing the crystals, openness to of all the psychic occurrences, and acknowledging synchronicity to do as Spirit led.

It was a short drive to the location just north of San Ignacio. Lucy and I shared a little bit with the others of our morning's experience. It was difficult talking over the wind, so we really didn't get to tell them all of it.

Both Laneta and Rachel also had an experience to share. They had talked long into the night. They called it the "night with no end," as time seemed to have stopped for them and they also saw a very peculiar moon that night.

We drove up to the ferry docking area, pulled over and parked the Rover. We saw a couple of little thatched shelters with vendors selling their wares. Down at the riverside waited the ferryboat on which we would be placing our Rover. Amazing as it seems, they actually use a hand crank to pull the passenger-laden boat across the river.

As I got out of the Rover I spotted a man near the vendors. He seemed to stand out for some reason, glowed brighter somehow, and I was drawn towards him. I could see his deep Mayan features and small build even between the others standing around him. As I began to take a step in his direction he looked up at me, left his friends and other guide companions, and came quickly over to the side of the Rover to speak with me.

"Hello," he said cheerfully. "My name is Juan and I can be your Guide for the temple for $20.00 for an hour and a half."

In that instant I knew him, though I had never met him previously, not in *this* life anyway. There was an undeniable spirit connection. I had never met this man, yet I knew him and trusted him immediately.

"Juan," I asked, "is that $20.00 for each person?"

"No, NO!" he exclaimed. "Not each person, but for all you in the car." His flashing eyes sparkled as he spoke and waved his hand over the car.

"Juan, we might be longer than an hour and a half. We have come to do spiritual work."

"No problem—I want to learn!" His voice was rising, as he became even more excited. "Take as much time as you need! I can ride in the car and tell you all about the temple and the people," Juan promised.

We all felt an instant rapport with him; his joyful manner and lively spirit told us he really enjoyed his work and he would be an excellent guide. We hadn't planned on hiring anyone for this trip but he was hired!

We crossed the river without incident and started up the steep pathway that served as a road. Faith put on the four-wheel drive. Xunantunich is 250 feet above the valley and has a spectacular view, but the road to the top is a real trip. While Faith dodged the deep ruts, we were tossed about, but Juan didn't seem to notice and began to tell us of the history of Xunantunich.

"My family has always lived near here in this valley in the Mayan tradition. My cousin and I still practice the ancient Mayan religion and ways. When we reach the top, you will be able to see the villages from the temple site."

Once we arrived and parked the Rover in a level area we had to climb the rest of the way on foot. At the entranceway to the site, we stopped for a few minutes to rest and have a Coca Cola. They still use the tall green bottles of my youth. Much of Belize seems to have stopped in time, somewhere in the 1950's. In many ways, I like it. It reminds me of the beach area where I grew up in Florida.

We began another climb up the steep pathway, then up the wooden stairway that suddenly put us in a huge field. I stood frozen staring at the sight before me, astounded, as Juan began to speak.

"Now this is very unusual: the Maya, you see, always make the four pyramid configuretion. However, this site has a center pyramid mound—no one knows why they put the mound in the center of their field. And it is FLAT TOPPED. There is no other configuration like this in all of Maya land."

We were in the field of four pyramids—with a flat-topped pyramid mound in the center of the field! This was the field shown to me just this morning while I was in trance with Lucy.

"Juan, *I* know why," I thought. "It is the burial mound of the Atlantean. He has been released and is on top of that mound!" I turned around and pulled Lucy up the stairs next to me.

"Lucy, LOOK! " I whispered to her.

"Oh, my God, that's it," Lucy whispered to me. "That's the Atlantean!"

"Now what am I going to do?" I exclaimed to her.

"We're here! I'm not ready for this...think...don't panic. Use your intuition. Take command," I told myself.

I spoke to Juan taking him aside.

"Juan, you will be taking some of the others ahead to the rest of the site. Some of us are going to be on top of that mound. We have some work to do," I said to him firmly.

"OK," he said, "I will do that. We will meet you later."

He began to gather his group together and I mine. I felt as though I had an instant partnership with this vibrant man; he had come to help. As we walked toward the mound, Juan continued speaking.

"The Maya were very smart people. Instead of tearing down their temples when they needed to rebuild, they simply rebuilt over the old ones, leaving them underneath one another. There have been found as many as thirteen levels in the courtyards found by the archeologists. For them, this is very good as they can tell from the layered ruins the whole history of the people!"

So that's why we had so many layers to get through yesterday get to the Crystal Skull! Each layer held the energy of its age; no wonder it took such force to get us through. The Skull was probably under thirteen separate civilizations, each one sealed before the next was established upon the old ruins. Now I understood!

Looking up at the mound of the Atlantean, I had a lot of thoughts charging through my head. The menacing gray, stepped mound was really in front of me and the Atlantean awaited us up there.

All the universe was watching.

They had been watching us all during this trip. Could we do this? Would we do this?

It's one thing to have a dream or a vision during the night with a monster chasing you, but to wake up and find he's standing up there over your head. This was not a dream, not a child's bedtime fable…This was an Atlantean! I've never tackled an Atlantean before, at least not in this life.

"Lucy, in my vision there were four of us up there and we only have three who choose to take the invisibility feathers: me, you and Rachel. One other person must be with us. I have extra feathers."

"Who is it?" Lucy asked.

"I don't know!" I said as I pulled Racha-el aside and began to fully explain the night's vision and the instructions.

"Racha-el, we have to go up there and capture an Atlantean rogue spirit who has returned from the dead. He has somehow been released by the "El Bruto" I have been given instructions how to do this, but we need one other person."

Re entombment of the Atlantean that had been freed, many died.

She looked deeply at me as I spoke. I waited, watching her.

"First of all, will you do this with us?" I asked.

"Yes," she answered without a moment's hesitation. "And we'll ask Laneta to help."

She then went to Laneta and explained what was about to happen. Laneta agreed to come up with us. Amazing people they are! Can you imagine someone approaching you and telling you that you have just been selected to capture a rogue Atlantean?

Rob, Faith and Elisa went ahead with Juan while we prepared ourselves to go up the mound.

"We're going to need the crystals," I said as I pulled out my large crystals from my satchel handing one to Rachel, Vaneta and Lucy.

"Guess I'll need this, too." I took out my crystal skull although I was uncertain of how to use it in this situation. The skull just seemed to be the right one for the occasion.

"Here, Laneta," Racha-el offered, "take these."

She held out some of the invisibility feathers to Laneta. Laneta took them hesitantly. I unwrapped my feathers from the bird of invisibility who had given them to us. A word of thanks again went up.

"I'm not sure these are going to work for me," Laneta expressed her concerns as she considered the feathers in her hand.

"You know, I wasn't one of those originally moved to take the feathers. Will they protect me?"

"I am sure they will," Racha-el assured her of the protection and the nature of the feathers.

"Laneta, we need you! I am certain of their effectiveness," I convinced her, plus our need for a fourth person.

"We need four people for this. I saw there were four people just this morning in the vision with Lucy. That's how this has to be done." I continued, "The mound is rectangular; it will require one of us for each corner. We really need you!"

She then confidently took the feathers as I began.

"Remember: We are invisible to the Atlantean as promised by the vision. As long as we have the feathers and the TATA DUENDE's powers of invisibility; we are safe. I have that power. Remember the TATA DUENDE coconut I have? I have the cinders of the tree struck by lightning. I have captured his energy. The spirits and my Guides instructed Lucy and me completely this morning. All things were made possible for this to happen. There are no coincidences in any of this, and we will be able to do this!"

Once ready, feathers in our hair, we began to ascend the mound. I remembered OBED's words: *He will know you are coming as you ascend the mound.*

You cannot be seen, or harm will come."
I prayed.

We silently ascended the mound on the right side. We found a worn path to climb and reaching the top found a small circular ring of stones in the center.

"Look at this!" I exclaimed. "Coming out from the center ring of stones you can see a strange growth of grass on top of the mound. The grass is growing in a circular formation around the center."

It looked as if it were a spiral of grass, which grew out from beneath a spiraling energy.

"Of course, the energy of the Atlantean spiraled around like a tornado!" I explaineded aloud to them. "This really is the place!"

Standing on top of the mound we were directly in line with the El Castillo temple. Its impressive stature over us stood as a warning and I felt its imposing presence. Cool breezes stroked us as we stood. As we were taking in the valley views around us, I was struck by the ageless beauty of this country. It would be easy to disregard the dangers here, to be lulled into compliance and forgetfulness.

I was not aware of the Atlantean until we stood on the four outer corners of the mound. Once there, I began to feel the spinning energy.

"I call on the powers of the TATA DUENDE to hide us while we prepare the globe." I could just imagine him laughing hysterically. A trickster, we needed him now.

"It's been a long time since someone played with you, TATA!" I affectionately spoke to this entity.

Instantly I felt my energy strengthened. Aloud I prayed for strength and wisdom for all.

Rachel and I began to bring down the shimmering globe of light around all of us encasing the Atlantean. Suddenly Racha-el and Lucy were pushed backwards by the Atlantean energy. They had been seen. At that moment I called in the Archangels to assist us and they came.

"Archangel Michael, we need your sword!"

"The globe is in place!" I shouted. "Now, begin to walk in towards the center. The globe will begin to compress the Atlantean energy while we go forward."

Stepping forward cautiously, I felt the resistant energy of the Atlantean firmly beneath my hands. I also felt the strength of the crystal globe around me. Somehow the globe around us *was* us. We were the sides of the crystal globe, merged with it.

As we—the energy of the globe—moved forward, the compression of the space and Atlantean energy inside of it began. As it compacted, the energy of the Atlantean caused pain in my hands. Sharp pains went up my arms to my shoulders, then stopped mysteriously. "What's happening?" I wondered. Then I knew.

"I am the globe and the energy at my shoulders is pure energy," I thought. "That's why the pain goes no further. I can do this, there is no pain." I moved in. Then closer, another step closer. Each slow step brought us closer to the center, closer to the strength of its power.

After a few painful moments, we were all standing together around the small circle of stones in the center. The energy of the Atlantean was strong, solid and now compressed into a writhing ball beneath our hands. It clearly knew it was going down into its tomb.

"One more step. I've got to push it down into the mound tomb!"

As Lucy, Laneta and Racha-el held the energy in place, I took another step and I stood over the Atlantean. With both hands I began to push. Pushing the energy down was like pushing an elephant into a bottle.

It wouldn't go. Pain shot into my hands, electric shocks like lightning coursed through my hands and up my arms. The Atlantean was fighting back. Looking up at the others standing there I exclaimed,

"I can't get it in! My hand hurts so much I can't get it to go down!"

"What did the Maya do? How'd they get it in here?" I frantically thought.

"The Skull!"

The Guides actually shouted at me. Not just OBED, but a whole chorus of them.

"Use the Skull!"

They were as excited as I was.

A whole team and the universal cheering squad was back there!

Grabbing my crystal skull lying on the ground nearby, I placed it on top of the struggling Atlantean energy. Just like butter beneath the fired, hot, burning crystal skull, that beast just flowed down into the tomb.

Not expecting this to happen, the hand holding my crystal skull fell hard upon the center stones. The crystal skull was beaming and amplifying the energies flowing through me and held the energy down.

Holding the energy inside the tomb with the crystal skull on top, I could sense the slithering dark energy going back into its hold deep within the bowels of the earth.

I began to seal the tomb, to seal it down forever.

"It's in," I shouted, "it's in there now!

We've got to seal it, make it so this can never happen again!"

Excited and exhilarated, we began to seal the tomb.

For reasons of protection, we'll not tell how this was done, but it is completed. That beast which had the capability to terrorize the world has been returned into its tomb. The tomb is not the mound, the mound is just the marker the Maya had set up so long ago.

In a dark chamber, especially reserved for this one, there is a sarcophagus, vault-like and now sealed. It cannot harm the earth or its peoples any longer.

Susan Isabelle

"He will know you are coming as you ascend the mound.
You cannot be seen, or harm will come," said my Guide

Lucy
El Castillo in background overlooks the flat-topped Mound of the Atlantean.

The Atlantean had long ago decided it's own path of darkness and destruction.

10

One With Open Mouth

Racha-el, Lucy and Laneta sat and waited for the others to return. Going into the little store at the entrance of Xunantunich. I found a likeness of the stone formation on the beach of the Mopan River.

"Do you know who this is?" I asked the clerk as I held the little clay object in my hand. A small head lay in my hands. Its mouth was wide open.

"No. I know that it is one of the Maya Gods. One of the locals makes them," she answered. Too fragile to make it back home, I put it back up on the shelf just as Juan was bringing the others back from El Castillo.

After a few moments rest, he brought us into the museum of Xunantunich, a small thatched hut which enclosed two great stelae.

Juan began, "The stelae were used by the Maya to record the lives of their priests and kings. These two are still readable because they were beautifully preserved in the soil. This recorded their lives in great detail as you can see here."

Lucy quickly pushed past all of us. She went directly over to one of the great stelae, got down on her knees, and held the great stone within her hands. She began to rock, her head rolling from side to side.

We left her in her worshipful place, and did not disturb her. We could see she was greatly moved and somehow was connecting with her own past. We silently filed by her and back out into the shop area.

After a while Lucy came out of the shrine. We sat for a while together. Two great leaf cutter ants had attached themselves to her linen clothing and we worked hard to remove them, laughing at their tenacity to hang on, despite our efforts. We didn't speak of her experience with the stelae, but I know on some deep level Lucy had come home. There we stayed until it was time to return.

"What do the parrots mean to the Maya, Juan?" I asked Juan while walking back to the Rover.

"Oh, they are beautiful and have been used by the Maya for ceremonial purposes."

"I keep seeing them whenever I close my eyes, Juan. I am seeing them in a Great Tree. Last night one of them turned towards me and changed into a man-bird. He was half man and half bird!" He paled a bit as he answered.

"Oh, you have been visited by the Mayan Spirits!" he exclaimed. "In the past, the Gods would come to the people in the form of birds and animals to bring messages. That is a very good thing!" With that he quickly turned around and cut off the conversation.

"Getting too close to home," I thought and I went back to the group as we continued walking down the great hill.

Approaching him again, I asked, "Juan, how did you become a guide?"

"Oh, when I was a young man of 16 years I did not want to go to school, my father, he said to me, 'Then you must earn your life by the sweat of your brow!' You know what I mean?" Juan laughed.

"Yes, I do," I chuckled.

"Well then, I went to the place of Lubaantun where there was much work of excavation going on. You know about the place of the crystal skull?"

"Yes, I am familiar with it," I told him.

"I dug in the dirt, I worked with the archaeologists who liked me and taught me about my country. I worked for twenty years and worked the sites with them, going from one to another. I became very knowledgeable. You know, I work with the archeologists of University of New Hampshire, even now," he said. "I was even the guide for Queen Elizabeth when she came here."

"New Hampshire! Juan, that is where I live!" I was amazed at how such connections could happen.

"Then it is by the Gods!" he exclaimed.

"I have always loved archeology," I explained. "You have been very fortunate to have such an opportunity."

"Yes," he said "but the government requires we work through a license and the big companies hire us for not much money to be their guides. It is hard to make a living," he explained as we approached the Rover.

"Tomorrow is supposed to be a day off," I said to our small group as we stood around the Rover. We discussed our need for a guide should we decide to go to Tikal.

"We can choose to go to any of the different areas around us, or if you like, I was thinking of asking Juan if he could take us to Tikal."

"YES!" resounded from the group, and confirmed our next event.

"Juan, what would you charge to take us Tikal?" I asked. "Could you go with us tomorrow?"

"To take you all, you need passports, taxes, entrance fees and a big van. I can do this for $175.00 US. You cannot take your rental vehicle across the border, you know" he answered, "and it would not be safe to park it at the border either."

In the Rover driving down the bumpy road, I asked Juan if he would like some information about the skulls. I had brought extra materials for the group and had some copies and pictures of the Mitchell-Hedges skull which had been found in Belize as well as some others.

"Juan, have you ever seen a picture of the real Belize skull?" I asked.

"No," he answered.

"Well, I will bring one for you tomorrow!"

In dream-state later that night, I was later given this knowledge. Perhaps from the Bird-Man- Mayan God:

Long ago the ancient Maya had encountered him, the Atlantean. He embodied a personality, a body, who wrought much destruction on the peoples. They eventually caught him, beheaded him, and buried his spirit beneath this mound marker.

The ancient stelaes, or burial markers, had been placed around this mound holding the Priests who had contained him. The ancient priests stood guard over his spirit. The decorative symbols on the temple and the picture of the headless man told the ancient story of this one. They also displayed the warnings of danger. Shortly afterwards the Maya temples of sacrifice were abandoned.

Now, in more recent times, by a tragic mistake, an El Bruto, the ignorant one, using the powers of voodoo, had called and released him. His ancient powers of terrorism had infected different personalities of the population throughout the last fifty years. Not as in former times, but the potential for massive destruction was there. The spirits, ancient priests and the Mayan Gods had been waiting for us, someone, to come who would have the knowledge and energy to be able to return him to his tomb. We had been summoned.

The careful, deliberate events leading up to this moment were explained to me in great detail as I was given the vision to see the unfolding of the events. That day the old man sat by the side of the road had been planned far in advance of our coming. I know now that he, a Mayan close to his religion, knew of our coming. He had caught the bird and hung it on the fence in obedience to the Mayan Gods who watched over his land. He knew one day we would be coming for those feathers. He sat there every day in the hot sun and he waited for us. He knew and wanted to see who we were. Did he know that a very white woman of white goddess energy would be summoned from a place far away? I wonder… He had stood up to watch us, probably in amazement. But in nodding of his head to me, he accepted the fact, went on his way.

"I define in order to love Measuring loyalty"

On Assignment with Adama

The placement of the TATA DUENDE in the doorway of the San Ignacio motel had gone unnoticed for many, many years, until we came. The lightning summoned by the Maya Gods had struck and reduced to ashes a sacred tree that also waited.

Elisa had been consumed by the all-powerful need to go down that path, not tomorrow, not the next day, but that very moment. We weren't in the hotel half an hour when she fairly demanded we go. She moved the unmovable "me" by her insistence. We had to find the tree before the next morning. We were brought there by the power of the Mayan Gods who led us there step by step. The strong spirit of the TATA DUENDE had prevailed and brought us there. I now realized the plan and the completion of the task.

The Maya are about to move into the forefront of spirituality along with their energy and knowledge-keeper cousins, the Incas. The work of the Atlantean was to prevent that progression. He had done that before, terrorizing the people and instituting bloodletting sacrifice, which was abhorrent to the populace and the Maya Spirit Gods. They suffered greatly under his rule, his possession of leaders. That will not happen now. His containment is completed.

I expect the country of Belize to enter the 21st century gloriously. It will come forth into new prosperity and peace. The ancients are free to lead us into the new age of truth and knowledge. Belize is a gift to the world just waiting to be opened. It holds many wondrous healing plants and its beautiful spirituality awaits us. I learned much of that spirituality in the days and weeks to come.

"I am guided by the power of death"

11

And So It Is, Ixchel

Thursday Night,
the Night of WESAK

On the way home, we searched for a place to celebrate the evening of WESAK. To assist you in the understanding of WESAK and its importance to the world, I highly recommend reading the works of Alice Bailey. In summary, during the WESAK festival three are honored: Melchizedek, the planetary Logos, who is the Lord of the World, or Sanat Kumara; Buddha, the Illumined One; and Christ, the Son of the Father, the World Savior and the Redeemer. During the time of WESAK, these three work together to transmit to humanity powerful spiritual Truths. These energies are designed to assist mankind in understanding divinity. This takes place on the <u>May Full Moon</u> in conjunction with the Tibetans celebration of the Buddha. Together they focus and give the energies to the disciples and those seeking enlightenment.

From Alice Bailey's works:

WESAK Festival at the time of the Full Moon of May, links the major Eastern religion with the major Western faith, it esoterically provides the key to the open door between Shambhala and the Hierarchy.

After dark we went outside the motel on a grassy ledge high above the valley. Carrying my crystals, the dish of water, and mats, we found a perfect area to begin the celebration.

First I drew a large circle on the ground and placed large crystals in the North, South, West and East position. We each chose one of these positions to sit in.

I then placed a large upright crystal in the center of the circle in the plate of water, representing the Tibetan practice to invite the Buddha energy to our location.

I drew out all the symbols I knew on the ground within the circle. Due to our location this was done on the grass. Using my palm chakra energy, I began to activate each symbol by drawing it out again with the energy beams coming from my hands. The energy actually began to come up so powerfully it was a bit painful as I activated each one. I had to move up higher above the symbols. Moving about the circle I repeated the names of the symbols in a soft chant. Over and over again their sacred names were sung in my heart and mind, and with my voice.

Soon the symbols were rising upward to the stars on waves of energy. Standing before the crystal grid, I took my Master crystal and began to activate the grid with this chant:

"I fill you with love, I fill you with Peace, I fill you with Light, the True Light
I fill you with love, I fill you with Peace, I fill you with Light, the True Light
I fill you with love, I fill you with Peace, I fill you with Light, the True Light"

We stood around the now-pulsing crystals, and I prayed to the Divine. I Invited all the Masters, the Mahatma, Pure Unconditional Love from the Source of Love, and the Christ Light.

"I pray for all the indigenous tribes of the world, for those who have held the Truth of the ancients, those who have suffered much at the hands of the ignorant, you are honored. Your presence is invited here as we also represent you here in this place. I pray for your strength, your love and care of the Mother Earth, as We love you...

I pray for peace for all the peoples of the world...for the country of Belize in which the bough of Peace rests from the Sacred Dove.

I pray for healing of the Earth...forgiveness for those who abuse her love.

I pray for the Mother, nurturer and keeper of us all in our lives upon her breast.

I pray for the establishment this night of the Pillar of Peace of the Divine Feminine Grid, for its never-ending standard in this country of Belize. We represent the world here in this Grid; there are none others here.

I pray for the balancing of the energies with its placement and the end of suffering on the Earth and of the Earth.

I pray that as this Pillar is formed its Light will shine forth out into the Universes as a beacon of Feminine Love and Justice."

And then I sent the energy into the crystals. A great beam of energy went up into the sky, pulsing the energy of all the Shambhala symbols, our prayers, and our love of the Earth and all its peoples.

We stood, formed and connected the energy ring that would now form the basis of the new Grid formation here in Belize. This ring is one of many being shaped all over our globe. As each ring interconnects with the others, the Hologram of Love is being created in the physical realm. The Hologram is actually the Flower of Life globe, representing pure feminine energies. Soon this globe will be complete. It will encircle the earth. A pillar was needed here in Belize. Tonight it was established.

Two years previously, I had been instructed by my Guides to begin to form the rings. Each class stood and shaped the ring, then sent it upward into the atmosphere to join others that had already been established above the earth. At the time, I did not know what we were actually doing.

The Flower of Life globe contains all the platonic solids. These ancient globes have been found etched into the pyramids and in places of knowledge all over the earth. They are structured by sacred geometry, containing the linear lines of the masculine within. The sacred geometry of all creation is contained within that sphere. Once again, the feminine contains all of creation. As above, so below.

We sent it up the great Pillar, which was now beaming into the night sky.

Now we were ready for the Buddha to come for our initiation. As the blessing from the Buddha washed over us, we lost our physical form in the outpouring of energy. Unable to stand at first, we were pulsing and tingling from head to foot. Consumed in the energies, unable to sit or stand, we lay on the ground.

As I looked up into the night sky, I was full of the love and the light. I looked up to see a great circle cut from the clouds above us. The great beam, The Pillar of Belize was flowing out into the universe all the way up to the stars.

The Pillar beam of energy was cutting away the clouds. I could see the stars twinkling above us through a great hole where a short while before was a fully-clouded sky. I could hear the astonished gasps of the others as they lay on the ground around the crystals seeing this great sight above them. From the heavens we must have looked like a great seven-spoke star upon the earth. We were glowing!

After a few minutes, days, or maybe hours—we could not tell as we all lay suspended in waves of joy—the clouds that had covered the full moon opened to bathe us in beautiful silver moonbeams. Impossible as it seemed, even more blessings and energy began to flow to us. Now it was the pure feminine energy of the moon.

Ixchel, the Moon Goddess, is the Goddess of all medicine, all healing. She is the feminine, silvery beauty of the night sky. Her blessings fell on us. I remembered the legend.

Once Ixchel had been in love with the Sun God, Ahkin. He became very possessive and Ixchel fled from his control into the realm of the underworld. It is said she died there for a period of thirteen days and nights, establishing the thirteen moons of the year. The Sun God continues to chase after her every day and night, but finally, he has recognized and respected her beauty.

It reminded me of our present situation in the world: The feminine has been controlled and harnessed by the male energies. Feminine intuition, gifts of life, nurturing, and natural healing skills for the earth and humanity have been held in captivity. As women, we have sought refuge from the heat of the sun's chase.

Now in this time of transition, we have begun to realize and reestablish our true power. We are joining one another and restoring our feminine power, not a copy of men, but as women.

Women are the creators of life on the earth. Women who understand this have power and honor in society. Women: have confidence and strength in that knowledge. Use it! We have forgotten, and we must now teach our young. We will need to establish a healthy balance on the earth.

The ring of feminine energy we had sent up on the beam had joined the other rings forming across the globe. We were making the new Flower of Life hologram and the Grid of Feminine Energy upon a pillar here in Belize. It is symbolic of the women of this world—we must join one another to be strong in the Light. It was now being bathed in the pure platinum glow of the Moon. Bathed in Ixchel's blessings.

"Let's stand," I managed to say.
"I can't," whispered Lucy. "I don't have any legs, they're not here. I have no body."
We waited until she was able to stand, whispering about the awesome events to one another.
"We need to focus the moon's energy. It's blessing us and we need to bring that in to the Earth plane and into GAIA," I spoke in hushed tones.

"We need to become the focusing Angels, to direct the blessings to the Earth. Now reach back and touch your wings with the back of your hands," I instructed.

There were little "Ooohs and Ahs" as for some it was the first time they had contacted their wings. The energy present this night was so powerful, I did not have to open their wings for them as I usually do in our classes. They had already activated.
"Touch them and begin to raise up your hands, all the way up over your heads," I continued. *"Pull them open......EXTEND!"*
Once opened and up over our heads I showed them how to use their precious wing tips to focus the beams coming in from the cosmos.

"Oh, my!" someone said as the Moon Energy of Ixchel began to come in through the wing lenses. Its force made her loose her footing momentarily.

"That's it," I said, "now you've got it! Let's do it again, but this time we will turn toward the moon! Be sure to ground and secure your feet to the earth!"

We all turned to the huge glowing full Flowering Moon of May that hung glorious in front of us. Standing there on the ledge I felt as though I was standing on the edge of the earth. Beneath me was the darkness of the valley and above me the entire galaxy.

Once again we solemnly raised our wings. We focused the energy rays of the full moon that were now bathing the earth, and condensed the rays into one great ray that beamed down behind us into the Grid. Seven Rays of seven focusing angels on the night of WESAK concentrating the Divine Feminine energies, we shone silver in the night. I don't know that I have ever seen anything so beautiful. Behind us the seven rays flooded into the grid in preparation for the goddess energy to manifest. The force once again pulled us backward.

"Now we will begin using the sacred chants to secure them to the Earth Plane."

Together we sang softly, inviting the Goddess on the wings of the chants. As we finished the chants, one by one Lucy, Rachel, Rob, and Elisa lay back down on the grass looking up into the sky, traveling, I am sure, each to their home planet once again. I sat before the grid absorbing the pulsing energy and the joy was beyond all joy.

I saw Elisa rise up again from the ground. She was filled with a luminous light and beamed with joy, a peace I'd never seen in her before. She began a sacred, ritual dance.

"She is Divine Feminine", I heard. She is allowing the Divine energies to perform this ritual through her, I realized as she began to move. She performed a beautiful dance of pure spirit, beyond words, as she began to sway with the energy. The energies of Divine Mother, Ixchel's energies, were flowing through her. In the silvery light she shone brightly.

Raising her crystal to the Moon in one hand, her silvery robe flowing out from her, she danced the energy down and directed the elixir into the Earth with a crystal she held in her other hand. She then sent the energy upward to the sky, the home of the newly forming grid above us. Her movements were slow and full of grace. Very beautiful! I am honored to have been allowed to observe the bringing in of the feminine energy by one that carries the Goddess energy, one who was chosen for this task.

A Priestess of the Divine Feminine Energy was with us that night!

When she completed her Dance of the Goddess, I was guided that it was time to receive the downloading of the crystals held within the grid.

"It is now time for the crystals to give their blessings to us." Those still lying on the grass began to arise.

"Take the crystal closest to you," I said, "and hold it gently in your hands."

They each reached out to take one of the glowing, vibrating, pulsing, energy-charged crystals. Once each had made their selection, I continued as guided.

"Now the crystal has information that can only be given during the times of intense universal transmission of energy, like the energy tonight. They have been pre-programmed to release their record keeping files directly into you with tonight's activation."

As each considered the words, they more carefully considered the crystals they held in their hands. I could see their thoughts as each wondered what they had selected.

"Take the crystal and bring it up to your third eye as close as is comfortable for you, and allow the energy to flow into you."

Once again we began to sway, now with the downloading of the crystals directly over and into our third eye. Warm and flowing, my cells began to vibrate a higher pitch; the sound within my ears became deafening in its tones. The purple, gold, and the blue swirling vibrations flowed into me bringing a wealth of knowledge directly into my cells. At the proper time, that information will surface into my consciousness and the consciousness of the others.

After a while it was time to close, to come back from our sacred space. We would always hold these memories. As we arose to return to the motel, Elisa exclaimed,
"Look at the Moon! It's the TATA DUENDE!"

We looked up again to the beautiful moon above us. There before us over the moon was a perfect cloud formation of the TATA DUENDE. Exquisite in its likeness, he revealed himself to us in the shining glow of the moon upon the clouds. He had come to us to confirm, and perhaps thank us, for our work with him. I honored him.

"I have never felt anything so incredible as tonight," Elisa continued. "My whole being became the feminine energies. I filled with the energies and transmitted them into the earth. I felt the milk flow, the tears, the essence of life-blood as it sanctified the earth. My body actually hurts from the physicalness of the experience!" We walked back to the hotel.
"Elisa, I believe that this was one of the most beautiful nights I have ever witnessed and I thank you!"
The whole world will thank her one day for her work tonight in this, and for those things to come. I hugged her goodnight.

"Ixchel, I thank you. We received your attuning energies tonight, we carry them," I said to her as I said goodnight to the beautiful full moon from my bedroom door.

Racha-el and Laneta began to share their experience while seated outside the door. I fell into bed. I could hear Racha-el's voice as I left in sleep....
"*As I lay on the ground, I was taken through the roots of the Ceiba tree, deep into the earth where I met a Shaman...*" she began.

I seal the process of heart.

12

Tikal Magic

May 19, 2000
Mayan Calendar Day: Blue Overtone Monkey
        "I empower in order to play
        Commanding illusion
        I seal the process of magic
        With the overtone of radiance
        I am guided by the power of self-generation"

    We rose early to meet Juan who was coming to take us to the Temples of Tikal in Guatemala. He drove up with another man who spoke only Spanish. The van was colorfully decorated with scapular medals of the Virgin and bore Guatemalan tags.

    We had a two-hour drive ahead of us. It was overcast and looked as though there would be rain to contend with.

    Once we were underway we stopped on the road going into Xunantunich to meet the young man who was making an image of Kulkulcan for me. There he was ready and waiting for us as we drove up. I was delighted to see the beautiful piece of artwork he had just completed for me. Packing it away, we continued our trip.

I pulled out the paperwork for the Mitchell-Hedges skull and gave the information to Juan. He read it carefully and made comments from time to time.

"I didn't realize it was so big," he said. "It's almost the size of a human being!"

"Yes, all the skulls that have been found are quite large. They have no tooling marks and have not been made by human hands."

"Why skulls?" Juan asked

"The skull is a repository of information. The skull of a human holds knowledge and the skull-shape of these tells us that they contain information, they hold knowledge. Imagine that many ages ago you wanted to preserve information, a record of history for the people. You could see into the future and knew that all the earth was going to be destroyed. You would need to find a way for the future people to understand you were passing that knowledge along. It would have to be something clear, easy to interpret. You would need a symbol. What symbol or shape would you use?"

"The skull," he said tapping his own.

"Yes, by using the symbol of the skull, they believed we would understand that's where the knowledge is contained. Unfortunately in our culture the skull has represented a symbol of death, not knowledge. There has been a misinterpretation. They knew one day someone would find the skull. There are five skulls that have been identified and it Is rumored that the Hopi Indians and the Indians of Peru also have a crystal skull."

"What do they do with them then?"

"They are believed to have been left here by another culture not from this planet. They are supposed to hold all the information about the creation of the universe and our planet. The day will come that a great prophecy will be fulfilled."

"A prophecy?"

"Yes, Juan, in the future all the skulls will be found and be reactivated. When all come together—all thirteen—they will speak to us. I am afraid that one of the skulls may have been lost, however."

"What happened?"

"There is a written legend that when Cortez's invaders came they found one of the skulls and broke it into pieces thinking it was the devil's work. Because they didn't understand its value to the world, we lost a great gift. It is said the Maya stood and cried loudly, and were inconsolable at its loss. Ever since the Indians have known to keep their valuable skulls hidden until the time of the Nine Hells, or the Veils of Tears, were lifted."

"Nine veils? What do you mean by nine veils?"

"Yes, Nine Veils, or Nine Hells of Tears. The five hundred years since the invasion were foretold long ago in several cultures. Now that time is over and the time of Quetzalcoatl is upon us. These are exciting times!"

He became quiet and went back to his reading and I looked out the window enjoying the beautiful countryside.

Soon we were at the border of Guatemala. This is not a pleasant place. It looks third-world and I wondered about proceeding. Busy, dusty, dirty, and chaotic, it was a sad introduction to this beautiful country. The moneychangers were at every window of the van. Juan took our passports and fees, and went into the building just ahead of us. A few minutes later he came out and motioned to us to take everything out of the car with us. Carrying our gear, we followed a tense Juan back into the building.

"There is a problem," he said, "I am not a licensed guide for Guatemala; the law has changed."

"What do we have to do?" I asked

"We will have to agree to hire a guide in Tikal."

"That is fine, Juan," I agreed. We were then given permission to pass. We went through a short line for customs. Fortunately I did not have to explain my crystals; the officer did not examine my bag. I had forgotten my clerical ID.

Once cleared to pass, we went over a small bridge with a lift gate and then we were in Guatemala. Tikal was just ahead. It began to pour rain, buckets full at a time. Juan leaned back saying to me, "Pouring rain, a blessing—it is a blessing! You will see!"

Arriving at the entrance to the Tikal temple site, we ran seeking cover from the downpour in the lobby of a great thatched area. Here there were many vendors who shared their colorful wares. There were cloth and textiles hanging all round and beautiful works of art from the native population.

Under the main room there was a model of the great structures of Tikal. As we began to ask Juan questions, he explained he would not be able to act as our guide. He appeared to be emotionally distressed. He disappeared for a few moments and returned with a young man.

"I have found a guide for you," he said. "He only asks $50.00."

"Juan, will you be able to come with us, too?" we asked.

"Yes, I can come!" he said, surprised. He was very pleased to be with us and excitedly began to speak of the temple site.

We hired the Guatemalan guide. The young man was an archeology student at one of the country's universities and very kind. As soon as the rain subsided to a drizzle we decided to go ahead and begin the walk. I think that if I had known we were going to be walking for eight hours, I would have taken the short route, or not gone!

I had strange feelings about this place as soon as we came to the border. I heard my Guide say to me,

"For you, do not touch anything here. Walk, see, but do not touch! You will do nothing here, but observe."

This was strange, I knew this was meant for me only. I was not to direct any of the group otherwise. I didn't understand, but that's OK with me. I have come to trust my guides. They've kept me out of a few situations!

13

Just Ask

As we started up one of the paths, Juan pointed out a tree that reached up into heaven.

"This," he said proudly, "is the Ceiba Tree. It is sacred to the Maya."

We stopped to look at the tree. It had a massive trunk of soft white bark, clear of lower branches that rose straight up and out of the earth.

"That's the tree I've been seeing when I close my eyes," I said to them.

At the top of the two hundred-foot tree were the umbrella shaped branches that reached far out into the Belizean sky. Its roots fanned out around the base as a wide cape sinking into the earth.

> "The Ceiba Tree represents the Worlds of Maya Gods and man," Juan began. "The roots of the tree go down into the earth to the Lower Worlds. The trunk of the tree is the Middle World where we as humans live.
> The branches are the dwelling place of the Higher Gods. It is very sacred," he repeated looking at me.

> "The tree is called the Madre Ceiba, the mother of the children of humanity, and holds all the wisdom of the Maya peoples. These trees are planned in the center of our villages to protect the people. The good winds come here and the top always has butterflies, people are happy here under her.
>
> The sacred Ceiba is also the way to the thirteen Upper Worlds. To go down is to enter the Nine Underworlds of the dead. One must survive the Underworld to begin to go up the tree into the Upper World, to become a Shaman."

I got the message. My man-bird parrot is a Maya God, who has been observing me. Had I begun the path of the Shaman? Is that why he would be observing me? I'd been in a few hells before!

We walked and we walked and we walked. It poured intermittently. Under our plastic raincoats we were in a steam bath. Finally we all just took off the rain ponchos and let the cooling rain flow over us. Yes, at that moment, the rain was a blessing! The young guide watched us stripping and said,

"The rain—it is a blessing!"

Well, we were certainly being blessed! Now I understood. The ancient Maya believed the earth was created by three bolts of thunder. They call upon the Chacs, their rain gods, in many of their rituals to bless them for their crops and also the water-like substances of the earth. The sap of the copal tree is sacred, as are tears and the rain. They are blessings, the fluids of the Earth Goddess!

We had missed, by a few weeks, one of their most important rituals. May 3rd is known as the Day of the Holy Cross. On that day the villagers go to the local water source carrying blue-green crosses. Three crosses are placed by the water to honor the spirits of the water and to seek plentiful water for the crops after the long dry spell. The whole ritual is feminine nature, as the women are believed to own the waters of the earth. From women flow the life-giving forces of all nature: mother's milk, tears of joy and sorrow, the life-giving blood. By the look of things around us, and the very wet experience I was having, their prayers had been heard. We were being blessed!

We saw miles of temple areas that were breathtaking. Monkeys screamed above us and swung from tree to tree; parrots squawked loudly as we approached.

I stopped to put the energizing symbols from Merlin on my feet: I was happy that he had given them before this trip. I needed them now and they worked!

In one of our Master classes he had come to give them stating, "You will need these to climb the temples."

The hovering gray ghostly temples were magnified in the murky mist that hung everywhere. Looking up at the steep steps rising several hundred feet to the next temple, I knew I'd not be going up there. They loomed over us and silently watched the whole area below, just as they had done for at least a thousand years.

As soon as we arrived in the largest temple area, a few of us were ready for a long rest. Juan, seeing our exhaustion, directed Lucy, Rachael and I over to a covered thatched roof picnic area with large tables. Elisa, Rob, Faith and Vaneta went to climb the massive structures.

I climbed up on one of the tables, lay back under the coolness of the thatched roof, and put my head on my pack.

"Ah, that feels good! Hard as a rock but wonderful!"

As soon as I thought this, I heard my Guide say,

"Offer him a treatment."

"WHO?!"

"Juan."

"What? *I* need a treatment! *I'm* the one that's exhausted!"

"Give him a treatment."

I could barely move, but rolled over on my side and called to Juan who was a few feet away sitting at another table.

"Juan, would you like to have some healing energy?" I asked.

"What's that?"

"Well, you just lay up here on the table and I'll show you!" I said, sliding off the table, energized.

Like a wonderful, excited child, he jumped up in my place on the table.

"Racha-el, Lucy, we're going to give Juan a treatment," I called. I got a few 'You've got to be kidding' looks from them, but they came right over.

As we gathered around him on the table he said,

"Ah, to be sacrificed by three women!" and laughed with us.

"Now, Juan, just relax. Let the warmth of my hands enter and bring deep relaxation. This is very nice and gentle. That's it, relax."

I could see him begin to take in the energy from all three of us and start to go into that wonderful Shambhala sleep of pure bliss. He went deep. After about fifteen minutes Juan was traveling far and was not on this earth plane anymore. We stopped and sat back to watch him. About half an hour later I saw his eyelids begin to move, then his eyes opened. Unable to move, he looked a bit panicked. I stood up and approached him speaking softly,

"That's good, Juan, you did beautifully, Take your time and come back slowly. Don't try to move. You'll be able to move again in a few minutes."

He slightly nodded and closed his eyes again. After a while Juan was able to sit up.

"What was that?" he asked.

I explained to him the healing energy. He agreed he felt very good and by the look on his smiling face, he certainly was feeling quite well. Just then the rest of the group came down the path to meet us.

"Sue, while I was up on the temple I felt the energy of something, something that wanted to pull us down," said Elisa. "I was able to use the symbols to sanctify the area and we changed the forces up there!"

"Awesome! You guys are great!" I exclaimed. This was their opportunity!

They excitedly spoke of their new abilities and the incredible view from the platform at the top of the temple. I felt a momentary regret at not taking the opportunity to go up to the highest and most well known temple in Guatemala, nor of participating in its cleansing.

Once again I heard the inner message that this work was not for me in this place at this time. Also confirmed was the fact I am here to activate others to the energies; they will continue the work.

Now we were about to walk the rest of the way back to the main entrance from which we had started out about six hours before. Along the way back down, I walked upon the white walkways of the ancient Maya. Cobbled stones formed the ancient passageways and roads. I felt their presence. I was directed to pick up several stones along the way. White and chalky, they melted away in my hands. I wondered why I was guided to pick them up. As I held the stones I began to understand. The illusions of time and existence were melting away. I held the symbol in my hands.

Back at the main entrance we all fell exhausted into the waiting chairs. Because my hiking boots had disappeared from the porch the night before, I had worn sandals during our walk. My feet had been worn smooth with the wet sandy clay that rubbed against my skin. I sent healing energy into my sore feet and legs.

We ordered the finest coffee in the entire world that afternoon. Deep, rich, dark Guatemalan coffee...the finest! A lover of excellent coffee, this was a treat I will never forget.

Juan came over, "I must pay the guide now for his services; it is $50.00."

By the expression on his face, I could see that the $50.00 to be paid to the unexpected guide was likely Juan's whole profit for this trip. He would have to pay the driver of the van, all our entrance fees, and taxes. There would be nothing left. He had spent the entire day with us sharing and acting as a guide for us for nothing. He did so with joy, without any complaint. I was amazed by him.

"Here is the fee for the Guide," I said handing him $50.00. "And here is your $175.00," I added.

He looked up, astonished, "Thank you!"

Back in the van Juan approached the Guatemalan driver excitedly, speaking in Spanish, "Estas mujered me estan resando I yo estaba paralisado no me podia mover," as he motioned toward us. "Estas mujered me estan resando I yo estaba paralisado no me podia mover."

Lucy leaned over to me giggling and whispered,

"He said, 'These ladies were praying for me and I was paralyzed!' He's telling the driver all about it."

Juan had indeed experienced something he'd not soon forget.

"We will take you to a place where you can buy very good textiles." Juan declared. "It is just before the border, if you'd like to go."

"We'd love to see it," we all agreed, knowing we were in for a special treat.

We drove to a small village to make purchases. On laden shelves were textiles, works of art. We were in awe at their beauty. In those simple thatched huts and houses we had seen along the way, many hands had worked the looms to create the treasures before us.

The Kulkulcan/Quetzalcoatl bird was prominently displayed in many of the designs. In one of the back rooms there were brightly painted clay forms of the Mayan gods. Masks of all types were hung for purchase. Shelf after shelf held clay skulls, the size of human skulls. I wondered what the locals use these for, as it was unlikely tourists often came here.

When we arrived back at our hotel, Juan approached me privately.

"I want to tell you, I have never met people like you before. The night before we met, I was awakened by a voice. It said, 'Poncho, they are coming!' Poncho is my family's name for me, no one uses it, but they called me Poncho! The voice meant you."

He continued speaking quietly,

"I must tell you this. I know a man from Guatemala who says he has a skull, a crystal skull. I could speak to him and see if he would let you see it."

"Oh, Juan, please tell him if he will come, we would be happy to pay him well for his time!"

"I must go to Mexico tomorrow, at noon I must leave," he said sadly. "I will not be back before you leave. I can see you tomorrow morning at Cahal Pech at 8:00 am. I will bring him then, if he wants to show you."

"We will be there!" I answered.

I told the others at dinner. We were all excited to have the opportunity to see a real Guatemalan crystal skull and we all looked forward to the next morning's adventure!

14

The Maya: Lords of Light

May 20 2000
Cahal Pech
Mayan Calendar Day: Yellow Rhythmic Human
"I organize in order to influence
Balancing wisdom
I seal the process of free will
With the rhythmic tone of equality
I am guided by my own power doubled."

We were at the entrance of Cahal Pech early in the morning. I sat under the tree at the entrance gate awaiting Juan's arrival. While there, I began to feel the energies enfold me. Slowly, gently I slipped into the white mist now filling my being. I closed my eyes and let the attunement energies enfold me.

"This is wonderful," I thought. "So gentle, so caressing, so blissful!"

My aura began to fill with the Light of Peace. Expanding, expanding, I was being filled. I became aware of a presence beside me.

"Sue, don't you think we ought to go inside the gate to wait?" the presence asked

"No, I want to stay here," I mumbled.

"But, I feel we ought to wait inside the park," this one spoke again, insistent.

"No, you go ahead," I said.

I went back into the soft glow once again. A few minutes later the presence, in another form this time, was back.

"Don't you think we ought to go inside the gate to wait?" I was asked again.

"No, I want to stay here, I'll wait for Juan here,"

I answered back from the Light of the energies flooding me.

"Let's go in," it implored me.

"I am not moving from this spot," I said firmly. The presence left.

I continued to bask in the energies. I was so full! Only a few times in this life have I been so filled. It is so wonderful there. The Light, the Peace. This was going to be a very special attunement. Just then my eyes popped open.

"He is coming," I heard the voice of a Guide say.

I stood and could see a small car struggling up the hill. It stopped, and Juan and another man stepped out of the car. Juan practically ran to gave me a big hug.

"This is my friend," he said. "He has the stone!"

I was introduced to one of the most humble men who walk the earth. Gentleness poured from him.

"I am honored," I said to him.

Together we walked into Cahal Pech, dodging the multitude of anthills outside the main temple area. Juan led us to a stepped area where we sat while he began to explain the ancient history of Cahal Pech. After a few minutes, as he paused, I interrupted.

"Juan, we have to do an attunement here today at Cahal Pech so we will need to do this first if we are to be finished by noontime."

"Oh, I know just the place for the ceremony!"

A delighted Juan led us into what was obviously a favorite place of his. It was secluded and completely walled in with a large center tree. Juan explained we would be under the sacred copal tree as we did the ceremony. Handing him the camera, both he and his friend climbed the steps overlooking the area to watch. They would be taking pictures of us during the ceremony. Both appeared delighted with this arrangement.

I opened my bag of crystals and began to place them in the center of the courtyard. Elisa started to burn incense and consecrate the area. After laying the large towering crystal stones in the North, South, East, and West positions, I arranged the thirteen inner silvery moonstones representing the feminine energies. Then the outer 20 golden citrines were placed in the outer circle, representing the male energies.

Inside the circular layout of the stones, I reverently placed my crystal skull with seven crystals radiating out from the skull. This represented the seven spirits of wisdom. The seven were around the crystal skull, the repository of knowledge. All these numbers—7, 9, 13, 20—were sacred to the Maya, I realized as I lay them out. They had been sacred to me before ever knowing anything of the Maya. The ancients all had the same knowledge at one time. We all have much in common if we only take the time to notice and acknowledge one another.

Standing, I performed the ancient smudging ceremony. I held the abalone shell—the ocean turtle shell—a symbol of Mother Earth. I filled it with burning copal, the flowing sap of the copal tree, the feminine. The rising smoke cleansed and purified the aura. This is done to release any residue of negativity, bad spirits and prepare us for the anointing of the Spirit. It also is very similar to the burning of incense in the Catholic Church. Same idea, different location, that's all.

As we lined up and began the ceremony, two large vultures arrived and stood guard in the tree overhead.

"I miss my ravens on this trip," I thought. They were always with me.

Their constant companionship back home was a comfort. Now we had two large black vultures. As Elisa saw them, she was taken aback.

"Is that a bad sign?" she asked. "Should we make them go away?"

"No, actually the vulture is a sign of death and resurrection to Native American Indians, and in other cultures. It is appropriate that they are here and is actually a confirmation of what we are doing here today," I answered to the whole group.

As I finished the next to the last person, I looked up at the two men seated on the steps watching us intently in absolute silence. I motioned for them to come down. Without a moments' hesitation, they literally ran down the steps and stood at the end of the line waiting for their turn to be smudged. As I began to lift the shell up with its billowing smoke around Juan, I could hear OBED's voice.

"Susan, it is their time. It is desired they have the anointing."

"Am I to give them the Earth Healer attunement?" I asked incredulously.

"No, you are to give Shambhala."

"WOW! OBED, that's going to be a tricky. I'll have to shift the energies," I exclaimed in my mind as I finished the smudging.

"We will assist," was the final communication.

"Juan, would you and your friend like to join us in the ceremony?"

"Oh, yes, we would!" he replied eagerly.

"Juan, when I do this you will have an empowerment, a gift, you have never had before. I will be assisting Spirit to bring you the gift of healing. You will have the gift of healing in your hands. I will touch you on your head, hands, heart, and feet. Do you understand this?"

"Yes," he answered, "I will explain this to my friend."

On Assignment with Adama

After a few moments of excited Spanish, they were both standing in front of me with glowing smiles. They were ready. I motioned to them to take their place with the others who were seated around the crystals.

They found their places to sit in the circle. They each pulled from their pockets a stone. Juan placed his in the center. The friend handed me his stone. He carried it gently. As I took it in my hand, I could see it was a small tooled glass head about the size of a half dollar. It was filled with air bubbles, a sure sign of a poured-glass object. This was the crystal skull Juan had told me about.

I could tell as he held it with great reverence, that he believed this was the "real deal." It was not a crystal skull as he believed, but looked like pure glass. However, it was very precious to this man.

I felt momentary sadness, then placed it in the center and moved my crystal skull to its side, giving the glass object the place of honor.

"Today," I thought, "this little glass head will be activated with energy like never before!" I could see he was pleased.

"I guess they really were ready, "I thought, as I began the attunement ceremony.

I took my Master crystal and began to activate all the crystals and circulate the energies in their formation. It is a representation of our own Merkaba fields around us.

"I fill you with love, I fill you with Peace, I fill you with Light, the True Light,
I fill you with love, I fill you with Peace, I fill you with Light, the True Light,
I fill you with love, I fill you with Peace, I fill you with Light, the True Light.
I activate the Divine Feminine Energies,
I Activate the Divine Masculine Energies,
I Activate and Bring Forth the Creative Energy of the Christ-Light,
With these I activate the Seven Spirits of Wisdom and Creative Power."

With the swirling energies activated and growing outward, expanding, we were ready for the next activation.

"I pray for all the ancestors, the indigenous tribes of the world, for those who have held the truth of the ancients, those who have suffered much at the hands of the ignorant, you are honored. Your presence is invited here as we also represent you here in this place."

With this prayer the whole place began to fill with the spirits of the past. They were standing all around us. Lighting more copal incense, I made prayer offerings to all four directions honoring their spirits.

"I honor you of the South, those who have remained here to watch, to guide, to protect. I honor those who have given of themselves for all the ages. For this day, I honor you. I honor your generations, your lives, the height of your summer seasons of life, your coming of age, your children and you."

The sound of rattles released the prayers upon the winds and the drawing near of the ancient spirits was once again upon us.

"To those of the West, I honor you of the West, those who have remained here to watch, to guide, to protect. I honor those who have given of themselves for all the ages. For this day, I honor you. I honor your generations, your lives, the height of your giving of self through the seasons of your life, your maturity of age, your children and you."

"I honor you of the North, those who have remained here to watch, to guide, to protect. I honor those who have given of themselves for all the ages. For this day, I honor you. I honor your generations, your lives, the coming of the elders, the teachers of your seasons of life, your transitions of form, your children and you."

"I honor you of the East, the place of the Rising Son, those who have remained here to watch, to guide, to protect. I honor those who have given of themselves for all the ages. For this day, I honor you. I honor your generations, your

lives, the coming seasons of life renewed, your ascension, your children and you."

I began to pray to the Divine, Source of all Love, for Its energies to fill us and prepare us for this attunement, this initiation, into the energies of Shambhala and the Earth Healers through GAIA, the Mother who supports, nourishes us and cares for all our needs.

I invited all the Ascended Masters, the Mahatma, Pure Unconditional Love from the Source of Love, and the Christ Light to fill us. Then raising my hands, I asked for the empowerment of Melchizedek to fill them. My hands began to glow with the energies. I was prepared to begin.

"I am open now to channel the Divine to each one here as appropriate for their Divine purpose on Earth and the Creator's will," I stated aloud to all present.

Going behind the first initiate I laid my hands upon the head, saying

"I activate the Divine energies of Shambhala, Mahatma, Pure Unconditional Love, and the Christ Light."

As the energies began to flow I went to each initiate, anointing him or her in the Spirit and giving the appropriate attunement for each. True to their promise, my Guides helped me make the necessary adjustments in the energy flow for each. I could feel the warmth come into Juan's and his friend's hands as I attuned them. They both began to rock back and forth as the energies entered them. Tears of joy began to flow down their cheeks.

"They will be great healers and teachers among the people," I heard.

As I prepared to give the Earth Healer's attunement, once again Lady GAIA came to give it herself. Again I was simply the channel for her powerful message.
"I AM LADY GAIA."

The energies came up from the center of her heart, the center of the Earth, up my feet, legs and back, flowing out my hands to those being initiated. Three blasts of her energy are given to each initiate, sealing in her energies and the new ability of the Earth Healer.

Standing before each participant, I placed my fingers on their third eye and prayed.

"Open by the Power of God, The Holy Spirit, Shekinah, and the Christ Light."

With the invocation, the flowing White Light filled each one activating their pineal and pituitary glands. I felt the pulsing begin as the glands filled with Light, expanding and activating. The glands continue to grow in size and are more sensitive to the Divine energies coming into each one. The Light of the Divine expansion of these glands will even cause physical transformation of the initiates heads and features.

This gives each one highly increased powers of perception and psychic abilities. As each was attuned to the energies, the symbols, and the empowerments, they would now be able to see and use these incredible gifts.

Going to the heart Chakra, each was opened, sealed to the energies of Love, sealed with the Pure Love of God. This love is to be shared with all the people of the Earth. Unconditionally, they will now give to all with whom they come into contact.

I knelt before each initiate. The attunement of the hands was next. Holding them up to God I said,

"I consecrate and dedicate these hands to the receiving and the giving of theenergies of Shambhala, Mahatma, Unconditional Love and the Christ Light. I ask for the special gifts that are for each."

Great rocking waves of these energies flowed through me into the waiting hands. I was rocked back and forth as wave after wave flowed through me to them. Together we moved in unison, swaying to the motions of the incoming forces. Warmth flowed through me and into them in wonderful coupling. They received the energies both in their hands and their hearts. Additional gifts were given as their hands were lifted to God and He filled them. All were greatly blessed.

Finally everyone's feet were opened to the energy. The energy flowed through their bodies and was placed into the Earth Star beneath each initiate. These new energies were also given to the Earth who has waited long for us to return and activate them. The energies were safely secured to the center of the Earth from the Earth Star.

"With each step we take, we now bless the earth. We hold and channel these energies which are the life-giving energy of the future.
We give thanks to those Beings of Light who are here for our highest good, those of you who have walked with us as our Guides, our teachers. You have held our hands, praying for this day to come.
To you and to the Source of all Love, we confirm before all, we will use our gifts for the highest good of mankind.
I give thanks to Lady GAIA who has shared her wondrous gifts, to St. Germain who has made this possible, and to Melchizedek who has brought forth the attuning energies, we give thanks."

We sat together absorbing the gifts, the blessings, the activations, and the total wonder. For several minutes we sat in silence, each with our own worshipful, deep thoughts. Some of us journeyed inwardly to sacred places where we met with our Guides, communed with them, and received instructions.

The a-tune-ment, or attunement, brought each to the Oneness of Divinity. It is a process of being one with the Divine. The activations are profound and are felt on a level that is impossible to describe.

I know the ancients were watching us in this place. They had waited centuries. The energy of Cahal Pech was much different from the other temples. There was no need for clearing and lost or trapped spirits were not present. When I had sat at the entrance of Cahal Pech they brought gifts, many gifts to me. I was filled. Somehow Cahal Pech had been spared the indignity of the past that had been wrought on the rest of the temple areas.

Susan Isabelle

Perhaps it had something to do with the name, Cahal Pech, which means 'the place of ticks.' Sometimes the smallest irritants can prevent us from large-scale suffering. Maybe because of this affliction of ticks on the populace here prevented mass murder by keeping the population numbers down? A speculation, that's all.

15

Activation of the Skulls

After a while I could see each person beginning to come back into the physical, into conscious awareness once again.

"Now we will activate the crystal skulls by bringing in the Pillar of Light," I explained to Juan and his guest, and our wonderful group of Lightworkers.

"We are going to 'tone' a symbol which calls in the Divine energies and activate the crystal skulls in the center. Is that OK with you?"

"Oh, yes," they both responded and nodded their heads enthusiastically.

"It will also establish a pillar of Light in this place which will remain here, sanctifying the whole area for eternity."

As I looked to them for approval, they nodded again. I then explained,

"We will first draw down the energies and then tone, or sing, the Song of the Angels. The Song is a long tone, of specific sounds, that solidifies and connects the Pillar to the Earth Plane."

I gave them a demonstration of the tone we would use, then we all began the long tone. The men joined in just about the time the angels did. Holding their heads back they let the tone flow though them. Once you tone this you can never be the same! The sound reverberates throughout all your cells, lifting you and joining both the physical and the spirit through the tone. Scripture says:

"In the beginning was the Word (tone/vibration), *The Word was with God, and not anything that was made was made but by the Word."*

There is power in the Word. Creative power is in the sound. The Word is known as the Christ who is TONE, is CREATOR energies. He is the at-tone-ment. Meditate on that! Through tone comes creation. We were about to create.

As we channeled the Song of the Angels, the Divine was called, and came. The long tone reverberated throughout the area. Its vibration was felt deep in the earth, it awoke the sleeping ones, and they sang with us!

Three times it was sung, as we did so my crystal skull in the center began to glow, shining out the energies that were being sung into it. All crystal skulls are set to tones and when the proper tones are sung to them, they will activate. There was so much energy being channeled into the center from all nine of us that my crystal skull and the glass head were shining bright, sending out rays of Divine Energy. The seven crystals around them glowed, channeling the energy outward, and established the energies of Divine wisdom in a great circle in which we were all bathed. A great Light filled the whole area.

When we had finished the song we all were wiping away tears of complete joy. Our ceremony was complete. I went over to Juan and his friend, who was still crying softly. I spent a few minutes showing Juan and his friend how to use their new gifts.

"Hold your hands out like this and will the energy to flow out from your palms. It comes in through the top of your head and out through here," I said, touching the palm chakras.

"I can feel it! I can feel it in my hands and in my head!" they exclaimed through joyous tears.

"Now feel the aura, or spirit, of each other. You can feel the energy coming from each of you and the energy centers of the body."

On Assignment with Adama

I motioned to them, sweeping over them, demonstrating the location of the chakras, then let them explore on their own. Their hands shook as waves of tingling energy were felt by each man as they swept the other's aura.

"When someone is ill, these will be weak, close to the body."

I demonstrated each chakra and assisted them in locating them, touching their chakras in demonstration.

"All you have to do is give more energy to make the chakras strong again. Pray and ask for the energy to come, and it will."

"Yes, yes, we can feel this, it shines beneath our hands," Juan exclaimed.

Both men were smiling, and very excited about this gift they had received. Lucy came over and, in Spanish, explained further details for the use of their new energy gifts. I had admired her fluency and great skill with people on several occasions during this trip, especially now. She taught with great love and compassion. I could see the need for her special talents and all the people she could teach shine in a vision before me. Lucy, you are needed; multitudes await!

Lucy came over. "He would like to speak with you," she said motioning to Juan's friend. "He wants you to take the head. He was very moved and wants you to take it."

I went over to where they were sitting. In broken English, he said,

"I want you to have the head, you know how to use it. I found it under the sacred Ceiba tree, at the roots. It is old and worth money."

I told him, "I can understand that you had hoped to gain money. I cannot do that. If it were an ancient piece, the country would have to have it. But, I have to be honest with you...I do not believe it is old."

He looked surprised.

"I have seen it and I believe it is a kind of a glass."

He was shocked, but I went on, picking up both my crystal skull and the head.

"See, here is a real crystal skull I have, and this is the other one you have. You can see the air bubbles and the tool marks on the head you have found." He saw and nodded.

"It is also flat on the bottom."

"If it was real, these would not be here," I said.

I pointed to the bubbles and the tool marks.

"Feel the difference and the weight. Real crystal has no air bubbles like this. It is heavy, cold to the touch, and can warm slowly with the energy, glass does not. I am sorry to have to tell you this, but it is a poured glass head. A visiting tourist must have left it there. We have things that look like this at home, it is called molten glass." I said this very gently.

"I am sorry to disappoint you, but I am happy to pay you for coming, for giving us your time, but I cannot buy it."

There was a flurry of discussion in Spanish as the man considered the facts. He clearly was disappointed. He is a Guatemalan. We had seen their country, extreme poverty abounds everywhere you look.

He sadly told us that he had thought he had found something that would at last help his family. He was the father of several children and had hoped to send his children to college on the money gained. He had much difficulty finding work. I felt so much compassion for him on his situation. He had found something he thought was akin to our finding a million dollars or winning the lottery, only to find it was a fake. To have had such a wonderful attunement, then such a disappointment.

He told us how his village shaman used objects to heal and he had thought this one was like the one the shaman used. He told us how the shaman put the crystals in rum to see what the spirits would say about the patient.

We were fascinated with his stories about life in Guatemala and had many questions. Lucy explained to him that with his new gift of healing, he, too, could become a chiclero—shamanic healer—to his people. Maybe he wouldn't have to go try to find work after all.

"I will speak to my family," he said, solemnly. "I will contact you later."

I never expected to see him again as he walked away.

Later that night at the motel, I had a visitor.

" I thank you for the powerful gift you have given me in my hands this day," he spoke gently in his broken English.

"I am moved. I told my family of the difference. I talked with them. We want you to have this. You may have this as you will know how to use it."

With that he freely handed me the little glass head.

I was deeply touched and could hardly speak. He had just handed me his treasure that wasn't a treasure. If he had been a dishonest man, this would not have happened. He may have sold it to someone else for a high price.

"I would like to help your family," I said.

"I would like to pay for the wonderful teaching you gave us today. May I do this?"

"Yes," he answered softly.

I love this man for all that he is and his gentle goodness, I realized. I told him I would help his family as I could.

In another way, the glass head had prospered him far beyond what money could buy. He now had within him an ability to heal both himself and the members of his village. Perhaps in time he will enlighten all Guatemala!

Cahal Peck   Receiving the Skull

16

Plumed Serpent's Return

The sun was shining brightly. Its rays beat down upon and into us. The angels (or angles of light) beamed something into us new in this age. Those seated around were not aware of it, but a miracle was occurring. There were *no shadows*! The hour of the noon alignment had arrived, and the rays were upon us.

High above in the cosmos a connection had occurred. Belize and Mexico were now in direct alignment with the sun and the Pleiades. It was a time for magic. We were bathed in its Light and the Light of the Mayan Spirits around us.

Earlier I had handed out to the group a paper compiled from the writings of several contemporary authors, including John Major Jenkins, author of *Maya Cosmogenesis 2012*. I highly recommend his book to anyone seeking more detailed information. He believes, and supports in his writings, that Kulkulcan/Quetzalcoatl is the Plumed Serpent symbol of the sun/Pleiades conjunction. He also shows clearly that the temple of Chichén Itzá is a processional clock.

It is my belief, based upon his writings and that of others, that it meant this day—May 20, 2000—heralded the return of the Plumed Serpent. Jenkins claims the temple of Chichén Itzá was built in 830 A.D. for this very purpose.

This whole area was witnessing the beginning of the 12-year countdown to the spectacular alignment predicted for May 20, 2012.

The zenith—or the return of Kulkulcan/Quetzalcoatl, he sun/Pleiades unification—is when the throne is taken, when the peak, or zenith, is reached in what is called the Heart of Heaven.

On that day—May 20, 2012—above Chichén Itzá's temple a great astronomical event will occur. There will be a solar eclipse all across Central America and western North America. *The Sun and the Pleiades will pass over the zenith with the moon.*

The calendar date is 10 Chicchan, meaning the Serpent.

Quetzalcoatl, indeed, is returning. This little group assembled here has been bathed in the first rays of the coming. I know in time they will each be called into service. To what service, I do not know, but it shall be revealed.

Walking back from the ceremony, Juan held Racha-el back to speak with her before he was to leave for Mexico as this was likely the last time he would see her. He professed his deep admiration and devotion to her. He was to be the first of many.

I remembered Chuen, under the sign of Venus, Goddess of Love. It was to Chuen she had given the lottery tickets back in Belize City. He had indeed given something in return. Racha-el spent the rest of the day walking around holding her heart humming,

"*I am Full. I used to be I AM, but now, I AM Full!*" She glowed.

I expanded so much in the Light that day that I was taller- and much wider than usual. I was much bigger than the male guide and my cousin who is taller than I.
Chal Pech
Susan Isabelle expanded in Light on the day of 5/20/2000

17

Telos Portal

We were running out of time in San Ignacio. We had one more very important project to complete before leaving: The Telos Portal. The portal had to be located at the waterfalls. Everywhere we had asked about waterfalls.

No one knew anything about the waterfalls at El Pilar. We had prior direction from Spirit that the portal would be at the waterfalls at El Pilar. They had to be opened before we left in the morning for Belize City. We decided to stop back at our hotel for lunch before going to El Pilar. We looked at the large map on the wall at San Ignacio Hotel

"I don't see any waterfalls on the map," said Elisa. "There just aren't any."

"No," I answered. "The thousand-foot waterfalls we had expected to visit just don't seem to be the right direction. No, they are connected with El Pilar somehow, I know."

We all sat down around the table on the deck overlooking the jungle and Mopan River to consider our plight. Angel, our waiter, came over to the table and began to take our orders.

"So, you are all leaving tomorrow," he said. "It's been real!"

"Angel, do you know where the waterfalls are at El Pilar?" I asked.

"Oh, no, there are no waterfalls at El Pilar, but there are some nearby."

"Where?!" we all cried together, startling him.

"They're not on any map, as the tourists do not go there. Only the locals go there."

He said shaking his head, uncertain if he should say more.

"Angel, we have to go there today. It is very important. Please tell us how to get there," Elisa pleaded with him.

"You will never find them," he said. "I will ask if I can get out of work to take you there. They are deep in the jungle."

He then served our meal as we waited for his boss to decide if Angel could take us. He pulled up a chair next to Faith.

"And so, Little One, why do you want to go to the waterfalls?" he asked.

"We have to open something up there for all of Belize."

"And what is that?" he playfully inquired.

"Angel, we do spiritual work and this will open Belize to the Light and Love of God once again," I answered. "We have to go."

He got up and went back into the kitchen, returning a few minutes later saying,

"I will go with you to take you there. Explain to me what you do."

I explained to him about the healing energy of Shambhala. He asked many questions and was very interested.

"Angel, would you like to have an attunement to the Shambhala energies?"

"Oh, yes! I'll take you today to the falls and be here tonight after work to meet you!"

We were back in the Rover to begin the trip to our waterfalls. Following Angel's little car, we discussed how Spirit had miraculously provided for us once again. At the last moment an 'Angel' had come to direct us...amazing!

We drove over the bridge crossing the Mopan River. We followed him up the side of a hill on a narrow dirt road, down through a farmer's pasture, and entered the thick green jungle. Faith drove the Rover through a stream and lots of mud, and parked on the side of a hill. We could go no further in the car. The rest of the trip would be on foot. While we were taking our gear from the car, Angel came up to us.

"It's not much further now. It's just through the jungle up there." He pointed through some thick growth.

"Well, here we go again!" I hoisted my pack of crystals up onto my back. We made our way through the thick vegetation and came out into a clearing. It was flat and surrounded by jungle rising up on each side of us. We could hear the falls, but they were hidden from our immediate view.

"They're right down here," directed Angel.

He took us over to a ledge where we looked down, thrilled. Just beneath us were several falls flowing from what appeared to be a man-made channel. Man-made, but not in the past thousand years or so.

The water making up the falls flowed from the hills around us, across the clearing in a channel, and had been directed into six waterfalls which splashed down into three large tiled tiers, one over the other, in pools of water. The uppermost pool was a stream that was surrounded by five-foot high Peace Lilies. White and towering on their stems, they waved white blossoms to welcome us.

Tumbling down from here was a second level which formed six waterfalls with alternating forced water jets, just like massage jets. We took turns sitting beneath the multitude of sprays. Cold and invigorating, they felt wonderful.

Faith, Elisa and Rob took advantage of the third level down, a beautiful diving pool complete with waterslide. Diving and sliding from the second level they plunged into the deep blue-green waters. Little handholds carved centuries ago guided them back up the stone walls to join us. We were in paradise.

Angel laughed as he watched us play in the waters. Coming over to me he said,

"This is my most favorite place in all of Belize!"

"Angel, it is a paradise! Thank you for bringing us here!" He nodded.

"Angel, would you like to have your attunement here?"

His face lit up. "Oh yes," he breathed. "What do I have to do?"

"Just take off your shoes. Here's a perfect place for you to sit on this rock," I answered.

He sat surrounded by the sounds of gentle waterfalls and waving Peace Lilies as he removed his shoes. Elisa, Laneta, Racha-el and Faith gathered around him as I gave him his attunement, sending him the energies.

Angel glowed. He simply glowed. His face truly was that of an angel as the energies entered him. He lifted his face upward in rapture toward heaven. His black skin shone with the sunlight and the Son-Light. So enraptured by the Light, I could not at first open Angel's hands. I waited, then saw he was prepared. I took his hands in mine and raised them to the Light to be filled…

We all cried. He was *so* radiant, *so* beautiful. He stayed there a long while. We waited, then his eyes opened. He seemed surprised to see us all there upon his return to the physical. He certainly hadn't been with us.

After a few minutes, he realized what he had been doing and he was a bit embarrassed as we looked at him with obvious adoration. He grinned widely, saying,

"Yes, we are fine. There's only one way in, so only one way out!" We laughed again, waving goodbye to an angel.

"That was verrrry nice, verrrry interesting!"

Then he began to laugh joyfully and we laughed with him.

"Oh, I must be getting back! I am late, I will see you this evening!" He said as he hurried down the path. "You are sure you can find your way back?"

18

Heed the Message

Now it was time for us to complete our mission. I went up above the falls to find a place for the opening of the Telos portal here in Belize. Following the channel of water back across the clearing I saw a large towering mound with trees growing all over it. Covered in centuries of jungle growth was an ancient Mayan temple. We had been playing in the fountains and waterfalls at the base of the courtyard of a temple...how perfect.

Looking across the way through the dense jungle, I could see the three other temples that surrounded our playground. In all the other temple areas we had visited, the courtyard was always free of structures. Courtyards were flat, grassy fields. The only other courtyard to have a structure had been the place of the Atlantean tomb mound.

Now here was another beautiful example of an area dedicated to something special; not to death, but Life. The Waters of Life! Full of life and beauty, this temple had once been the Lemurians to visit and enjoy its pleasurable waters. Here we would reopen that gateway.

At the base of the temple we set up our blankets to sit on. I passed out the remaining symbols and instructed the group.

"We will be setting up the symbol to first send this to Telos at Mt. Shasta. Once we have established the connection there, we will connect to a location near your home. Don't send this into your house, however. A couple of weeks ago we did this in an Advanced Master class and one young woman decided to send the energy to her house. People don't listen to me sometimes!" They laughed.

"While she and her brother were playing cards later that night, something got their attention. There were lights flickering and moving around in the living room plants. They also had an Indian visit them in the night."

"What did they do?"

"The next day we had to spend class time to go back out to the site to close it down. I want you to know I won't be sending anyone back here for a while, so choose carefully where you want to send this!"

They thought about it for a few minutes then when everyone was ready we began.

"Put your hands down on the ground," I began.

"Ouch! Move! Everybody MOVE!" shouted Faith from the other side.

"They're coming!"

A large red 'blanket' was moving across the ground. Advancing directly toward us were army ants, a billion of them, moving as one. We gathered everything and ran as close to the waterfalls as we could, and sat down again.

"Gee, Juan was right!" Rob said. "He told us, 'When they come, people have to move out of their way. Sometimes they come right through their houses and the people just stand outside waiting for them to pass.'"

"They won't get any argument from us today," I laughed.

"OK. Now let's get back to work. Put your hands down on the ground and begin the long tone." I looked down at my hands firmly pressed against the ground.

There on top of my hand was a single red ant looking up at me. Then I knew; I knew! We had been in the wrong spot. We were at the base of the temple.

The portal site was at the *waterfalls*. The ants—these little red beings—had been summoned to charge us, forcing us to relocate to our proper position. I began to laugh; how wonderful! As the others began the tone, I could hardly contain my glee. Even the ants, the tiniest creatures, hear and obey the great design. How wonderful is our God, our Source and how loving! I let the little being stay atop my hand as I began the tone. He, too, was a part of this!

The great tones sailed across the jungle. We filled the air, the sky and the earth. Beneath us the earth began to open her doorways, creaky with age. The oil of Spirit, of Light, flowed into the ancient passageways.
All the way to Mt. Shasta they opened to the flowing tones.
The tunnels of Adama, the Light, of the Lemurians opened and were restored.
At the moment of the transition, some twelve years away, they will be used.
We have done it!

The sound of our tones wafted out over the land; we could hear them sounding out stronger than our voices could carry them. Tones were lifting, but not from us. Up in the treetops they rose. From the trees surrounding us, and all across the countryside, something amazing was happening. The *PARROTS* were sounding the ancient tones! We sat back and listened in wonder. The beautiful green parrots up in the trees, and the Mayan Spirits were joining us!

The Vision

As they toned, I began to have a vision. As I entered the vision, I shared as best I could what was being shown to me.

"I am being shown this land as it was in the distant past. Adama is with me, he is my escort.
All around us are children with their mothers. They are enjoying the wondrous beauty of this place. It is so natural to them. Such joy. They are happy and playing. Such peace here, so much happiness!
The temple rises high behind us; it is white and sparkles in the sun.

The courtyard where you are sitting is white stone. All around us there are flowers   blossoming everywhere and I can smell their fragrance. I have never seen such beauty anywhere on this earth!"

"I am being drawn upwards and I know I am entering the realm of the future.
I am above the earth and I can see below.
They are showing me a vision of the future earth," I managed to say.
"There are no cities; there are no oceans.
Many, many lakes are here among the trees; all is tropical, all is beautiful, green, with small villages of white in between.

The people...the people walk freely; there are no cars, no roads.
There are huge pyramids that rise up into the sky all over the earth. They are stark white."

"What are these?" I asked my Guides.

"These are the power sources which shall come;
they will empower the planet.
The new technology is that which will free the earth and its peoples."

The pyramids shone in the sun, white and sharp above the green of the towering tress surrounding them.

Coming out from the four sides of the pyramids I could see interconnecting highways of pure white. They joined all the other pyramids across the globe.

"And what are these?" I asked Adama.

"These are the 'higher-ways',
the result of the balance of spirituality and that of technology.
It is your contribution to this time.
You are seeing the result of your efforts on behalf of the Earth and All its peoples."

Then I was returned to my body.

I know I have been unable to convey the enormity and glory of this vision as shown to me, as it truly exists in our future.
Sometimes when the way is difficult, and I feel as though I've worked for something that no one could possibly understand, I bring myself back to this place. I have literally released all for this vision of a future Earth of LOVE.

Of all the gifts I could ever desire to give to my family, my children,
to you, to the earth,
this is what I would want for all of you. It makes everything I endure worthwhile.

***I just want it.
NOW!***

EL ALEATOR

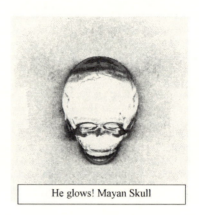

He glows! Mayan Skull

19

Sastun

The day's work and my vision had drained all my physical strength. My spirit was forever altered, heightened. There is nothing that could ever dissuade me from this path I have undertaken. The vision confirmed my purpose and my life's mission.
This is the future. I will do my part to see it happens.
All thirty-six sites will be opened. Somehow it will happen.

I retired to my room as soon as I could manage it. I reflected on the day, then I fell into much-needed sleep.

Later that night I was awakened from sound sleep by a strange sensation. My flesh, my skin became tightly drawn as if it didn't fit my body any longer. I had rippling sensations up and down my legs. It also felt as though someone, unseen, was squeezing my legs.

"What's this?" I thought. "I don't sense anything in the room."

I turned over to try to go back to sleep. About an hour later, I felt the top of my head pulsing so hard, I felt as if I was going to be sucked up and out!

"Now what?" I scanned the room. "All clear. This has to be my imagination, I'm so tired I'm out of my mind!" I thought and pulled up the sheets.

The pulsing on the top of my head was actually spiraling the crown chakra so fast I began to fight to stay in my body. I sat up.

"What is going on?" I got up and walked around the room. It seemed once I was standing the pulsing subsided.

"Something is causing this and I have to find it now or I'll never get any sleep," I complained. I went over to my backpack which I'd placed by the head of my bed.

"That thing is pulsing! I'll move it further down," I thought sleepily as I laid down. I pushed it under the bed away from my head and dropped back to sleep. A few minutes later I was feeling my solar plexus chakra going wild.

"I'm never going to get any sleep! What the hell is going on!"

Angry with exhaustion, I reached under the bed to pull the bag forward again. It was still pulsing with energy.

"What is in this thing?" As I started to open the bag, I remembered and spoke to myself, "I have two activated skulls in this bag! Oh, Boy!
Plus seven activated wisdom crystals!"

I began to attune the whole bag to the energy of Shambhala and the Christ Light just in case something else had gotten into my backpack. It took the energy just as if a human was having an attunement.

It was calmer now, so I pushed it back down near the foot of the bed. I fell back asleep only to awaken an hour later with my feet feeling as though they were extended all the way across the room. They were tingling, extended and pulsing.

"OK," I thought, "I'll attune it again! Last time that worked." I gave it another attunement. This time I got up and I put the whole bag in the bathroom and closed the door just in case.

"That ought to do it!"

Back to bed again. Up again after just a few minutes, the energy now pouring in from the bathroom. I sealed off the doorway and put protection around the room. This didn't feel 'bad' or 'dark,' but I did not feel in control. I like to be in control of my crystals and don't like surprises like this.

"I don't like this!" I thought. "This is very strong and I am not happy!"

I looked around the room again. Everyone was sleeping very peacefully. It apparently wasn't bothering them.

"No, I don't understand this!" I thought as I lay back down on the bed. Eyes fully open and awake, I stood watch. Things in the room began to change, the darkness of the room became bright, then velvet darkness everywhere. Electric blue swirls of energy began filling the space like galaxies hung in the room. Pulsing, pulsing the energy built to a high pitch. It felt as though I was on a hallucinogenic.

One by one they entered. They spun furiously then took on shapes. The spirals exploded in midair: first the parrot came; brightly colored, vibrant red and blue and flew across the bed, then returned to the swirling electric blue energy which hung above the room.

Right through the wall the enormous panther walked into the room. His mammoth form came right to the edge of my bed. He had golden yellow eyes which stared at me as I lay hiding beneath the covers. He snorted, turned and glided away, becoming the blue swirling mass.

"I must observe, I must observe, not partake." I told myself.

I watched all of this in total amazement trying to remain in observer mode, and tried not to think as I watched them. I knew what I was seeing was a demonstration of my power animals. They had come! I tried not to move, not to breathe; I waited.

The golden skinned deer with a mighty, towering rack bounded through the velvet night and was gone. A sleek, spotted jaguar prowled throughout the room as though looking for prey, then suddenly transformed back to one of the electric blue swirls hanging above me.

Then the cold darkness came. The soft velvet turned to coarse coal, black as pitch. The VOID. With it came frightening forms of nighttime specters and I was definitely afraid. Specters of death, of hatred, of fearful shape, of fear...

"My God, what are these?" I prayed for the Light.

"I must overcome the fear! I cannot give into the fear!"

"Breathe in the Light, be the Light!" I heard.

Breathing in the Light, I obeyed. I became Light.

"I AM Light, I AM Love."

I refused the fear and became the observer. I watched as they passed, saw their masks, their deformed specter shapes. Not coming to possess, they came to perform, to show themselves as the keepers of darkness. I avoided the impulse to feel trapped in this place of the void, but I wanted out.

"I know who you are. I do not belong in this place," I thought. I prayed even more. As soon as the words were spoken, the room changed. The soft velvet reappeared, The void was gone.

Calling upon the Christ Light, the electric blue spirals once again appeared hanging in the darkness of the velvet room. I watched as these mighty spirals began to spin vibrantly, expanding, filling the room with their light.

They became the purest white as they transformed into the Mayan Lords of Light.

The Nine Spirits of the Maya came as the Nine Benevolent Spirits of Peace to present themselves.

Beautiful, feathered, and Shimmering White!

Garbed in sparkling white skins and flowing tunics with cords wrapped about the waist, these Maya were glowing golden amidst the purity of the white light which they emitted.

I spoke with them as if one of them.

I was lifted from up my bed to greet them in my Light body.

20

Red Resonant Skywalker

May 21, 2000
Mayan Calendar Day: Red Resonant Skywalker
Dreamspell:
> "I channel in order to explore
> Inspiring wakefulness
> I seal the output of space
> With the resonant tone of attunement
> I am guided by the power of life force."

"Sue, it's time to get up, we're off to Belize City. Got to get there in time for our boat trip and snorkeling!" I awoke to find the others moving about the room in the early morning dawn. Wiping away the remnants of sleep, I recalled the night's events.

"Was that a dream?" I thought reaching over to grab my backpack at the head of the bed where I had placed it the night before.

"It's not there!" I hung upside down over the edge to peer under the bed.

"It's not there!" I jumped up and ran into the bathroom.

There the backpack sat, where I had secured it during the night when all this had begun. I picked it up. It was quiet now, finally at rest.

"No, that was not a dream," I thought as I sat on the edge of the bed holding the pack in my arms. I wondered as I sat there contemplating the situation.

I didn't even dare open the pack. I began to ask myself a few questions.

What did we do at Cahal Pech?
Was my crystal skull the cause of this?
Was it the other glass head?
...Something really is in my pack!
What have I got?
What is this?
What am I going to do now?
Do I even want this?
...I was up all night—until the Mayan Spirits came, then I went with them!
Where did I go?
...I have no memory!
...I don't like not being in control!
Whatever it is, can I give it back?

I was quiet, thinking deeply as we drove back to Belize City. My emotions were conflicted. I didn't want to leave this wonderful, magical place! San Ignacio, I'll miss you!

Now back in Belize City, I registered our group at the hotel while Elisa and the others prepared to go on the snorkeling trip and the boat.

Up in the room at last, I sat out on the balcony rocking. I had so much to consider and to digest. The night before had been the most extreme of all my experiences. I had gone with the Mayan Gods and I had no memory of it. I just wanted to rest, to reflect, and maybe float around in the pool at most. I begged off the boating trip.

"Sue, I'll stay with you," said Lucy. "I don't want to go either."
"Are you sure, Lucy? It's a once in a lifetime chance!"

"I will stay." The others left the room and headed toward the dock.

I was happy to have Lucy to talk with about my experiences during the night. I needed to discuss it with someone. I told her what had happened, and of my turmoil.

Together we opened my backpack and took out the crystals to examine them. The seven crystals were still humming from all their activity, but something had definitely happened to my crystal skull, I examined it more closely.

"See here, Lucy? Look at this! All across the top of the skull there are lines and clouds inside. I never saw those before!"

We turned and touched the warming skull. It was really activated and humming.

"And look at this! There's a rainbow above his right eye. Wow, that wasn't there before."

We took out the glass head and looked at it. It seemed to have a turquoise glow around it. Like little kids we took it into the bathroom and shut off the light to see if it still glowed.

"No, I guess it must just be the light reflection in the room from the curtains." I said, packing it away. It was cold and non-responsive.

We cleansed and attuned the beautiful stones Lucy had purchased in Belize and Guatemala, then headed downstairs to the pool. It was a great afternoon and I slept under the shade and blossoms of a beautiful red hibiscus tree along with a big iguana.

That night we all gathered together in the Radisson dining room to reflect on our trip and share one last meal together. In the morning we each would go our separate ways. We shared our day's events.

We laughed with Racha-el's story of how the driver of the boat had formed an instant attraction to her. He spent the whole day teaching her. She ended up giving him her boat shoes. He was thrilled.

A native flutist was playing the most extraordinary tunes on his little carved flute while we ate our dinner. He danced the sounds to Racha-el in particular, then sent the music out over us with a wave of his hand. He was amazing. He played several songs of pure love to Racha-el, dancing around her.

"I AM Full!" was all she could say, as she held her heart. Chuen was at it again!

21

White Galactic Wizard

May 22, 2000
Mayan Calendar Day: White Galactic Wizard
Dreamspell:

> "I harmonize in order to enchant
> Modeling receptivity
> I seal the output of timelessness
> With the galactic tone of integrity
> I am guided by the power of endlessness."

Sastun

As I wandered around the airport waiting for our flight, I was attracted to a book high up on the top shelf of one of the small vendors. I reached up and removed it from its cradle. I read the title: *Sastun*. "What is that?" I wondered. Flipping through the pages, I found that it had been written by a woman named Rosita Arvigo. I opened to a page, which read:

"When they first opened the tomb at Xunantunich, the workers fell to the ground in a stupor. Just before passing out they heard hmmmmmmm-mmmmmmmmm. Some of the workers died."

That got my attention; I bought the book. Was this the freeing of the Atlantean? I wondered? Was this the El Bruto?

When they opened the tomb they must have released it!

I was to learn a lot more as I read the entire book on the flight to the States. It was about her work, and her five-year apprenticeship with a Mayan healer called Don Elijio Panti.

Most importantly, I was to learn about the use of crystals as healing and communication tools of the ancient Mayan Spirit Gods.

I learned that my little crystal skull, brought from the States to this faraway land, had most likely been infused with the Mayan Spirits on May 20th under the Sun/Pleiades conjunction at Cahal Pech.

That was the 'Day of no Shadows', the day of the beginning of the twelve- year countdown to the return of Kulkulcan. We brought down the Divine Energies and toned the connection. That's why that night I had such a strange and eerie experience. They had come to introduce themselves to me and show their power.

The Mayan Spirits choose whether or not to inhabit an object for an initiate. In other words, I have been given a very special gift from the Mayan Spirits themselves. Not often are these given to other than devoted Mayan Shamans. I am honored and I thank them!

The stone would only work for the one the Spirits had chosen. They would teach me how to use the stone in a specific manner for healing others, and for discernment in my healing practice.

One of the primary uses of the Sastun was to assist the healer and owner of the stone in the work of healing others and to help guide the holder's path.

The healer washed marble Sastuns in rum and sought answers to his patients' ailments and cures for them.

By checking the alterations, lines and other markings in the crystal, the Spirits may communicate to the Shaman. Many prayers and rituals are also associated with the Spirits. I now diligently honor them and their help to me.

I realized what I have been given by the Mayan Spirits. I had been given the answers to questions about the little glass head I had received. Now I understood the new lines and markings in my crystal skull. This was certainly ethereal! Melchizedek had promised otherworldly knowledge. This fit the description!

White Galactic Wizard
I harmonize in order to enchant
Modeling receptivity
I seal the output of timelessness
With the galactic tone of integrity
I am guided by the power of endlessness

I am now a White Galactic Wizard.

They are Sastun! Now the adventure would begin! There are just 34 more sites to open and seal!

P.S. Racha-el has recently had a proposal of marriage! Prince William, the son of Prince Charles and the late Princess Diana recently graduated. He went directly to Belize.

Adama, What's Next?

Sastun! On!

From the Word of Melchizedek,
I, Al'lat Le Andro Melchizedek, am to tell the people:

"Melchizedek is the Eternal Lord of Light, Sovereign of Light, in charge of organizing the levels of the heavenly worlds of YHWH for the transit into new creation."*

*this quote is also found in " The Keys of Enoch," by Dr. J. J. Hurtak

I have come to awaken, anoint and fulfill my role as an anointed Melchizedek. I will, as a Priest of El Elyon, The Most High God, as guided, administer the Shekinah to you and instruct you in the ways of YHWH. The way is simple. It is of faith in the only Universal Father, Creator and Nurturer/Teacher of all and that of Love to self and one another. The Shekinah, the Feminine Spirit is being given to those of the Priesthood in sacred anointing and the gifts are being made manifest to the Sons of Light. I have given myself to the transmission and service of Spirit to do this for the people of Earth at this time. Many diverse gifts are given and are tangible, real empowerments.

I have received instructions directly from Melchizedek and the Priesthood. I am here to teach the spiritual principles and coordinate with the High Priest Melchizedek, the work of the Christ to the Earth and its peoples. The Male Merkaba energies and the Female Flower of Life energies are taught now to bring understanding of the sacred truths. These truths are now being revealed to humanity in the last days of this age. I am here to anoint many of the Sons of Light. Others, of the Priesthood of Melchizedek, to awaken you, to bring guidance, restoration, and direction of purpose so you may effectively perform what you have come here to do. I have also come during this time to embody the female aspect of the Melchizedek energies to bring balance and restore these female energies to Earth.

I have also come as the Earth Healer, the One to restore the sacred sites of the Earth. The Michael Pillar of Light knowledge has been given to me now to release the earth of many burdens. I am to teach selected individuals and give them the attunement and ability to complete this work. Over the centuries many souls have passed onto death in vibrations that were so low. Because of their low vibration and not having the transformative energies needed to ascend, they have remained close to the earth plane. As Melchizedeks, we have the responsibility to assist these souls. They remain and wander the earth in grief, sorrow and pain, often reliving the trauma of their death or seeking past love. Their plight is one that draws our love and compassion to them. The Light is ever there for them, however they have not the strength or esteem to transcend this state. Their energies not only burden Mother Earth, they also hinder the ascension of Mother Earth. She will be freed from this in one way or another.

The Pillar is guided and overseen by Archangel Michael. He stands near to hold the space and prevents any disrupter energies from hindering the ascension of these dear ones! As the Pillar is connected to Heaven and Earth, it forms a direct pathway into the Creative Light of the Christ. Archangel Michael is called upon to direct souls into the Light. Guides and family of the past join as the souls are lifted into the Light. The captives are set free as they realize the time of ascension is now and all is released in the Light of Christ, they are now free.

"Melchizedek is in charge of the heavenly Order Brotherhood of Melchizedek and the spiritual and planetary priesthood of Melchizedek (Ps 110:4 Heb 7:1-3,15,24) Jehovah will prepare the world for deliverance through Melchizedek and the Order of Melchizedek (110:4-7 Judges 5:19-21 Heb 5:9-12 Melchizedek is a manifestation of a Son of God -Heb 7:3" Keys of Enoch, Scriptures

At the end of time, The Sons of Light as the Order of Melchizedek will return to Earth to reunite the scattered brotherhood of Melchizedek and establish the Kingdom of God with the Christ who is the Eternal Son and High Priest after the Order of Melchizedek (Heb 6:20)

Through Attunements and Initiations, I am empowered and given the responsibility to activate as many as are called to come for the re-gathering of the Melchizedek brotherhood. This purpose is to usher in the Kingdom of God in preparation for the embodiment of the Christ Priest Reign upon the Earth and the glorification of the Earth throughout the Universes.

The elect of the Order of Melchizedek are Sons of Light who come to manifest into the world of third dimensional form and manifest the sovereignty of God in transmuting the Earth and other planetary systems to higher dimensional forms. They work implementing the truths of God. The Melchizedek Order administers to man through the Merkaba. In this way the architectonic models in the heavens can be built on the earth, and those other systems, to the many levels of universal creation. The Melchizedek Order is after the Order of the Son of God

Together we will establish and activate the new unity consciousness grid (the architectonic model) over planet Earth to restore balance and universal understanding to all the Children of Light. Once this has been established and correlated, all of creation will recognize the Earth as a planetary entity whose time has come to ascend and become part of the Universal community of the Pure Light under the order of Melchizedek and the Universal Christ.

The Melchizedek Order governs, oversees, the quadrants of the planetary worlds. Wherever the Adamic seed has been transplanted, they administer spiritual, progressive knowledge, and transmutation of energies; dimensional systems changes, to these worlds.

I have incarnated here from my position in the System of Andromeda to complete the work here on the Earth planetary "crisis." A crisis worker, you might say, the Melchizedeks assist worlds in their transition phases and ascension processes. It is important at this time that I come and do the work to ensure the transition of not only your planet Earth, but also of the Twelve Galaxies which make up the Andromedan System. As the Over Light Being of this system I am responsible to see that they too pass through into the new Universe.

It holds the keys to the opening of the heavens with respect to the contact areas on the earth

I have begun the work of opening the Heavens to bring in and center the energies contained of heaven and of the new grid forming above the Earth at this time. Those who work with me are actively anchoring the energies now in those specific areas of the globe as they have been so taught. Using our activated Merkaba we anchor the Light to the Earth in preparation has the ability to commune with the celestial communities of the Brotherhood of Light throughout the Father universes coordinating the work of the Christ in the heavens and on the Earth.

During the Karmic Contract readings, direct contact has been made through me to the Brotherhood for the purpose of clarifying the roles of the Melchizedeks on the Earth. Direct guidance and instruction are given to those who are of the Priesthood. These are not psychic readings, but are rather word from the Melchizedek realm to the Sons of Light.

The Order is Eternal (Heb 7:3) and has foreordained its Priests and Programs before the world was.

Vesica Piscis
The Cross
The Fish
The Only Begotten of the Father/Mother
The Christ
The Vishnu
All Creation is Given Unto Him
Flower of Life
Tone
Vibration
The Light
"No one comes unto the Father, but through Him"

The Seven Sacred Directions; Divine Thought: The basis of Creation of the Vesica Piscis, the Light from which all creation has sprung, all platonic solids.

Codex
Sacred Manuscript Teaching
The Law of Life,   The Law of Love

We are not alone, Guides and Angels are with us
Gifts of the Spirit are for this day
Universal Love is meant to be shared with one another
Universal Love is always with us
Karmic illnesses exist….Spiritual cleansing heals
Mandala, Geometric form creates an energy signature
We are learning so as to use our gifts
We each have a separate path
Not all are of the same Spirit
Sometimes you need to make a stand for Spirit
Contact with the departed and Ancients is possible
Ask and you shall receive
Ravens and animal guides assist bring messages
Psychic Gifts can develop later in life
Some of our most difficult challenges can come from family
Downloading occurs at night...write!
Crisis and opportunity come hand in hand
Geometric form creates gateways
We learn so that we may Use our gifts
Practice gratefulness
Cellular memory requires release
Share the knowledge being given to you
Illness teaches, changes DNA
The more you give, the more you receive
You will always have free choice
You cannot own Spirit
Guides can and do, manifest in physical form
Stones are useful in healing
People have their own agendas, karma to work out
Entire countries are in need of releasing karma
Sites exist from ancient times and hold energy
Nature spirits work with us
Prayer, tone and symbols work!
Spirit requires sacred space
Spirit will provide for you

WE can and do alter time at will
Storms, events carry strong emotion
Energy grids can protect
We are just learning now
We are the Children
Elderly death process very important to the soul
Angels do intervene in events
Guides assist us in death
Departed see clearly on the other side
There is no real death
Compassion is to be expressed to all
We are various species from across the universe
Forget nothing, all is vital
Stones and crystals are programmable
You can access crystal programming
Use ALL your tools
You may access other dimensions
When you receive information, act on it
Prayer seeks the Creator first
Create through tone
Prophesy will be fulfilled
Ascended beings exist in/around Earth
Mankind did 'fall'
Creator's Light is power
They will come

As you can now see, even in the everyday moment there are sacred truths to be found.
Find your truths.

Susan Isabelle

Word of the Living Codex

*To Every Master seeking Shambhala
The Holy City of Light,
The Lemurians and Your Future, We Speak;*

*"Despise not your trials for they are
Initiations into Higher Truth
And will raise the consciousness of
All of Humanity as you surpass the trials*

*Hold Fast to the truth You Hold Within
At times, it may dim,
But even a spark of the Light of God
That shines brightly in you, Lights the World*

*Speak the Word of the Shekhina,
Her Loving Peace,
Her Strength, Her Compassion, Her Wisdom,
For She is the Beloved of God,
Build Her Temple within you*

*Angels seek to guard and protect the Beloved of God.
Let Her be found within;
No harm shall ever befall you.*

*Then,
You shall find the Holy Gate
And Enter into Shambhala
Even as We,
Your Brothers and Sisters Before You"
Adama*

As channeled to Susan Isabelle March 4, 2005

Bibliography

ANDREWS, TED, *Animal-Speak: The Spiritual & Magical Powers of Creatures Great & Small*

ARGÜELLES, JOSÉ, *The Mayan Factor: Path Beyond Technology*

CARROLL, LEE, *The Journey Home*

MELCHIZEDEK, DRUNVALO, *The Ancient Secret of the Golden Flower of Life*

FREIDEL, DAVID; SCHELE, LINDA; PARKER, JOY, *Maya Cosmos: Three Thousand Years on the Shaman's Path*

GILBERT, ADRIAN, *The Mayan Prophecies: Unlocking the Secrets of a Lost Civilization*

HANCOCK, GRAHAM, *Fingerprints of the Gods*

HURTAK, J. J., DR., *The Book of Knowledge: The Keys of Enoch*

JENKINS, JOHN MAJOR, *Maya Cosmogenesis 2012, The True Meaning of the Maya Calendar End-Date*

MINI, JOHN, *Day of Destiny: Where Will You Be August 13, 1999?*

MORTON, CHRIS and THOMAS, CERI LOUISE, *The Mystery of the Crystal Skulls: A Real Life Detective Story of the Ancient World*

MURRAY, KATHLEEN, *The Divine Spark of Creation: The Skull Speaks*

ROBBINS, DIANNE, *Telos: The Call Goes Out — Telepathic Messages from Adama*
    Revised edition, 2003 *Messages From the Hollow Earth*

SPILSBURY, ARIEL and BRYNER, MICHAEL, *The Mayan Oracle: Return Path to the Stars*, Chapter 2

Rosita Arvigo, *Sastun My Apprenticeship with A Maya Healer*

Andrews, Shirley, *Atlantis and Lemuria*

Jones, Louise, *Telos*

Susan Isabelle
International Teacher
of the Master Teachers
Founder, REV. BS, LSW,
Certified Advanced Hypnotherapist
Al'lat Le Andro Melchizedek

Stonehenge, England

Incredible Experiences!
For book orders, or to register for sessions
or classes, call
**530.964.3129
Shambhala Center
and
Gaila Goddess Specialty Shoppe
530.964.2333**

Email:
Shambhalatemple@ aol.com
Web: http://www.Shambhalatemple.
com
PO Box 1093
Mc Cloud California 96057

International Institute Melchizedek Method of Shambhala Training Certification Program and Classes

Levels 1&2 Shambhala Practitioner
2 days each class, 7 incredible symbols
Complete instruction: Chakra, Auric, Light, Color,
Multidimensional healing: Scanning, Meridians
22 point Initiation to the Energies
DNA Alteration to Light
3rd Eye and Melchizedek's Gift of the Halo Opening

Level 3 Therapist
2 days, 5 symbols
Full training: Mandalas, Stargates, Crystals, Crystal Skulls,
Gemstones, Sacred Merkaba Activation,
Lemurian Contact, Advanced Psychic

Level 4 Advanced Master/Earth Healer
2 days, 5 symbols St Germaine & Lady Gaia
The NEW GAIA Earth Healer Attunement;
Fieldwork, trips, and Activation or
Advanced Alternative Healing Techniques

Level 5 Master Teacher
Ongoing support for new teachers!
The 22 Atlantean Master Symbols, Michael's Pillar,
Personalized Initiations on the Mountain

Level 6 Maha Karuna
Put it ALL TOGETHER! Work with the Elementals, restore the Earth! Long toning and Angelic chants are taught with 13 amazing symbols!

Level 7 Rainbow Masters
Receive the NEW Spectra Symbols which bring in Divine Feminine from the Feminine Aspect of God. Seven KEYS exist which open the Secrets of the Universe to the Feminine Aspect Powers. Work with the Six Goddess Energies!
Goddess Initiations and Training

Masters' Monthly Planetary Support Group
Certificates and Comprehensive Manuals

Watch for Susan's next book,

We, The Lemurians, Shall Come
The next assignments from Adama were to take Susan to distant lands! England, Canada,
Montauk, Long Island, The Indians and Florida connect in the most unusual way....
Due out in July 2005!